Jeremiah 30–52
and
Lamentations

Westminster Bible Companion

Series Editors

Patrick D. Miller
David L. Bartlett

Jeremiah 30–52
and
Lamentations

JOHN M. BRACKE

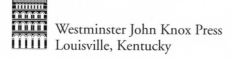

Westminster John Knox Press
Louisville, Kentucky

Book design by Publishers' WorkGroup
Cover design by Drew Stevens

First edition

Published by Westminster John Knox Press
Louisville, Kentucky

This book is printed on acid-free paper that meets the American National Standards Institute Z39.48 standard. ∞

PRINTED IN THE UNITED STATES OF AMERICA

00 01 02 03 04 05 06 07 08 09 — 10 9 8 7 6 5 4 3 2 1

Library of Congress Cataloging-in-Publication Data

Bracke, John M. (John Martin), 1947–
    Jeremiah 30–52 and Lamentations / John M. Bracke. — 1st ed.
        p.   cm. — (Westminster Bible companion)
    Includes bibliographical references.
    ISBN 0-664-25583-3 (alk. paper)
        1. Bible. O.T. Jeremiah XXX–LII—Commentaries.   2. Bible.
    O.T. Lamentations—Commentaries.   I. Title.   II. Series.
    BS1525.3.B732   1999
    224' .2077—dc21   99-43129

Contents

LAMENTATIONS

Series Foreword

This series of study guides to the Bible is offered to the church and more specifically to the laity. In daily devotions, in church school classes, and in listening to the preached word, individual Christians turn to the Bible for a sustaining word, a challenging word, and a sense of direction. The word that scripture brings may be highly personal as one deals with the demands and surprises, the joys and sorrows, of daily life. It also may have broader dimensions as people wrestle with moral and theological issues that involve us all. In every congregation and denomination, controversies arise that send ministry and laity alike back to the Word of God to find direction for dealing with difficult matters that confront us.

A significant number of lay women and men in the church also find themselves called to the service of teaching. Most of the time they will be teaching the Bible. In many churches, the primary sustained attention to the Bible and the discovery of its riches for our lives have come from the ongoing teaching of the Bible by persons who have not engaged in formal theological education. They have been willing, and often eager, to study the Bible in order to help others drink from its living water.

This volume is part of a series of books, the Westminster Bible Companion, intended to help the laity of the church read the Bible more clearly and intelligently. Whether such reading is for personal direction or for the teaching of others, the reader cannot avoid the difficulties of trying to understand these words from long ago. The scriptures are clear and clearly available to everyone as they call us to faith in the God who is revealed in Jesus Christ and as they offer to every human being the word of salvation. No companion volumes are necessary in order to hear such words truly. Yet every reader of scripture who pauses to ponder and think further about any text has questions that are not immediately answerable simply by reading the text of scripture. Such questions may be about historical and geographical details or about words that are obscure or so loaded with meaning that one cannot tell at a glance what is at stake. They may be about the fundamental meaning of a passage or about what connection a particular text might have to our contemporary world. Or a teacher preparing for a church school class may simply want to know: What should I say about this biblical passage when I have to teach it next Sunday? It is our hope that these volumes, written by teachers and pastors with long experience studying and teaching the Bible in the Church, will help members of the church who want and need to study the Bible with their questions.

The New Revised Standard Version of the Bible is the basis for the interpretive comments that each author provides. The NRSV text is presented at the beginning of the discussion so that the reader may have at hand in a single volume both the scripture passage and the exposition of its meaning. In some instances, where inclusion of the entire passage is not necessary for understanding either the text or the interpreter's discussion, the presentation of the NRSV text may be abbreviated. Usually, the whole of the biblical text is given.

We hope this series will serve the community of faith, opening the Word of God to all the people, so that they may be sustained and guided by it.

Jeremiah 30–52

"I Will Restore the Fortunes of My People"
Jeremiah 30–33

Jeremiah 30–33 is often referred to as the "Book of Comfort." There is a dramatic shift of emphasis in these four chapters from Jeremiah 1–29. Although the first twenty-nine chapters of Jeremiah do contain some material that look to God's eventual restoration of Israel and Judah (for instance, 3:15–18; 12:14–17; 16:14–15; 23:1–8; 24:4–7; 29:10–14), the emphasis of these chapters is decidedly upon God's judgment. Jeremiah 30–33 assumes judgment but looks beyond judgment to the time when "God will restore the fortunes" (30:3, anticipated in 29:14) of Israel and Judah.

The material contained in Jeremiah 30–33 has been collected and placed in these chapters because of its concern for God's restoration. The prophet Jeremiah likely delivered some of the oracles now recorded in Jeremiah 30–33 at different times during his career. For instance, texts such as Jeremiah 30:10–11 and 31:7–9 suggest a reunification of the northern and southern kingdoms, Israel and Judah. These texts may reflect Jeremiah's support for the reforms of Judah's King Josiah, which included efforts to reunite Israel, the northern kingdom destroyed by Assyria in 722 B.C., with Judah, the southern kingdom. Other material may reflect Jeremiah's vision for Judah's future even as the Babylonian invasion was underway (32:1–15). Some scholars, noting that portions of the material in Jeremiah 30–33 are written in a style and use vocabulary that is very different from that found in speeches or poems from Jeremiah himself, have suggested that parts of Jeremiah 30–33 were added by later editors of the book (for instance, 31:27–30, which resembles Ezek. 18:25–29; 31:10–14, which sounds like the latter parts of the book of Isaiah; or 31:38–40, whose rebuilding theme is like Zech. 14:10–11 and Ezek. 40–48).

In the way it has come to us, Jeremiah 30–33 provides the most sustained articulation in the book of Jeremiah of the hope that God will "restore the fortunes" of Israel and Judah following judgment.

Jeremiah 30:1–3

30:1 **The word that came to Jeremiah from the LORD:** [2] **Thus says the LORD, the God of Israel: Write in a book all the words that I have spoken to you.** [3] **For the days are surely coming, says the LORD, when I will restore the fortunes of my people, Israel and Judah, says the LORD, and I will bring them back to the land that I gave to their ancestors and they shall take possession of it.**

These verses function as the introduction to Jeremiah 30–33. The word of the Lord that is the focus of this section of the book concerns the "coming" days, that is, the future of Israel and Judah (v. 3). God commands that Jeremiah write this word of the Lord in a book. The implication is that the "coming" days will be well in the future. The word needed to be written down so that it could be remembered over a long period of time (compare a similar instruction, though about God's judgment, in Isa. 8:16–18, 30:8). Although these chapters offer hope to Israel and Judah, they do not negate God's judgment, as the prophet Hananiah had tried to do (Jer. 28).

God's word about the coming days is the promise that "I will restore the fortunes of my people" (30:3). We are given a hint about what God's restoration of the fortunes of Israel and Judah might involve when, in the last half of verse 3, God promises to bring Israel and Judah back to the land of their ancestors. In Jeremiah 1–29, we hear repeatedly that God's judgment will mean the loss of the land of promise. God's promised restoration will reverse this judgment, and the land lost through judgment will be restored. As we will see throughout these chapters, the meaning of "restore the fortunes" is the reversal of God's judgment and the restoration of Israel and Judah as they were prior to the exile.

"Restore the fortunes" is the theme of Jeremiah 30–33. This theme is anticipated in Jeremiah's letter to the exiles in the prior chapter (29:14). The restoration of the fortunes of Israel and Judah is identified as the content of God's word in these first verses of Jeremiah 30. The promise that God will restore the fortunes of Israel and Judah occurs at several places throughout these chapters (30:18; 31:23; 32:44; 33:11) and is used at the very end of these chapters in Jeremiah 33:26.

It may be a surprise that Jeremiah announces a word of hope and restoration, inasmuch as he has been in severe conflict with other optimistic prophets who have offered Judah hope. In fact, we hear a prolonged condemnation of such optimistic prophets throughout Jeremiah 27–29. Notice, however, the difference between Jeremiah's announcement of God's restoration and the promises of the optimistic prophets Jeremiah condemns. The optimistic prophets announce a promise that attempts to undermine God's judgment and make light of God's intentions to pluck up and tear down (1:10), to destroy Judah through Babylon. In only "two years," says Hananiah, the Babylonian threat will be over (28:3). The optimistic prophets do not take seriously God's judgment of Judah. The promise of restoration introduced in Jeremiah 30:1–3 assumes the full force of God's judgment, the loss of the land, and a long period before God might restore Israel and Judah. Jeremiah announces building and planting, but not before God's plucking up and tearing down (1:10) has cleared the way for a new beginning between God and God's people.

In the church, God's Easter triumph over death is joyfully celebrated, and rightly so. However, the celebration of Easter Sunday assumes the cost and pain of Good Friday when God contended on the cross with the powers of death and evil. God's Easter building and planting assume Good Friday's plucking up and tearing down. Long before Jesus' death and resurrection, Jeremiah knew that Good Friday was essential to Easter. As we read Jeremiah 30–33, we will need to remember that God's promised restoration assumes God's judgment.

Jeremiah 30:4–9

30:4 **These are the words that the LORD spoke concerning Israel and Judah:**
5 **Thus says the LORD:**
  We have heard a cry of panic,
  of terror, and no peace.
6 **Ask now, and see,**
  can a man bear a child?
  Why then do I see every man
  with his hands on his loins like a woman in labor?
  Why has every face turned pale?
7 **Alas! that day is so great**
  there is none like it;
  it is a time of distress for Jacob;
  yet he shall be rescued from it.
8 **On that day, says the LORD of hosts, I will break the yoke from off his neck, and I will burst his bonds, and strangers shall no more make a servant of him.** 9 **But they shall serve the LORD their God and David their king, whom I will raise up for them.**
10 **But as for you, have no fear, my servant Jacob, says the LORD,**
  and do not be dismayed, O Israel;
  for I am going to save you from far away,
  and your offspring from the land of their captivity.

Jacob shall return and have quiet and ease,
and no one shall make him afraid.
11 For I am with you, says the LORD, to save you;
I will make an end of all the nations
among which I scattered you,
but of you I will not make an end.
I will chastise you in just measure,
and I will by no means leave you unpunished.

While Jeremiah 30–33 is about God's promised restoration, the initial poem of these chapters begins with a portrayal of the day of the Lord. The day of the Lord was, in the popular thought of ancient Israel and Judah, a day when God would finally set the world right and the enemies of God's people would be judged. Among Israel's prophets, however, the day of the Lord was imagined as an occasion when God would call to account Israel and Judah, and not their enemies. This is clearest in Amos, where the prophet asks why Israel wants the day of the Lord since it will be "darkness, not light; as if someone fled from a lion, and was met by a bear" (Amos 5:18–19; also see Isa. 2:12–21 and Zeph. 1:14–18). In verses 5–7, the day of the Lord is presented much as it is in Amos, as a day of judgment, "a time of distress for Jacob" (v. 7). Central to the portrayal of the day of the Lord in these verses is the image of men writhing like women in labor, in pain from which there will be no escape (v. 6). Their condition reflects the terror of the day in which there will be no evidence of "peace" (well-being, wholeness; compare uses of this word in Jeremiah 29) for Judah. Earlier in the book of Jeremiah, the image of a woman in labor is used to portray the anguish of Judah as an invader approaches (4:31 and 13:21). The images of verses 5–7 summarize what has been imagined about God's judgment in Jeremiah 1–29.

However, at the end of verse 7 God promises "rescue" for the people from this day "so great there is none like it." While God's judgment is presented with all of its horror, these verses look beyond judgment to restoration. The promise that God will "break the yoke" from the neck of God's people refers to Jeremiah 27 and 28. Jeremiah has placed a yoke on his neck to symbolize servitude to Babylon by Judah and the nations (27:1–11). Jeremiah has condemned Hananiah because he has broken the yoke off Jeremiah's neck, an action that indicates Hananiah's anticipation of an early end to the Babylonian captivity. By contrast, the promise in Jeremiah 30 that God will break the yoke from the neck of God's people overtly recognizes the severity of God's judgment (vv. 5–7) and the long delay of any restoration (v. 3). God's removal of the yoke from Judah's neck will mean that Judah will be able to serve God and the Davidic king whom God will "raise up" (v. 9). Of course, the Davidic kings are charged by Jeremiah with leading Judah away from the Lord, and the judgment God has threatened through Jeremiah includes the removal of Judah's kings. The restoration promised in verses 8–9 is a reversal of the judgments of God threatened in Jeremiah 1–29.

The reversal of the judgments threatened in Jeremiah 1–29 is also very evident in the promises of verses 10–11. The promise that God will "save" the people is repeated twice (vv. 10 and 11), and both times God's saving is connected with the end of captivity. Captivity or exile in Babylon is, of course, a central way that God's people will experience God's judgment. In verse 10, the promise to save is elaborated to mean that Jacob will "return and have quiet and ease." In Jeremiah 1–29, God threatens judgment against Judah because they refuse to "return," that is, repent (see, for instance, 3:14, 22; 4:1). The people will not return, but finally, God promises to return them to their land. In verse 11, the promise to save is elaborated to mean that God will make "an end of all the nations" but not of Jacob. The claim that God will severely punish but not make a "full end" of Judah (v. 11) occurs earlier in the Book (see 4:27; 5:10, 18) to anticipate that beyond judgment God intends restoration. In verse 11, the promise not to make a "full end" serves as a reminder not to hear God's promised restoration apart from judgment. So, God's promise not to make a full end of Jacob leads to the assertion that the Lord will "chastise" and not leave Judah "unpunished" (v. 11).

God's reversals of Judah's fortunes, so important in these verses and throughout the Book of Jeremiah, remind us of the way Mary's song in Luke's gospel envisions God turning the world upside down through Jesus. Mary sings of God who will bring "down the powerful from their thrones" (Luke 1:52) and send "the rich empty away" (Luke 1:53). Jeremiah 1–29 imagines this kind of reversal. Judah is portrayed in these earlier chapters of the book as secure in their assurance that God will protect them and will never allow Judah or Jerusalem to fall; or, confident that through idols and political and military cleverness, they can keep themselves secure. God's judgment threatens to bring low the exalted leaders of Judah and to send them empty away to Babylon. Mary also affirms that God will "lift up the lowly" and fill "the hungry with good things" (Luke 1:52–53). God's restoration promised that finally Judah, humbled through exile, would be lifted up from captivity by God and restored.

The book of Jeremiah thus invites us to reflect in our time who is exalted that God might in judgment humble; and who is lowly, that God might restore and exalt.

Jeremiah 30:12–17

¹² **For thus says the LORD:**
   Your hurt is incurable,
   your wound is grievous.
¹³ **There is no one to uphold your cause,**
   no medicine for your wound,
   no healing for you.
¹⁴ **All your lovers have forgotten you;**
   they care nothing for you;
   for I have dealt you the blow of an enemy,
   the punishment of a merciless foe,
   because your guilt is great,
   because your sins are so numerous.
¹⁵ **Why do you cry out over your hurt?**
   Your pain is incurable.
   Because your guilt is great,
   because your sins are so numerous,
   I have done these things to you.
¹⁶ **Therefore all who devour you shall be devoured,**
   and all your foes, everyone of them, shall go into captivity;
   those who plunder you shall be plundered,
   and all who prey on you I will make a prey.
¹⁷ **For I will restore health to you,**
   and your wounds I will heal,
   says the LORD,
   because they have called you an outcast:
   "It is Zion; no one cares for her!"

Medical images are used in this passage, which continues the theme of God's judgment and restoration of Judah and Israel. As these verses begin, the diagnosis for God's people is bleak and shared forthrightly with them: "your hurt . . . incurable," "your wound . . . grievous, "no medicine . . . no healing for you" (vv. 12–13). Then, the news gets worse in several ways.

Jeremiah announces to God's people that they are abandoned and without support. Their "lovers," their political allies to whom they have turned for help, have forgotten them and no longer care for them (v. 14). Jeremiah links ominous medical images with stark political realism to describe God's judgment.

Still worse, this poem is clear that it is God who has inflicted the wound upon Judah, but for good reason, so there is no cause for complaint. The sequence of statements in verses 14–15 is carefully arranged to emphasize God's harsh judgment and the hopeless condition of the people:

    a. God said, "*I have dealt* you the blow of an enemy";

       b. This is followed immediately by God's justification of this action, "*because your guilt is great . . . your sins are many*";

          c. God then chides, "Why do you cry out . . ." and reiterates the terminal diagnosis, "Your pain is incurable."

       b. The reason for this incurable pain is then again given, "*because your guilt is great . . . your sins are so numerous*";

    a. God concludes by announcing, "*I have done* these things to you."

The people of Judah have brought judgment upon themselves, their situation is hopeless, and they should not complain about it. It is as if a physician treating a patient with heart disease were to say, "You ate fatty foods and didn't exercise for years, so your illness is your own fault and don't complain about it!" The political and theological realism of these verses is blunt about God's judgment and leaves little room for optimism about the future of Judah.

Thus, the reversals described in verse 16, which conclude in verse 17 with God's promise "I will restore health to you," are surprising and nearly unbelievable. It is even difficult to understand the sense of the word "therefore" at the beginning of verse 16, which suggests that what follows is the logical conclusion of what has come before. There is nothing in verses 12–15 to prepare us for the conclusion that those who have devoured God's people will be devoured or that those who have made Judah a prey will themselves be made a prey. Nor does God's announcement that "your wound is grievous" (v. 12; see 14:17 where this phrase is connected with judgment) in any way prepare us for the promise that "your wounds I will heal" (v. 17). There has been considerable speculation that the word "therefore" with which verse 16 begins is a mistake, perhaps a copying error by a scribe. By what logic are we to understand the connection between the hopeless condition of the people presented in verses 12–15 and God's promises to restore Judah in verses 16–17?

The key to this puzzle is found in the last lines of verse 17, in which God justifies the decision to restore the health of the people. Earlier in these verses, God justifies striking Judah with "the blow of an enemy" by saying it is "because your guilt is great, because your sins are numerous" (said twice in vv. 14–15). Similarly, when God promises to restore health to Judah, God gives the reason by saying "because . . ." (v. 17). The nations, God indicates, called Judah "an outcast" and said of Zion, "no one cares for her." While God has already indicated that the political allies of God's people, her "lovers," no longer "care" for her (v. 14), the taunt of the nations that "no one cares for her" suggest that even God no longer cares. Such a perception and accusation are more than God can allow. "Therefore" (v. 16), God is moved by the very consequences of God's own judgment to the decision to restore health to Israel and Judah. At several places in the book of Jeremiah we have seen that God feels deep anguish at having to punish God's people (for instance, 4:19–22; 8:18–9:3). In this text, the Lord witnesses the consequences the "blow" God's own judgment has inflicted, and having heard the taunt, "No one cares," is moved to a fresh decision about Israel and Judah.

Jeremiah 30:18–22

30:18 **Thus says the LORD:**
> **I am going to restore the fortunes of the tents of Jacob,**
> **and have compassion on his dwellings;**
> **the city shall be rebuilt upon its mound,**
> **and the citadel set on its rightful site.**
> [19] **Out of them shall come thanksgiving,**
> **and the sound of merrymakers.**
> **I will make them many, and they shall not be few;**
> **I will make them honored, and they shall not be disdained.**
> [20] **Their children shall be as of old,**
> **their congregation shall be established before me;**
> **and I will punish all who oppress them.**
> [21] **Their prince shall be one of their own,**
> **their ruler shall come from their midst;**
> **I will bring him near, and he shall approach me,**
> **for who would otherwise dare to approach me?**
> **says the LORD.**
> [22] **And you shall be my people,**
> **and I will be your God.**

These chapters tend to alternate between bold, sweeping statements of God's intentions for Judah and Israel and more specific descriptions of what restoration will be like. Jeremiah 30:12–17 probes the logic of God's decision to "heal" God's people. The present text is more specific and imagines God's restoration in concrete terms.

These verses begin with a restatement of the theme of Jeremiah 30–33, that God will "restore the fortunes" of the people (see 29:14; 30:3). The promised restoration is linked to God's decision to have "compassion" on

Israel and Judah. The emphasis of these verses then falls upon the specific ways in which "restoration" is to occur and God's compassion will be expressed. Again, what is imagined is a series of events that will reverse the consequences of God's judgment.

Throughout Jeremiah 1–29, God's threatened judgment includes the destruction of Jerusalem and the Temple. In judgment Jerusalem will be made "a desolation" (for instance, 6:9; 9:11; 12:10) and the Temple destroyed like the ancient worship site at Shiloh (7:14; 26:9). In these verses, the vision of God's promised restoration includes the city "rebuilt upon its mound" and "the citadel set on its rightful site" (v. 18). In Jeremiah 1–29, God's threatened judgment is seen as resulting in lamentation and weeping (see 6:26; 9:10–11; 17–19), the end of celebrations and mirth (see 7:34; 16:9), and the depopulation of the land (see 10:20; 15:8; 16:4; 18:21). The vision of God's restoration offered here sees the consequences of judgment reversed: "the sound of merrymakers," an increase in population, children who live to an old age (compare Isa. 65:20), a re-gathered congregation, and God's punishment upon those who have oppressed Judah. There may well be some reference to the covenant blessings of the book of Deuteronomy suggested here (see Deut. 28:1–14).

It is interesting that this vision of restoration does not include a "king," but a "prince" (v. 21). It could be that what was imagined for restored Israel was not a monarchy but another form of government where God's rule would be more direct (that is, a theocracy). Early in Israel's life, there were no kings (see, for instance, Judg. 8:23). Further, kings had been a primary reason for God's judgment (Jer. 21:11–23:8 offers a long indictment of kings). Verse 22 may have in mind something like a priest-prince instead of a king. Such an idea can be found in other Old Testament material from the time of the exile (for instance, in Ezekiel 45:7–9).

The conclusion of this section (v. 22) affirms a renewed relationship between God and the people. The phrase "you shall be my people, I will be your God," repeated often in the Old Testament and in the book of Jeremiah, has been called a "covenant formula." As the conclusion of these verses, verse 22 affirms in succinct form that the goal of God's restoration is a renewed relationship between God and the people. Early in Israel's history, the Promised Land was the tangible sign of relationship between God and Israel. In the text we are examining, what is important about the restoration of Jerusalem and the Temple, and the restoration of normal and ordered life in Judah, is that these again give concrete expression to the restored relationship between the LORD and the people of Israel and Judah.

Jesus announced and through his life gave expression to God's reign (the kingdom of God). Just as the text we have been examining is concrete in thinking about God's restoration of Judah and Israel, Jesus was also concrete in thinking about what God's reign will mean. So, for instance, we can hear in the Beatitudes in Luke 6 a concrete expression of what God's reign will be like for the poor and hungry as well as the well-to-do:

> [20]Then he looked up at his disciples and said:
> "Blessed are you who are poor,
>> for yours is the kingdom of God.
> [21]"Blessed are you who are hungry now,
>> for you will be filled.
> "Blessed are you who weep now,
>> for you will laugh.

Jeremiah 30:23–31:1

> 30:23 **Look, the storm of the LORD!**
>   **Wrath has gone forth,**
>   **a whirling tempest;**
>   **it will burst upon the head of the wicked.**
>   24 **The fierce anger of the LORD will not turn back**
>   **until he has executed and accomplished**
>   **the intents of his mind.**
>   **In the latter days you will understand this.**
>   31:1 **At that time, says the LORD, I will be the God of all the families of Israel, and they shall be my people.**

This material occurs in almost identical form in Jeremiah 23:19–20. In Jeremiah 23, these verses are used to distinguish the optimistic prophets, who announce that all will be well with Judah, from prophets like Jeremiah, who announce God's judgment. When read as part of Jeremiah 23, these verses assert, against the optimistic prophets, that God's intention is to judge Judah. Only when the exile has occurred will Judah finally understand God's intentions about judgment.

When read as part of Jeremiah 30, these verses have a broader meaning than in Jeremiah 23. Jeremiah 30 has indicated that God's judgment makes restoration a possibility; plucking up and tearing down make building and planting possible. In Jeremiah 30, "the intents [of God's] mind" that God's fierce anger is to accomplish need to be understood as the restoration of Judah and Israel. There have been hints throughout the book that beyond judgment, God intends restoration. The restoration God intends beyond judgment is the focus of Jeremiah 30.

Jeremiah 30:24 and Jeremiah 31:1 are linked as both use an expression for some future time: "In the latter days" (v. 24) and "At that time" (v. 1). The intent of God's mind that Judah will understand "in the latter days" (v. 24) is specified in Jeremiah 31:1. They will understand that God intended a renewed relationship, that "I will be God . . . and they shall be my people." This affirmation of relationship in 31:1 echoes 30:22.

Taken together, the verses of Jeremiah 30:23–31:1 provide an appropriate summary for Jeremiah 30, but also a fitting introduction to Jeremiah 31. Beyond judgment, God intends restoration, a restoration of Israel and Judah in their land, and a restoration of the relationship between God and the people.

Jeremiah 31:2–6

31:2 **Thus says the LORD:**
The people who survived the sword
found grace in the wilderness;
when Israel sought for rest,
3 **the LORD appeared to him from far away.**
I have loved you with an everlasting love;
therefore I have continued my faithfulness to you.
4 **Again I will build you, and you shall be built,**
O virgin Israel!
Again you shall take your tambourines,
and go forth in the dance of the merrymakers.
5 **Again you shall plant vineyards**
on the mountains of Samaria;
the planters shall plant,
and shall enjoy the fruit.
6 **For there shall be a day when sentinels will call**
in the hill country of Ephraim:
"Come, let us go up to Zion,
to the LORD our God."

The vision offered in this material develops the affirmation of the prior verses that God's ultimate intention is restoration beyond judgment. God's judgment of Judah is assumed. In verses 2–3, God's people are described as "the people who survived the sword" (remember the pervasive threat of "sword, famine and pestilence" in Jer. 1–29) and as people to whom the Lord appeared "from far away" (the sense of distance suggesting exile). However, the stress of this passage is not on the judgment that has occurred but on God's relationship with Judah and Israel that is to follow judgment:

a. The affirmation that "the people who survived the sword found grace in the wilderness" (v. 2) reminds us of the initial description of God's relationship with Israel in the book of Jeremiah. Jeremiah 2:1–3 describes Israel as a faithful bride who followed Yahweh in the wilderness. The idolatry of Israel shattered that initial relationship and led to judgment (the point of Jeremiah 1–29, though particularly Jeremiah 2–3). The present text takes us beyond "the sword," God's judgment, and announces that in the wilderness, the people will find "grace," that is, God's favor. The relationship between God and the people is thus imagined to have come full circle. The wilderness was the place where God's relationship with Israel began, and will be the place for the restoration of the relationship between God and Israel (for a similar view of restoration after judgment, see Hos. 2:14).

b. The end of verse 2 and beginning of verse 3 assume a spatial distance between God and the people which God bridges by appearing to Israel "from far away." The book of Jeremiah presents the initial relationship between God and Israel as one in which the people followed after God (2:2–3). However, Israel went far from God (2:5) and followed after idols (2:8, 15). Israel's decision to distance themselves from God brought judgment, and the judgment of exile had an obvious spatial dimension as Israel was removed from the land (the spatial aspect of Israel's sin and God's judgment is most evident in Ezekiel; see especially Ezek. 1, 8–11, and 43). The affirmation that God appeared to Israel "from far away" again suggests that God took initiative after the exile to restore relationship with the people, to close the gap between God and a people who went "far" from God (2:4) to pursue idols (2:8, 25).

c. Verse 3 concludes with two statements by God which re-affirm the basis of God's continuing relationship with the people after the exile. God affirms "everlasting love" and continuing "faithfulness." Interestingly, in the description of the initial relationship between God and Israel in Jeremiah 2:2–3, Israel's "love" and "devotion" (the same Hebrew word translated as "faithfulness" in this passage) for God are affirmed. What Jeremiah 1–29 makes clear is that Israel's "love" is not "everlasting" nor is Israel's "devotion" continuing. As these verses anticipate God's restoration of Israel and Judah, the restoration is to be grounded no longer in Israel's love and devotion but in God's.

Judah and Israel broke the relationship with God and had no way of restoring the relationship. The initiative for the restoration is with God— God who extends grace to the people who survived the sword, seeks them out from afar, and extends them "everlasting love" and continuing "faithfulness." However, because of God's initiative, after plucking up and breaking down there will be "building" (v. 4) and "planting" (v. 5) for God's people. Verses 4–6 again present the building and planting of restoration as the reversal of the judgment of Judah: the dance of merry-makers (v. 4) will replace the wail of mourning women (9:17–22); the land that had become desolate like a desert (12:7–13) will again be planted with vineyards producing fruit (v. 5). Zion, about whom it was said, "no one cares" (30:17), will again be the place where the people worship (v. 6). God's initiative to restore relationship will have tangible consequences for the people and the land.

It is God's faithfulness that these verses of the book of Jeremiah affirm as the basis for hope about Judah's building and planting. The emphasis of these verses on God's faithfulness touches a theme that runs throughout the Bible. In Psalm 145, the enduring faithfulness of God is connected with God's concern for those who are afflicted and bowed down, like Judah in exile, but then also to the food that we living creatures eat daily:

> The Lord is faithful in all his words,
>   and gracious is all his deeds.
> The Lord upholds all who are falling,
>   and raises up all who are bowed down.
> The eyes of all look to you,
>   And you give them their food in due season.
> You open your hand,
>   satisfying the desire of every living thing.
> (Psalm 145:13b–16)

Even in the simple act of receiving our daily bread, the psalmist reminds us that we are participating in a profound theological reality, the faithfulness of God whose graciousness sustains our lives in seasons of plenty and of want.

Jeremiah 31:7–9

31:7 **For thus says the LORD:**
Sing aloud with gladness for Jacob,
and raise shouts for the chief of the nations;
proclaim, give praise, and say,
"Save, O LORD, your people,
the remnant of Israel."
  8 **See, I am going to bring them from the land of the north,**
and gather them from the farthest parts of the earth,
among them the blind and the lame,
those with child and those in labor, together;
a great company, they shall return here.

⁹ **With weeping they shall come,**
and with consolations I will lead them back,
I will let them walk by brooks of water,
in a straight path in which they shall not stumble;
for I have become a father to Israel,
and Ephraim is my firstborn.

In rich poetic language that is much like that found in the book of Isaiah (see, for instance, Isaiah 35), these verses announce that God will "save . . . the remnant of Israel" (v. 7). One affirmation of these verses is the promise that God will bring the people back from Babylon, "from the land of the north . . . the farthest parts of the earth" (v. 8), to their land. This promise of a homecoming is expressed by a series of statements about what God will do, and, as a result, what will happen to God's people. Thus, the promise of homecoming is carried through these verses by alternating statements by God ("I") and about the people ("they"):

"I am going to bring them from the land of the north . . . and gather them" (v. 8)
"they shall return here" (v. 8)
"I will lead them back, I will let them walk by brooks of water" (v. 9)
"they shall not stumble" (v. 9)

The exile was to end, and God's people were to return home.

Three other features of the promise of homecoming in these verses are worth noting. First, there is an affirmation that God will see to it that even those who are weak and vulnerable will be included in the journey home: "the blind and lame" and even pregnant women in labor (v. 8). That no one will be excluded from this homecoming would certainly have been a powerful assurance for those who had been in Babylonian exile for many years. Second, there is the promise that the journey "from the land of the north" will be a much easier journey than the post-exodus trek through the wilderness, and so a much more glorious event. God will lead the people "by brooks of water" (compare the lack of water in the wilderness after the exodus, Exod. 17:1–8) and in a straight path (remember that Israel wandered 40 years in the wilderness to reach the promised land the first time). Third, with the promise of a homecoming, the weeping of God's people will end (v. 9, and in Jeremiah 1–29 the lamentation caused by God's judgment, for instance in 9:10–11, 17–19), and instead, they will sing, shout and give God praise (v. 7; compare the singing of God's people after their deliverance from Egypt, Exod. 15:1–18, 20–21).

Finally, the conclusion of this poem is quite important in that it provides the rationale for God's decision to end the exile and bring Israel and Judah home. God's relationship with Israel and Judah is affirmed using the image of a father and son: "I have become a father to Israel, and Ephraim is my firstborn" (v. 9). Early in the book of Jeremiah, reflecting about what a relationship with Israel and Judah might entail, God muses, "I thought you would call me, My Father, and would not turn from following me" (3:19). However, the people would not follow, and they turned to the baals; God's judgment, exile, was the result. The promise of homecoming for Israel and Judah is rooted in God's reaffirmation of relationship, "I have become a Father to Israel."

Every time we pray, "Our Father, who art in heaven . . . ," we are reminded that the ground of our life and hope is God's decision to be parent to us and graciously consider us children.

Jeremiah 31:10–14

31:10   Hear the word of the LORD, O nations,
     and declare it in the coastlands far away;
     say, "He who scattered Israel will gather him,
     and will keep him as a shepherd a flock."
 11 For the LORD has ransomed Jacob,
     and has redeemed him from hands too strong for him.
 12 They shall come and sing aloud on the height of Zion,
     and they shall be radiant over the goodness of the LORD,
     over the grain, the wine, and the oil,
     and over the young of the flock and the herd;
     their life shall become like a watered garden,
     and they shall never languish again.
 13 Then shall the young women rejoice in the dance,
     and the young men and the old shall be merry.
     I will turn their mourning into joy,
     I will comfort them, and give them gladness for sorrow.
 14 I will give the priests their fill of fatness,
     and my people shall be satisfied with my bounty,
     says the LORD.

God's announcement of homecoming shared with Israel and Judah was also heralded among the nations. God was sovereign over the nations, and had shown sovereignty in using the nations as agents of judgment to pluck up and tear down Judah and scatter them in exile. However, God the shepherd who had allowed the flock to be scattered, intends to gather the flock again (v. 10). It is important to remember that in the Old Testament and in the book of Jeremiah, kings were called shepherds, so God's claim to be a shepherd is about being sovereign, the King of Israel and the nations.

The description of what God intends for the re-gathered flock stresses the fertility of the land, the land as a place of blessing. Of course, blessing is what God had intended for Israel and Judah in the land even though they had frustrated this intent:

> I brought you into a plentiful land to eat its fruits and its good things.
> But when you entered you defiled my land,
>   and made my heritage an abomination.
>
> (2:7)

Because of the admonitions of the people, God's judgment was that the "plentiful land" became a waste and a desolation (the description of the drought in Jeremiah 14 is especially significant) and was finally lost. In Jeremiah 18, the once plentiful land is described as

> a horror, a thing to be hissed at forever.
> All who passed by it are horrified and shake their heads.
>   (18:16; also see 19:8)

Among the covenant curses in Deuteronomy is the threat that God's people would become an object of horror to all the kingdoms of the earth" (Deut. 28:25). In judgment, God had brought curse on Judah, the land became a desolation, and Judah became a "horror" to the nations.

This poem looks beyond judgment to God's restoration, to what God intends (30:24), but what is not yet (so v. 13, which indicates by the word "then" that what is imagined in these verses is still in the future; compare 30:3: "the days are surely coming"). Restoration will end the curse and result in blessings to be heralded among the nations. God's people will be "radiant over the goodness of the LORD " (v. 12) and "satisfied with my bounty" (v. 14). God's blessing, goodness, and bounty will be evident in grain, wine, oil, herds, and "life . . . like a watered garden" (v. 12; compare the descriptions of God's blessings in Deut. 28:1–14). Little wonder that among God's people mourning will be turned to joy (v. 13). While the text does not say it directly, the proclamation of this vision of God's intentions among the nations suggests that the horror of the nations at desolate Judah will be turned to awe when they view restored Judah.

Yet, this poem is clear that the bounty and blessing of restored Judah will have everything to do with God's resolve and little to do with Judah's merits. The nations are to see and understand that God has scattered but will gather, ransom, and redeem, will comfort and give gladness, will give fatness and satisfy God's people. God is sovereign in plucking up and tearing down and will be sovereign in building and planting as well.

Jeremiah 31:15–22

31:15 Thus says the LORD:
 A voice is heard in Ramah,
 lamentation and bitter weeping.
 Rachel is weeping for her children;
 she refuses to be comforted for her children,
 because they are no more.
16 Thus says the LORD:
 Keep your voice from weeping,
 and your eyes from tears;
 for there is a reward for your work,
 says the LORD:
 they shall come back from the land of the enemy;
17 there is hope for your future,
 says the LORD:
 your children shall come back to their own country.
18 Indeed I heard Ephraim pleading:
 "You disciplined me, and I took the discipline;
 I was like a calf untrained.
 Bring me back, let me come back,
 for you are the LORD my God.
19 For after I had turned away I repented;
 and after I was discovered, I struck my thigh;
 I was ashamed, and I was dismayed
 because I bore the disgrace of my youth."
20 Is Ephraim my dear son?
 Is he the child I delight in?
 As often as I speak against him,
 I still remember him.
 Therefore I am deeply moved for him;
 I will surely have mercy on him,
 says the LORD.
21 Set up road markers for yourself,
 make yourself guideposts;
 consider well the highway,
 the road by which you went.
 Return, O virgin Israel,
 return to these your cities.

> 22 **How long will you waver,**
> **O faithless daughter?**
> **For the LORD has created a new thing on the earth:**
> **a woman encompasses a man.**

This poem presents a conversation among Rachel, God, and one of Rachel's grandchildren, Ephraim. We hear Rachel's voice first as she cries in Ramah (v. 15). She was the wife of Jacob, and together they were the ancestral parents of God's people. The tribes of Israel bore the names of Jacob's sons, who included the several children Jacob had with Rachel. Jacob himself was also called "Israel" by God (Gen. 32:27–28). Ramah is a location traditionally associated with Rachel (see 1 Sam 10:2, which locates Rachel's tomb at Zelzah, a site near the town of Ramah north of Jerusalem). Rachel is weeping because her children are lost. Lamentation and weeping characterize the response of God's people to judgment in Jeremiah 1–29; in Jeremiah 30–31, it has been promised that restoration will turn weeping to joy (directly in 31:9, 13). Rachel's grief indicates the loss of the exile.

God speaks next, assuring grieving Rachel that her time of grief will end (v. 16) and that there is "hope for your future" (v. 17). God's assertion that there is hope for Rachel is surrounded by promises that make the hope specific: "they will come back from the land of the enemy" (v. 16); "your children shall come back to their own country" (v. 17). God promises Rachel that the lost children will "come back." The Hebrew word here translated "come back" is the same word God has used to call the people to repent, that is, "return" (see 3:11–14; 4:1–2). In other words, God promises to return the children who themselves have refused to return to God (or turn to God from the idols they have worshiped). An act of deliverance is described not unlike the exodus. Even as God had delivered the Hebrews "from" the land of Egypt and brought them "to" the land of milk and honey (Exod. 3:8), so God promises Rachel that her children will come back "from the land of an enemy" "to their own country" (very similar to vv. 7–9).

One of Rachel's grandchildren, Ephraim (the son of Rachel's son Joseph, see Gen. 30:24–25; 41:50–52), is heard in verses 18–20 pleading with God, "bring me back" (v. 18). He admits that he had "turned away" from God, but also claims that he has "repented" (v. 19). Ephraim's appeal uses different meanings of the same Hebrew word meaning "turn" or "return." Ephraim had turned from God, then turned back to God, and wants God to return him. Did Ephraim intend to return to the land or to relationship with God? It may well be both.

God responds to Rachel's weeping at once, but God does not respond immediately to Ephraim's distress. Instead, in verse 20 we hear God's musings about Ephraim, something like a soliloquy. God remembers Ephraim as a "dear son," is "deeply moved for him," and pledges to have "mercy" on him (in 30:18, the Hebrew word here translated as "mercy" is translated as "compassion"). In Jeremiah 1–29 we hear God's anguish as God contemplates the judgment of the people (for instance, 4:19–22; 8:18–9:1). Having heard the dismay of Ephraim, we hear again in verse 20 God's anguish, God "deeply moved" to have mercy on a dear son. Much as in Jeremiah 30:12–17, where the consequences of judgment move God to "heal" Zion, in these verses, too, the consequences of judgment on Ephraim have deep impact on God.

Finally, in verses 21–22, we again hear God speak, though neither Rachel nor Ephraim is addressed, but "Virgin Israel," that is, God's people who are personified as a woman. Despite this unexpected change in who is addressed, God's words reflect a concern for both Rachel and Ephraim. "Virgin Israel," that is, God's people—Ephraim and all of Rachel's lost children—are instructed to mark their way well ("set up road markers," "make yourself guideposts," v. 21) so they can "return." Rachel's children will come back and Ephraim will come back, too.

However, the conclusion of God's speech in verse 22 is exceedingly difficult to understand. The Old Testament scholar Bernhard Anderson has helpfully suggested that the meaning of verse 22 can best be determined by taking clues from the preceding verses ("The Lord Has Created Something New"). While the NRSV translates the location of God's creation as "on the earth," Jeremiah 30–31 suggests that the location of God's concern might be better understood to be the "land," a perfectly acceptable translation of the Hebrew of verse 22. So, we now need to ask what new thing God might have created in the land.

The answer of the text is still confusing—a woman encompasses (or embraces) a man! What can this mean? Remember that in these verses God is addressing "Virgin Israel," that is, God's people who are personified as a woman. What, then, might God's people embrace in the land? Well, Rachel is weeping for her lost children, and Ephraim, her grandson, wants to return to the land (and relationship with God). Anderson has proposed that the meaning of "a woman encompasses a man," when read as part of verses 18–22, is that the "Virgin Israel" will embrace a son. God's people, bereft of children and a future due to God's judgment, are promised by God that they will again have children, sons for their mothers to embrace. The vision of God's promised future in these verses is that in grief God will be moved to mercy, and grieving mothers will find their lost children. Israel will return home and have a future.

In reading these verses, you may have noticed that the focus is upon Ephraim, that is, the northern kingdom, Israel. Judah is not explicitly mentioned (compare 31:7–9 which is similar). In the context where we find this poem (as well as the poem in verses 7–9), amidst material concerned with the restoration of both Israel and Judah (30:3), we likely hear the promise of restoration applying to both Israel and Judah after the Babylonian exile. However, it may well be that these poems which are about Ephraim (or the northern kingdom, Israel) did not originally address the crisis of the Babylonian exile. The northern kingdom, Israel, had fallen to Assyria in 722 B.C. and had existed as a territory of the Assyrian empire until the collapse of that empire about the time Josiah became king in Judah (about 620 B.C.). It is widely recognized that Josiah's efforts to restore Judah after a century of Assyrian domination included an effort to reunite the former territory of Israel with Judah, thus reestablishing a nation equivalent to that ruled over by David and Solomon. This poem and perhaps the one found in Jeremiah 31:7–9 may have been associated originally with the effort of Josiah to reunite Judah and the former territory of Israel. However, in the complicated process by which the book of Jeremiah was formed, these poems have been included in such a way that they refer to restoration after the Babylonian exile.

Jeremiah 31:23–30

31:23 **Thus says the LORD of hosts, the God of Israel: Once more they will use these words in the land of Judah and in its towns when I restore their fortunes:**

> **"The LORD bless you, O abode of righteousness,**
> **O holy hill!"**

24 **And Judah and all its towns shall live there together, and the farmers and those who wander with their flocks.**

> 25 **I will satisfy the weary,**
> **and all who are faint I will replenish.**

26 **Thereupon I awoke and looked, and my sleep was pleasant to me.**
27 **The days are surely coming, says the LORD, when I will sow the house of Israel and the house of Judah with the seed of humans and the seed of animals.** 28 **And just as I have watched over them to pluck up and break down, to overthrow, destroy, and bring evil, so I will watch over them to build and to plant, says the LORD.** 29 **In those days they shall no longer say:**

> **"The parents have eaten sour grapes,**

and the children's teeth are set on edge."
[30] **But all shall die for their own sins; the teeth of everyone who eats sour grapes shall be set on edge.**

Both sections of this text, verses 23–26 and 27–30, imagine what life will be like for the people when God has finally restored them. The concern of this material for restoration is obvious in verse 28, which picks up a major theme of the book as a whole, God's plucking up and breaking down, God's building and planting. The Lord, who had watched over the word (see 1:12) to pluck up, would finally watch over the word to build.

The first section, verses 23–26, contains a quotation of what God's people *will say in praise of God* when they are restored to the land (v. 23). God will be acknowledged as the source of renewed blessing in the land. Verses 24–25 portray God's blessing upon the land in specific terms. The second section, verses 27–30, also quotes God's people after their restoration, but this quotation indicates what the people *will no longer say in complaint* against God after their restoration (v. 29). Grumbling about the fairness of God's judgment will cease, and the appropriateness of God's justice will be recognized (in Ezek. 18, this same quotation about the fathers eating sour grapes is cited as a complaint of those exiled). Through the use of these two quotations, the two sections are complementary in imagining how, when God has finally restored the people, they will come to a favorable view of God that was undoubtedly lacking during the exile itself.

Verse 26 is difficult to understand and thought by most to have been added by a later editor of the book. Some have related this verse to the vision of the prophet Zechariah (Zech. 4). Another possibility is that the verse is suggesting that restoration will result in the reversal of the covenant curse of Deuteronomy 28:65–67 and the possibility of fitful sleep.

Jeremiah 31:31–34

31:31 **The days are surely coming, says the LORD, when I will make a new covenant with the house of Israel and the house of Judah.** [32] **It will not be like the covenant that I made with their ancestors when I took them by the hand to bring them out of the land of Egypt—a covenant that they broke, though I was their husband, says the LORD.** [33] **But this is the covenant that I will make with the house of Israel after those days, says the LORD: I will put my law within them, and I will write it on their hearts; and I will be their God, and they shall be my people.** [34] **No longer shall they teach one another, or say to each other, "Know the LORD," for they shall all know me, from the least of them to the greatest, says the LORD; for I will forgive their iniquity, and remember their sin no more.**

This is undoubtedly one of the best known texts in the book of Jeremiah if not the entire Bible. As Christians, we have understood that God's new covenant with us is accomplished through Jesus. However, it is also important that we first hear God's promise of a new covenant within the book of Jeremiah itself.

God established a covenant with Israel at Sinai (Exodus 20–24). The covenant was based upon that which God had done for Israel: "I am the Lord your God who brought you out of the land of slavery, out of the house of slavery" (Ex. 20:1; but also see Jer. 11:6–7). The covenant stipulated how the people were to shape their community in response to God (the purpose, for instance, of the Ten Commandments in Exod. 20: 2–17). The first and most basic commandment or covenant stipulation was that Yahweh, the God who had freed Israel from slavery, was alone to be Israel's God (Ex. 20:3).

Within Jeremiah 1–29, the people are accused of breaking God's covenant and bringing upon themselves covenant curse because they have not obeyed; that is, they have not responded to God appropriately (11:1–13; 14:21; 22:9). In particular, Israel and Judah are accused of forsaking God for the baals (1:16; 2:13, 17; 5:7, 19; 9:13; 12:7; 16:11; 17:13; 19:4; 22:9). Interestingly, the word "baal" also means husband or master. So God's covenant with Israel established God as Israel's master (husband, "baal"), but Israel forsook their rightful master for another (see particularly 2:14–19).

Thus, verses 31–34 are about the coming days when God will establish a "new covenant" with the people. The assumption of these verses is that judgment occurred because the people broke covenant by forsaking God for another husband (master, or "baal"; v. 32). If God intends to restore Israel and Judah, then a new covenant is needed to replace the one that had been broken. Or to say this in another way, if the reason for God's plucking up and tearing down is that Israel and Judah have broken covenant, then building and planting will require a new covenant.

The new covenant that is imagined in these verses differs in one significant way from the old covenant that had been broken. The first, broken covenant was written on tablets of stone. With the new covenant, God will write the covenant and its stipulations on the heart of the people. In Jeremiah 1–29, concerned with why God's judgment had occurred, a problem with the "heart" of God's people is often identified. Remember that for ancient Israel, the "heart" was not, as we often think of it, the seat of emotions, but instead the seat of human will or volition. The problem with God's people, Jeremiah charges, is that they have a bad heart, they will the wrong things and rebel against God. One passage is particularly significant as we look at God's promise of a new covenant. In Jeremiah 17:1, Jeremiah charges, "The sin of Judah is written with an iron pen; with a diamond point it is engraved on the tablet of their hearts . . ." No wonder God's people broke covenant! Their hearts were overwritten with sin that led them away from God. If the people are to enter into a new covenant, God will need to change their hearts and turn them back to God. That is exactly what verse 33 affirms that God will do: correct the "heart" problem of God's people.

With a new "heart," God and the people will again be in relationship: "I will be their God and they shall be my people (v. 33; see 30:22; 31:1). A consequence of the "new covenant" will be that at last all of the people will "know" God (v. 34). Throughout Jeremiah 1–29, the prophet has leveled the accusation that Israel and Judah did not or even refused to know God (2:8; 4:22; 5:4; 8:7; 9:3–6). "Knowledge" in the book of Jeremiah is not about an intellectual discernment of some fact about God; rather, to "know" God meant to be devoted to God and to obey God. Israel and Judah, according to Jeremiah, were neither devoted to God nor did they obey. Jeremiah 31:31–34 looks toward that day when God has established a new covenant and corrected the "heart" problem of the people so all will "know" God.

The last phrase of verse 34 provides the basis for God's promise of a "new covenant" and, more broadly, God's decision that after plucking up and tearing down there will be building and planting. The new covenant, along with the whole of God's promise to build and plant, is rooted in the inexplicable decision of God to forgive the "iniquity" of the people and remember their sin no more (v. 34). Building and planting, restoration to the land, and God's new covenant do not automatically follow plucking up and tearing down. The promised new covenant rests upon God's decision to forgive and not remember sin. God's decision opens the possibility for restoration, for building and planting, for a new covenant and a fresh start between God and the people.

We need to be careful about how we hear this powerful promise of God. In the book of Jeremiah, the promise is given to those who experienced the exile of 587 B.C. Those exiled experienced in very specific ways God's plucking up and tearing down, and this promise offers the hope of a new relationship and a fresh opportunity to be God's devoted and obedient people. The promise of a "new covenant" is not about Jesus or about God's gathering of the church, but about newness offered by God after Judah's Babylonian exile.

Of course, the writers of the New Testament affirm that in Jesus, God entered into a new covenant with humanity. This view is held particularly in Hebrews 8:8–13; 9:15–22; and 10:16—17, but it is also found in Paul (2 Corinthians 3) and in the words of institution of the Lord's Supper (Matt. 26:28; 1 Cor. 11:25). As Christians, we surely want to affirm that through Jesus, God has established a new relationship with humanity, which includes even us "Gentiles." As one commentator on this passage said, "To know Christ is to know God according to the spirit of Jer. 31:31–34" (Habel, p. 249). However, God's promise of a "new covenant" was not made first to Christians but to the Jewish survivors of the Babylonian exile. As Christians, we may borrow the idea of a "new covenant" as a way to express the newness that in God's grace we have experienced in Jesus. Still, "new covenant" does not belong to Christians exclusively, but it is also to our Jewish brothers and sisters, to whom God's promise of newness was made first. Walter Brueggemann states the matter bluntly:

> At best we may say that Christians come derivatively and belatedly to share the promised newness. This is not to deny Christian participation in the newness, though Christian participation is utterly grounded in Jewish categories and claims, and can have participation on no other terms. (*Jeremiah 26–52*, p. 73)

Jeremiah 31:35–37

31:35 **Thus says the LORD,**
      who gives the sun for light by day
      and the fixed order of the moon and the stars for light by night,
      who stirs up the sea so that its waves roar—
      the LORD of hosts is his name:
  36 **If this fixed order were ever to cease**
      from my presence, says the LORD,
      then also the offspring of Israel would cease
      to be a nation before me forever.
  37 **Thus says the LORD:**
      If the heavens above can be measured,
      and the foundations of the earth below can be explored,
      then I will reject all the offspring of Israel
      because of all they have done,
      says the LORD.

Two examples are offered, one in verses 35–36 and the second in verse 37, that indicate the Lord's enduring commitment to Israel and Judah. The final passage in verses 38–40 will also make this same point.

Verse 35 celebrates the "fixed order" of God's creation: the moon, the stars, and the sea. We have encountered before in the book of Jeremiah the claim that God is sovereign not only over nations and kingdoms (1:10) but over the whole created order (8:7; 10:12; 14:1–6; 23:24; 27:5–6; compare Psalms 46–48). Verse 36 builds upon this quick, one verse reminder of God's cosmic sovereignty and affirms that the people will "cease to be a nation" only if God's "fixed order" were to cease. Though in our time we might be inclined to reflect about the fragile ecology of the world and the danger that human abuse might collapse the created order (these are important concerns, to be sure), the point of these verses is straightforward. God's creation is not likely to collapse anytime soon, and God's promised restoration of Judah and Israel will last a long time, too.

The second example in verse 37 makes the same point. The unfathomable expanse of God's creation is stressed. Only when someone is able to measure "the foundations of earth" (see Psalms 18:7, 15; 82:5; Isa. 24:18; 58:12) will God reject Israel. Of course, the thought of measuring the foundations of the earth is absurd, as absurd as the idea that God will ultimately reject Israel. Already in Jeremiah 31, we have heard God reflect about rebellious Ephraim, "I still remember him . . . I am deeply moved for him; I will surely have mercy on him" (v. 20).

Jeremiah 31:38–40

31:38 **The days are surely coming, says the LORD, when the city shall be rebuilt for the LORD from the tower of Hananel to the Corner Gate.** [39] **And the measuring line shall go out farther, straight to the hill Gareb, and shall then turn to Goah.** [40] **The whole valley of the dead bodies and the ashes, and all the fields as far as the Wadi Kidron, to the corner of the Horse Gate toward the east, shall be sacred to the LORD. It shall never again be uprooted or overthrown.**

Mount Zion, the Temple standing upon it, as well as the whole city of Jerusalem, symbolized for Judah the presence of God and God's enduring commitment to Judah. Jeremiah severely criticized Judah's smug self-assurance that God would not hold Judah accountable, that somehow the Temple would guarantee Judah's well-being even if they rejected God and exploited their neighbors. Judah's self-assured smugness was one of the causes of judgment, of God's decision to uproot and overthrow Judah, Jerusalem, the Temple, and all of those who falsely assumed that their relationship with God was inviolable.

God's restoration will bring a time when Jerusalem will be restored.

God will carefully measure out the city as a sacred place (in a similar vein, see Ezekiel 40–48). Even the places profaned by the dead (though not stated, one might assume the bodies are of those killed in Babylonian invasion of Judah, see 8:2; 16:4–6; 20:6; 22:19; 25:33) will again be "sacred to the Lord" (v. 40). When the city is restored, God promises, it will "never again be uprooted or overthrown."

At least for some within the Jewish community, a passage such as this one, especially in view of the horror of the Holocaust, has given impetus to Zionism, the movement within Judaism to establish Israel as a Jewish homeland. Within Christian scriptures, we see another direction. "Jerusalem" becomes a symbol for God's presence, sanctification, and coming reign (Heb. 12:18–24; Gal. 4:26; Revelation 21).

Jeremiah 32:1–15

32:1 **The word that came to Jeremiah from the LORD in the tenth year of King Zedekiah of Judah, which was the eighteenth year of Nebuchadrezzar.** [2] **At that time the army of the king of Babylon was besieging Jerusalem, and the prophet Jeremiah was confined in the court of the guard that was in the palace of the king of Judah,** [3] **where King Zedekiah of Judah had confined him. Zedekiah had said, "Why do you prophesy and say: Thus says the LORD: I am going to give this city into the hand of the king of Babylon, and he shall take it;** [4] **King Zedekiah of Judah shall not escape out of the hands of the Chaldeans, but shall surely be given into the hands of the king of Babylon, and shall speak with him face to face and see him eye to eye;** [5] **and he shall take Zedekiah to Babylon, and there he shall remain until I attend to him, says the LORD; though you fight against the Chaldeans, you shall not succeed?"**

[6] **Jeremiah said, The word of the LORD came to me:** [7] **Hanamel son of your uncle Shallum is going to come to you and say, "Buy my field that is at Anathoth, for the right of redemption by purchase is yours."** [8] **Then my cousin Hanamel came to me in the court of the guard, in accordance with the word of the LORD, and said to me, "Buy my field that is at Anathoth in the land of Benjamin, for the right of possession and redemption is yours; buy it for yourself." Then I knew that this was the word of the LORD.**

[9] **And I bought the field at Anathoth from my cousin Hanamel, and weighed out the money to him, seventeen shekels of silver.** [10] **I signed the deed, sealed it, got witnesses, and weighed the money on scales.** [11] **Then I took the sealed deed of purchase, containing the terms and conditions, and the open copy;** [12] **and I gave the deed of purchase to Baruch son of Neriah son of Mahseiah, in the presence of my cousin Hanamel, in the presence of the witnesses who signed the deed of purchase, and in the presence of all the Judeans who were sitting in the court of the guard.** [13] **In their presence I**

charged Baruch, saying, ¹⁴ Thus says the LORD of hosts, the God of Israel: — wait

charged Baruch, saying, [14] Thus says the LORD of hosts, the God of Israel: Take these deeds, both this sealed deed of purchase and this open deed, and put them in an earthenware jar, in order that they may last for a long time. [15] For thus says the LORD of hosts, the God of Israel: Houses and fields and vineyards shall again be bought in this land.

The story of Jeremiah's purchase of a family field in his home town, Anathoth, reports another symbolic action by the prophet similar to those we have already encountered in the book (for instance, the loin cloth in Jeremiah 13 or the yoke bars in 27–28). Through these symbolic actions, the prophet illustrated or gave symbolic expression to his preaching. Jeremiah's purchase of a field in Anathoth is a symbolic action that illustrates the prophet's confidence that God will eventually restore Judah, that God intends not only plucking up and tearing down but also building and planting (1:10).

We are introduced to this story in verses 1–5. First, we are informed of the historical setting for this story (vv. 1–2). It is the last year of the reign of King Zedekiah of Judah (he ruled Judah for ten years, from 597 to 587 B.C.) when Nebuchadrezzar, the king of Babylon, was besieging Jerusalem. This is a story that is set in the very last days before Judah fell to Babylon in 587 B.C. In the unfolding story of the book of Jeremiah, this story takes us right up to the moment of Judah's captivity (1:3). God had threatened to destroy Judah and Jerusalem, and with Nebuchadrezzar at the gates of Jerusalem, what God had threatened through Jeremiah is inevitable and all but accomplished. As this story begins, there can be no doubt that God will pluck up and tear down Judah.

Second, we are told that Jeremiah was confined in prison by King Zedekiah because Jeremiah had prophesied that God would allow the capture of Judah by Babylon (vv. 3–5). While we have seen that Jeremiah was often in conflict with the leadership of Judah (for instance, Jeremiah 26, where he was seized after speaking at the Temple), this is the first time we have been told Jeremiah was imprisoned. (Details of Jeremiah's imprisonment will follow in Jeremiah 37:11–21.) The significance of Jeremiah's imprisonment is that it demonstrated that the leadership of Judah, and especially the king, had indeed failed to heed God's word (see, for instance, 26:5–6; 29:19) and rejected God's prophet. With Babylon at the walls of Jerusalem, the introductory verses of this chapter make clear that God will fulfill the word of judgment announced through Jeremiah. As this story about Jeremiah's purchase of a family field begins, God is about to destroy Judah because Judah's leaders have not listened to or obeyed God's word.

There will be no escape from judgment; God will pluck up and tear down Judah.

With the scene set, the plot unfolds to emphasize that God's word will be fulfilled. We have heard this claim in the introduction to the story (vv. 1–5), and we encounter this claim again in verses 7–8. God tells Jeremiah that his cousin, Hanamel, will visit him and tell him, "Buy my field that is at Anathoth, for the right of redemption is yours" (v. 7). That is exactly what occurred (v. 8). God's word was fulfilled.

Some background about the right of redemption is helpful to understand this story. "Redemption" is described in Leviticus 25:25–28 as a transaction by which one buys back a piece of property that a relative has had to sell because of financial difficulty. In ancient Israel, this practice would have been especially important because the land a family possessed was considered an "inheritance" from God and a sacred trust. To lose a family field would have been to lose one's part of the promised land entrusted to one's family by God. It is difficult for us in our culture, where property is readily sold, to appreciate fully the significance of the loss of family property in a culture where property was viewed as a link to one's relationship with God. Redemption was a family obligation to buy back property lost by relatives because of economic distress. Only later was "redemption" related to God's activity, especially in the latter portions of the book of Isaiah where God is frequently called Israel's redeemer (Isa. 43:1; 44:22–23; 48:20; 52:9; 63:9).

In the case of our story, Hanamel, Jeremiah's cousin, must have lost a field in Anathoth because of financial difficulty. He comes to Jeremiah with the request that Jeremiah purchase the field, that is, "redeem" it. Given the circumstances in Judah at the time this request came to Jeremiah, to acquire land was not very prudent. After all, Babylon had surrounded Jerusalem, and Judah was about to be taken over by a foreign power. A real estate investment at such a moment could at best be called ill-advised. Yet Jeremiah, having been instructed by God to purchase the field, does so. Verses 9–14 provide exhausting detail about the transaction: the price of the field (v. 9; the cost is given in weighed silver; coins of specified value were not yet used); the execution of the deeds (vv. 10–11; one copy of the deed is sealed and one is public); the public signing of the deeds before witnesses (vv. 11–12; we are introduced to Jeremiah's secretary, Baruch); provision is even made for the storage of the deeds so that they will "last for a long time" (v. 14). The point of all of these details is to stress that Jeremiah's purchase of the field is to be public and witnessed and a record of the event is to be preserved.

But why? Remember that God had instructed Jeremiah to redeem his cousin's field, so the very public act is to be a way through which Jeremiah is to be God's spokesperson. At the very conclusion of the story, we finally come to the "punch line" of the event. God speaks through Jeremiah to announce, "Houses and fields and vineyards shall again be bought in this land" (v. 15). The beginning of this story stresses God's word of judgment and how God is about to fulfill that word. God will pluck up and tear down Judah's houses, fields, and vineyards as God has said. However, at the very moment when this word of judgment is to be fulfilled, God speaks through Jeremiah another word, a word about another day when God will restore life in the land. What appears to be a foolish real estate transaction is a sign that points to the future God intends for Judah. Even as the word of judgment has been fulfilled, so, too, will God in time fulfill this promise of restoration. Of course, for those in Jerusalem about to be overrun by the Babylonians, God's promise must have seemed as nonsensical as Jeremiah's purchase of real estate. Yet, through the purchase of this field, God has spoken a new word whose fulfillment, though not evident, is sure in the "coming" days. Thus, Jeremiah's purchase of the field, an act that announces God's promised restoration, needs to be public, witnessed, and carefully kept so that it will last a long time.

It is often difficult to see past the chaos and disarray of our world and our lives. The morning newspaper on the day I write this is filled with stories about two acts of terrorism in Israel through which many people have lost their lives or been maimed. Alongside the story of the terrorist act in Israel, the newspaper reports a tragic and senseless automobile accident that resulted in the death of a promising young high school athlete. My local church congregation mourns the premature death of one of our faithful saints. Our world is often a place of death and chaos. Yet that is not all. There is another word God speaks that is trusted in the church as God's word about what will be, even when it is beyond our imagination:

> And I heard a loud voice from the throne saying,
>> "See, the home of God is among mortals.
>> He will dwell with them as their God; they will be his people,
>>> and God himself will be with them;
>> he will wipe every tear from their eyes.
>> Death will be no more;
>> mourning and crying and pain will be no more,
>>> for the first things have passed away."
> And the one who was seated on the throne said, "See, I am making all things new." Also he said, "Write this, for these words are trustworthy and true."
>
> (Rev. 21:3–5)

Jeremiah 32:16–25

32:16 **After I had given the deed of purchase to Baruch son of Neriah, I prayed to the LORD, saying:** [17] **Ah LORD GOD! It is you who made the heavens and the earth by your great power and by your outstretched arm! Nothing is too hard for you.** [18] **You show steadfast love to the thousandth generation but repay the guilt of parents into the laps of their children after them, O great and mighty God whose name is the LORD of hosts,** [19] **great in counsel and mighty in deed; whose eyes are open to all the ways of mortals, rewarding all according to their ways and according to the fruit of their doings.** [20] **You showed signs and wonders in the land of Egypt, and to this day in Israel and among all humankind, and have made yourself a name that continues to this very day.** [21] **You brought your people Israel out of the land of Egypt with signs and wonders, with a strong hand and outstretched arm, and with great terror;** [22] **and you gave them this land, which you swore to their ancestors to give them, a land flowing with milk and honey;** [23] **and they entered and took possession of it. But they did not obey your voice or follow your law; of all you commanded them to do, they did nothing. Therefore you have made all these disasters come upon them.** [24] **See, the siege-ramps have been cast up against the city to take it, and the city, faced with sword, famine, and pestilence, has been given into the hands of the Chaldeans who are fighting against it. What you spoke has happened, as you yourself can see.** [25] **Yet you, O LORD God, have said to me, "Buy the field for money and get witnesses"—though the city has been given into the hands of the Chaldeans.**

Following the story of Jeremiah's purchase of the field at Anathoth, the remainder of Jeremiah 32 is a prayer of Jeremiah (vv. 16–25) and God's response to the prayer (vv. 26–44).

Jeremiah's prayer is in three parts. The prayer begins with an extensive reflection upon God's character and ways (vv. 17–22). Jeremiah's prayer affirms the scope of these deeds as well as the Lord's power to accomplish what God intends (for instance, "Nothing is too hard for you," v. 17). An affirmation of God's faithfulness ("steadfast love to the thousandth generation") balances the recognition of God's judgment (v. 19). Central to this part of Jeremiah's prayer is the prophet's remembrance of the exodus, the primary way Israel and Judah knew God. In this prayer, the remembrance of the exodus functions to illustrate the claims made about God's power at the prayer's beginning, that "nothing is too hard for you" (v. 17). A series of phrases in verses 20–22 summarize the exodus deliverance from slavery in Egypt which, like the world's creation, God accomplished with an "outstretched arm" (vv. 17, 21; compare Deut. 26:8, but also see Jer. 21:5; 27:5 where God's outstretched arm will be used in judgment). The memory of the land stresses that God makes and keeps promises (v. 22) and functions within Jeremiah 32 to complement the claim of the story of the purchase of the field, certainty that God's word will be fulfilled.

The second part of Jeremiah's prayer shifts the focus from what God did to what the people failed to do when they entered the land. Verse 23, with its condemnation of God's people, might well serve as a brief summary statement for much of the book of Jeremiah up to this point. In prayer, Jeremiah recognizes that the people have not obeyed God, and of all that God has commanded, they have done nothing; therefore, God has made "disasters" come upon them. Of course, Jeremiah has warned again and again that if Judah failed to obey God, "disaster" or "evil," specifically Babylonian captivity, would result (1:14; 2:13; 4:6; 6:1; 11:11; 18:11; 19:15). As Jeremiah prays, the Babylonians are besieging Jerusalem (v. 24). This second section of Jeremiah's prayer concludes with an affirmation about God that has been woven throughout Jeremiah 32: "What you spoke has happened" (v. 24). God told Jeremiah that his cousin would visit him, and he did (vv. 6–8); God promised land to Israel's ancestors and gave it (v. 22); the judgment God had threatened was executed (vv. 23–24); what God intended occurred, and nothing was too hard for God (v. 17). Jeremiah's prayer is not to request something from God but to praise God who spoke a word and fulfilled it.

Jeremiah's prayer concludes (v. 25) by returning to the purchase of the field in Anathoth, and one senses that through his prayer Jeremiah is testing the premise he has just affirmed: God fulfills God's word, and nothing is too hard for God. Jeremiah seems to be posing to God the question, Are you serious having me "buy the field for money" even as the Chaldeans are ready to take Jerusalem? The prophet and we readers await God's response.

Jeremiah 32:26–44

32:26 **The word of the LORD came to Jeremiah:** [27] **See, I am the LORD, the God of all flesh; is anything too hard for me?** [28] **Therefore, thus says the LORD: I am going to give this city into the hands of the Chaldeans and into the hand of King Nebuchadrezzar of Babylon, and he shall take it.** [29] **The Chaldeans who are fighting against this city shall come, set it on fire, and burn it, with the houses on whose roofs offerings have been made to Baal and libations have been poured out to other gods, to provoke me to anger.** [30] **For the people of Israel and the people of Judah have done nothing but evil in my sight from their youth; the people of Israel have done nothing but provoke me to anger by the work of their hands, says the LORD.** [31] **This city has aroused my anger and wrath, from the day it was built until this day, so that I will remove it from my sight** [32] **because of all the evil of the people of Israel and the people of Judah that they did to provoke me to anger—they, their kings and their officials, their priests** and their prophets, the citizens of Judah and the inhabitants of Jerusalem. [33] They have turned their backs to me, not their faces; though I have taught them persistently, they would not listen and accept correction. [34] They set up their abominations in the house that bears my name, and defiled it. [35] They built the high places of Baal in the valley of the son of Hinnom, to offer up their sons and daughters to Molech, though I did not command them, nor did it enter my mind that they should do this abomination, causing Judah to sin.

[36] Now therefore thus says the LORD, the God of Israel, concerning this city of which you say, "It is being given into the hand of the king of Babylon by the sword, by famine, and by pestilence": [37] See, I am going to gather them from all the lands to which I drove them in my anger and my wrath and in great indignation; I will bring them back to this place, and I will settle them in safety. [38] They shall be my people, and I will be their God. [39] I will give them one heart and one way, that they may fear me for all time, for their own good and the good of their children after them. [40] I will make an everlasting covenant with them, never to draw back from doing good to them; and I will put the fear of me in their hearts, so that they may not turn from me. [41] I will rejoice in doing good to them, and I will plant them in this land in faithfulness, with all my heart and all my soul.

[42] For thus says the LORD: Just as I have brought all this great disaster upon this people, so I will bring upon them all the good fortune that I now promise them. [43] Fields shall be bought in this land of which you are saying, It is a desolation, without human beings or animals; it has been given into the hands of the Chaldeans. [44] Fields shall be bought for money, and deeds shall be signed and sealed and witnessed, in the land of Benjamin, in the places around Jerusalem, and in the cities of Judah, of the hill country, of the Shephelah, and of the Negeb; for I will restore their fortunes, says the LORD.

God's response begins very similarly to Jeremiah's prayer and confirms that Jeremiah has been correct in his affirmations. Jeremiah has addressed God praying, "Ah, Lord God" (v. 17), and God responds saying, "I am the Lord" (v. 27). Jeremiah had affirmed that God made "the heavens and the earth" (v. 17); in response, God's self-identification is as "the God of all flesh" (v. 27). Jeremiah asserts that "Nothing is too hard for you" and God responds by turning the prophet's assertion into a question, "Is anything too hard for me?" a question whose answer is certainly to be, "No!" The way Jeremiah's prayer and God's response echo one another suggests that Jeremiah and God are at least thinking similarly.

The remainder of God's response is presented in three parts, all of which explore God's sovereign power for which nothing is too hard:

a. The first exploration of the claim that nothing is too hard for God concerns the judgment of Judah (vv. 28–36). Note how the word "therefore" connects the question "Is anything too hard for me" with God's declaration, "I am going to give this city into the hands of the Chaldeans" (vv. 27–28). We have seen repeatedly in the book of Jeremiah that Judah had been unable to imagine that God might destroy Jerusalem or that Babylon might serve God's purposes. Jeremiah was in prison for prophesying such a treasonous notion. God's judgment had been beyond Judah's imagining, but with Babylon at the gates of Jerusalem (v. 29), God's power to speak a word and fulfill it, to intend judgment and execute it, are beyond dispute. The long series of accusations in verses 30–35 again offer in summary charges that God has brought against Judah through Jeremiah throughout the book. Notable are the charges that God's people "would not listen" though God had taught them persistently (v. 33) and that they worshiped the baals in the valley of Hinnom though God had not commanded it. The people have ignored God's word and the result will be destruction by Babylon (v. 36).

b. The second exploration of the claim that nothing is too hard for the Lord concerns Judah's restoration (vv. 37–41). With Babylon besieging Jerusalem, God's restoration of Judah seemed unimaginable and "too hard" even for God. By placing promises for restoration right alongside of the announcement of judgment in verses 36 and 37, these verses stress how very unlikely restoration was. If God intends to give Jerusalem "into the hand of the king of Babylon," what hope can there be? Restoration is "too hard" to imagine from within the besieged walls of Jerusalem. However, God's response to Jeremiah insists upon restoration with the same vehemence with which God has insisted upon judgment.

God's announcement of restoration (vv. 37–41) provides a catalog of promises, many of which echo those found in Jeremiah 30–31 (and may be some later editors' elaboration of these prior chapters):

1. God promises to bring God's people back to their land (v. 37; compare 30:10; 31:8–9; 31:10–11).
2. God promises renewed relationship, "They shall be my people, I will be their God" (v. 38; compare 30:22; 31:1; 33).
3. God will give the people a "heart" so they will "fear" God (v. 39–40; compare 31:33–34).
4. God will establish an "everlasting covenant" with them (v. 40; compare 31:31–34).
5. God will do "good" for the people and "plant them" (v. 41; compare 29:10; 31:40).

Nothing is too hard for God, neither judgment nor restoration.

c. The third exploration of the claim that nothing is too hard for God concerns Jeremiah's purchase of the field at Anathoth (vv. 42–44). Jeremiah's prayer ends with a gentle quizzing of God about the purchase of the field (v. 25). God's response to Jeremiah also concludes by addressing the purchase of the field. The "disaster" that God had brought upon the land resulted in "desolation" (v. 43). However, disaster and desolation are not God's final word. God's final word is the promise "I will restore their fortunes" and the assurance that the normal transactions and affairs of life will resume in Jerusalem and all of Judah. Concretely, God's promise of restoration is expressed in the assurance "fields shall be bought for money" (v. 44).

God's response to Jeremiah's prayer affirms the necessity of God's judgment and justifies God's decision to pluck up and tear down (vv. 26–36). However, beyond plucking up and tearing down, God intends building and planting. God promises to "restore the fortunes" of the people (vv. 37–44) and assures them that "houses and fields and vineyards shall again be bought in this land" (vv. 1–15). For God, who made "the heavens and the earth" (v. 17) and who is sovereign of "all flesh" (v. 27), nothing is "too hard" (vv. 17, 27). Beyond the imagination of Judah's leaders, God can pluck up and tear down. Beyond the imagination of those exiled in Babylon, God can build and plant.

It is not difficult to imagine how preposterous this chapter must have seemed to those persons exiled to Babylon in 587 B.C. and for whom the book of Jeremiah was originally intended. While there was the assurance that God would restore them and that nothing was "too hard" for God, those exiled in Babylon must have strained to find these claims believable. Perhaps our situation is not so different. We in the church live in the promise of God's coming reign, but personal struggles, community problems, and global issues make it difficult to see signs of God's reign and live with hope. Yet Sunday by Sunday we pray, "thy kingdom come." To be a Christian is to believe with Jeremiah beyond our ability to imagine it that God, for whom nothing is "too hard," intends and acts for newness in our broken lives, communities, and world. As Christians, we believe that God's newness and reign will come because nothing is "too hard" for God: our personal brokenness, complex community problems, even massive global issues. Knowing that nothing is too hard for God gives us courage to join God in the struggle for justice and peace in our world.

Jeremiah 33:1–9

33:1 **The word of the LORD came to Jeremiah a second time, while he was still confined in the court of the guard:** 2 **Thus says the LORD who made the** earth, the LORD who formed it to establish it—the LORD is his name: ³ **Call to me and I will answer you, and will tell you great and hidden things that you have not known.** ⁴ **For thus says the LORD, the God of Israel, concerning the houses of this city and the houses of the kings of Judah that were torn down to make a defense against the siege-ramps and before the sword:** ⁵ **The Chaldeans are coming in to fight and to fill them with the dead bodies of those whom I shall strike down in my anger and my wrath, for I have hidden my face from this city because of all their wickedness.** ⁶ **I am going to bring it recovery and healing; I will heal them and reveal to them abundance of prosperity and security.** ⁷ **I will restore the fortunes of Judah and the fortunes of Israel, and rebuild them as they were at first.** ⁸ **I will cleanse them from all the guilt of their sin against me, and I will forgive all the guilt of their sin and rebellion against me.** ⁹ **And this city shall be to me a name of joy, a praise and a glory before all the nations of the earth who shall hear of all the good that I do for them; they shall fear and tremble because of all the good and all the prosperity I provide for it.**

Jeremiah 33:1 links this chapter to the prior chapter by indicating that while still a prisoner Jeremiah received a second word from the Lord (see 32:1). Many details of Jeremiah 33 build upon or expand issues and themes already introduced in Jeremiah 30–32. There is a lot of repetition. For instance, the affirmation that God "made the earth" (v. 3) is part of Jeremiah's prayer in the prior chapter (32:17); Jeremiah 32 is concerned with "houses, vineyards, and fields" (vv. 15, 25, 44), and Jeremiah 33 mentions houses torn down to defend Jerusalem (v. 4). The description of Judah in Jeremiah 32:44 and 33:13 is almost identical; God's restoration of governmental order is promised in Jeremiah 30:20–21 and is the concern of Jeremiah 33:14–28; the promise of God's enduring commitment to Israel and Judah in Jeremiah 33:19–26 is similar to the promises in Jeremiah 31:35–37; finally, God's promise to "restore the fortunes" of Judah, an important theme in Jeremiah 30–32 (30:3, 18; 31:23; 32:44) is repeated twice in Jeremiah 33 (vv. 11, 26). The repetition and/or elaboration of material from Jeremiah 30–32 suggest that Jeremiah 33 may have been added by editors of the book of Jeremiah to reinforce what they found already in the book or to give a particular point of view about certain matters.

Verses 1–9 are concerned with the restoration of God's people expressed through a series of statements in verses 6–9. These promises of restoration are the "great and terrible things that you have not known" about which God invites Jeremiah to inquire (v. 3). These verses concern that which is not yet evident, God's building and planting.

However, God's building and planting can be understood only against the backdrop of plucking up and tearing down. So God's first concern is to describe once more why plucking up and tearing down are occurring. The Lord who "made the earth" (v. 2) continues to direct the course of events on earth. The Chaldeans were agents to enact that which God had decided: "I will strike down in my wrath . . . for I have hidden my face from this city because of all their wickedness" (v. 5). In response to the city's wickedness, God's face is hidden. In the Old Testament, to speak of God's face is to acknowledge the Lord's presence and protection (Num. 6:25; Psalm 31:16); when God's face is hidden, persons, communities, and the creation are Godforsaken (Deut. 31:17–18; Psalms 27:9; 69:17; 143:7). If God who "made the heavens and the earth" hides God's face or abandons the creation, chaos results (compare 4:23–26, where in different language a similar idea is expressed). Verses 4–6 portray the chaos that was overwhelming Jerusalem because God's face was hidden.

Those who had experienced the exile and for whom the book of Jeremiah was originally intended may have imagined that God was powerless or had arbitrarily decided to abandon Judah. Verses 4–6 assert that God has indeed abandoned Jerusalem, but in response to the city's wickedness; the Chaldeans express God's decision to "strike down," and houses have been torn down in Jerusalem because the Lord intended it. Jeremiah would have well understood this explanation of God's decision to pluck up and tear down Judah and Jerusalem.

The "great and terrible" things the prophet has not known (v. 3) are God's decisions made after plucking up and tearing down expressed in four phrases in verses 6–9:

"I am going to bring it recovery and healing; I will heal them . . .
                    (v. 6; compare 30:12–17)

"I will restore the fortunes of Judah . . . and Israel"
                    (v. 7; compare 30:3, 18; 31:23; 32:44)

"I will cleanse them from all the guilt of their sin"
                    (v. 8; compare 31:34)

"I will forgive all the guilt of their sin and rebellion against me"
                                                              (v. 8)

These new decisions do not negate God's decision to pluck up and tear down but are decisions by which God moves beyond anger and wrath (v. 5). The city that through judgment has become a desolation will again know "prosperity" (v. 9). The city that had become "a horror, a thing to be hissed at forever" so that all who passed by were horrified and shook their heads (18:16) will become for God a "joy, a praise and a glory before all the nations of the earth who shall hear of all the good that I do for them" (v. 9). Through God's decision to heal, restore, cleanse and forgive, the people will experience renewal and prosperity. The nations that witness this restoration, will also be brought to a new relationship with God: "they shall fear and tremble" (v. 9).

Thus, God who made the heavens and the earth claims continuing sovereignty over the creation. God's sovereignty has been exercised in anger and wrath, but God will not turn God's face away forever. Beyond the decision to tear down, God will also exercise sovereignty in healing, restoring, cleansing, and forgiving. Ultimately, God intends to relate graciously to Israel and Judah and to all nations.

Jeremiah 33:10–11

33:10 **Thus says the LORD: In this place of which you say, "It is a waste without human beings or animals," in the towns of Judah and the streets of Jerusalem that are desolate, without inhabitants, human or animal, there shall once more be heard [11] the voice of mirth and the voice of gladness, the voice of the bridegroom and the voice of the bride, the voices of those who sing, as they bring thank offerings to the house of the LORD:**

> **"Give thanks to the LORD of hosts,**
> **for the LORD is good,**
> **for his steadfast love endures forever!"**

For I will restore the fortunes of the land as at first, says the LORD.

These verses assume that judgment has occurred. In announcing judgment, Jeremiah proclaims that in Judah and Jerusalem, God will bring desolation to the land and will "end the sound of mirth and gladness, the voice of the bride and bridegroom" (7:34; 16:9; 25:10). Marriages insure that communities will continue for another generation and have a future. Jeremiah's vision of Judah with no marriages means that Judah has no future. The sense of verse 10 is that life has ceased in Judah, and Jerusalem has become a city "without"—without human beings, animals, inhabitants.

Yet through Jeremiah we hear in these verses what God intends after Judah's destruction. Once more the mirth-filled and joyous voices of brides and bridegrooms will be heard in Judah singing thanks for God's goodness and "steadfast love." God promises that life that has ceased in Judah will begin again, and Judah will again have a future. Beyond plucking up and tearing down, God intends building and planting. The theme of Jeremiah 30–33 is sounded at the conclusion of verse 11: "I will restore the fortunes of the land as at first, says the Lord."

The hymn that is quoted in verse 11 is from Psalm 136:1, which recalls God's "steadfast love" as the basis for God's care and deliverance: in the creation (Psalm 136:4–9), in Israel's exodus from Egypt (Psalm 136:10–15), in leading Israel through the wilderness to the promised land (Psalm 136:16–22), and in the provision of food for all flesh (v. 25). Jeremiah announces that Judah and Israel will have a future, but only because of God's "steadfast love." In Jeremiah 2, God's people are remembered as once being "devoted" to God (2:2). The Hebrew word translated in Jeremiah 2:2 as "devotion" is the word translated for "steadfast love" in Psalm 136 as quoted in verse 11. It has been suggested that the sense of this Hebrew word is best expressed in English as "loyalty" (Sakenfeld, *Loyalty: Faithfulness in Action*). What has become clear through the Book of Jeremiah is that God's people are far from loyal or devoted to God. Any relationship between God and the people, and any future that might be possible, will need to depend upon God's loyalty, upon God's "steadfast love."

The psalmist knows that God's "steadfast love" is the basis of God's relationship with the creation from the beginning, the basis of Israel's relationship with God from the beginning, and the basis of God's relationship with all flesh. Jeremiah knows that if Judah is to have a future, that future will be grounded in God's "steadfast love." In writing about the relationship of Christians to God through baptism, the writer of 1 Peter declares:

By his great mercy he has given us a new birth into a living hope through the resurrection of Jesus Christ from the dead, 4and into an inheritance that is imperishable, undefiled, and unfading, kept in heaven for you, 5who are being protected by the power of God through faith for a salvation ready to be revealed in the last time.

(1 Peter 1:3–5)

The future of God's people has been and always will be grounded in God's "steadfast love," God's great mercy.

Jeremiah 33:12–13

33:12 **Thus says the LORD of hosts: In this place that is waste, without human beings or animals, and in all its towns there shall again be pasture for shepherds resting their flocks.** 13 **In the towns of the hill country, of the Shephelah, and of the Negeb, in the land of Benjamin, the places around Jerusalem, and in the towns of Judah, flocks shall again pass under the hands of the one who counts them, says the LORD.**

The beginning of verse 12 repeats the beginning of verse 10. Verses 12–13, like verses 10–11, assume that Judah has been destroyed and reduced by judgment to a "waste." As in much of Jeremiah 30–33, the promise given in these verses is that God will restore that which has been destroyed. So the land "without human beings or animals" will again become a place where in pastures shepherds will keep their flocks. In portraying God's judgment of Judah, Jeremiah announces drought, for instance, that will decimate pastures and flocks (14:1–6). After God's judgment, these verses imagine renewal of the land and resumption of herding. The geographic designations in verse 13 repeat those mentioned in Jeremiah 32:44 and indicate God's restoration of the entire land.

The phrase "flocks shall again pass under the hands of the one who counts them," at the end of verse 13 is interesting. It may only carry forward the pastoral images of these verses to suggest the tranquillity and order that will prevail when God restores Judah. However, the book of Jeremiah refers to Judah's kings as "shepherds" whose inattention to God's flock has resulted in the flock being scattered (that is, exiled; see 23:1–4). Verse 13 may suggest God's establishment of a new social order in Judah, namely, a new king or shepherd who will be attentive to the flock, God's people, in a way that the shepherds who allowed Judah to be exiled have not been (compare Ezekiel 34; John 10). This way of understanding verse 12 is also suggested because the material that follows in verses 14–26 is concerned with the God's restoration of the Davidic monarchy.

Jeremiah 33:14–18

33:14 **The days are surely coming, says the LORD, when I will fulfill the promise I made to the house of Israel and the house of Judah.** [15] **In those days and at that time I will cause a righteous Branch to spring up for David; and he shall execute justice and righteousness in the land.** [16] **In those days Judah will be saved and Jerusalem will live in safety. And this is the name by which it will be called: "The LORD is our righteousness."**

[17] **For thus says the LORD: David shall never lack a man to sit on the throne of the house of Israel,** [18] **and the levitical priests shall never lack a man in my presence to offer burnt offerings, to make grain offerings, and to make sacrifices for all time.**

Verses 14–18 concern God's restoration of the Davidic monarchy (and, to a much lesser extent, a Levitical priesthood) after judgment. Though charges against Judah's kings can be found throughout the book of Jeremiah, chapters 21:11–23:8 provide a significant concentration of material about the ways in which Judah's kings contributed to Judah's judgment.

However, in Jeremiah 23:5–8 there is a brief section indicating God's promise to restore the Davidic monarchy. The present section of Jeremiah 33 should be read as an expansion of God's promises to restore the Davidic monarchy first expressed in Jeremiah 23. Because these verses are not part of the Greek version of the book of Jeremiah, it is often suggested that they were a late addition to the book.

Verses 14–15 repeat Jeremiah 23:5–6 with one change. In Jeremiah 23 the *king* will be called "The Lord.is our righteousness," while in verses 14–15 it is *Jerusalem* (more will follow about this). The promise to which God refers in verse 14 is surely that of 2 Samuel 7:8–15. While God's promise to the house of David was "forever" (2 Sam. 7:13, 16), the Babylonian exile created a tension about God's promise that is reflected in the book of Jeremiah. God promises "forever," but Judah's destruction and the exile of Judah's last legitimate king, Jehoiachim, make God's promise suspect. One way that the book of Jeremiah tries to deal with God's seeming failure to keep promise with the house of David is to lay responsibility for the exile and what happened on Judah's kings themselves. The kings of Israel and Judah were charged to be God's agents of justice and righteousness (Psalm 72:1–4), and the failure of Judah's kings to fulfill this mandate resulted in judgment, exile, and the end of the monarchy (see especially 22:13–17).

Another way in which the book of Jeremiah tries to deal with what seems like God's broken promise to the house of David is found in these verses (and in Jeremiah 23), which announce that "the days are surely coming" when God will keep the promise and restore the monarchy. In contrast to the kings who were responsible for God's judgment, God will raise up a Davidic king who will "execute justice and righteousness in the land" (v. 15). Of course, the well-being of the whole land was a result of the righteousness of the king. Unjust kings brought destruction to the land (22:1–9), whereas a just and righteous king would bring blessing and prosperity to the land (Psalm 72). As the restoration of Judah is portrayed in Jeremiah 33, God's promise to establish a just and righteous king on the throne of David is connected with well-being in Judah and safety in Jerusalem. In other words, God will rightly order Jerusalem, and the city can appropriately be called, "The Lord is our righteousness" (v. 16).

Verses 17–18 may reflect developments in Judah many years after the exile had occurred. They envision the people ruled by both a Davidic king and a Levitical priest (on God's promises to the Levites, see Deut. 18:1–8). After the exile, priests had significant roles in shaping the life of Judah. These verses seem to reflect a situation in which the priest is more important than the king. In these verses, at least, the priests are assigned specific duties (making sacrifices) while the kings are assigned none. The community of God's people is presented in these verses more as a theocracy ruled by priests than a monarchy ruled by kings. In addition to reflecting the actual conditions of Judah after the exile, this perspective may reflect a negative view of kings who, according to the book of Jeremiah, bore considerable responsibility for the exile in the first place.

Jeremiah 33:19–26

33:19 **The word of the LORD came to Jeremiah:** [20] **Thus says the LORD: If any of you could break my covenant with the day and my covenant with the night, so that day and night would not come at their appointed time,** [21] **only then could my covenant with my servant David be broken, so that he would not have a son to reign on his throne, and my covenant with my ministers the Levites.** [22] **Just as the host of heaven cannot be numbered and the sands of the sea cannot be measured, so I will increase the offspring of my servant David, and the Levites who minister to me.**

[23] **The word of the LORD came to Jeremiah:** [24] **Have you not observed how these people say, "The two families that the LORD chose have been rejected by him,"** **and how they hold my people in such contempt that they no longer regard them as a nation?** [25] **Thus says the LORD : Only if I had not established my covenant with day and night and the ordinances of heaven and earth,** [26] **would I reject the offspring of Jacob and of my servant David and not choose any of his descendants as rulers over the offspring of Abraham, Isaac, and Jacob. For I will restore their fortunes, and will have mercy upon them.**

Verses 19–22 and 23–26 speak of God's enduring promise to the house of David and to the Levites (vv. 19–22) and to all of Israel (vv. 23–26). The phrase that holds this material together is "my covenant with the day and with the night" (vv. 19, 25). Verses 19–22 and 23–26 claim that only if God broke covenant with the day and night, in other words, allowed the entire order of creation to collapse, would God break covenant (v. 21) with David or the Levites, or "reject the offspring of Jacob" (v. 26, but also v. 24). The restoration that God intended would be enduring.

These verses draw upon a variety of Old Testament traditions about God's enduring promises. For instance, God's covenant with the day and the night remind us of Genesis 1 where day and night were created by God on the first day. Although covenant is not directly mentioned in Genesis 1, Jeremiah 33 uses the phrase "my covenant with the day and night" to express God's enduring commitment to God's creation. Perhaps we can also hear in these verses echoes of the story of the Flood (Genesis 6–9), after which God resolved to sustain the creation (Gen. 8:22) and made a covenant with Noah never again to "cut off" humanity by a flood (Gen 9:8–17). Finally, in verse 22 and then more directly in verse 26 there are references to God's promises to Israel's ancestors, to Abraham and Sarah. The language of verse 22 is similar to that used in God's promise to Abraham in Genesis 22:17 (compare Gen. 15:5) that he would have many offspring (see, too, Gen. 12:1–3, God's promise to bless Abraham). Reference to the promises to the ancestors is quite direct in verse 26, where God promises not to "reject" the offspring of Abraham, Isaac, and Jacob. Verses 22–26 recall God's enduring commitment to the creation, at the Flood, and to Jacob's ancestors.

Within Jeremiah 30–33, these verses are quite similar in intent to Jeremiah 31:35–40, which also indicate God's enduring commitment never again to uproot or overthrow (31:40). Further, the final verse of Jeremiah 33 restates the theme of Jeremiah 30–33, that God will "restore their fortunes" and so brings this section of the book to a conclusion with the same promise with which the Book of Comfort began (30:3). Judah's great guilt and numerous sins brought about God's decision to pluck up and tear down (30:14–15). God's "mercy" finally will result in another decision by God, to build and to plant and so "restore the fortunes of Israel and Judah."

"I Am Going to Give This City into the Hand of the King of Babylon"
Jeremiah 34–38

While Jeremiah 30–33 emphasizes God's intention to build and plant Israel and Judah, restoration is a possibility promised only after God's judgment. Jeremiah 34–38 again emphasizes God's intention to pluck up and tear down Judah because they had turned from God and failed to respond to God's prophet Jeremiah. God had called Judah to repent, but they had not, so God had threatened judgment. Jeremiah 34–38 takes us closer to the fulfillment of God's threat to pluck up and tear down Judah. The backdrop for Jeremiah 34–38 has "the foe from the North," Babylon, besieging Jerusalem.

Jeremiah 34–38 has as a major theme that God is handing Jerusalem over to the Babylonians, who will burn it with fire. The fiery destruction of Jerusalem is explicitly threatened in Jeremiah 34:2, 22; 36:32; 37:8, 10; 38:17–18, 23. Complementing the theme of the fiery destruction of Jerusalem is a continuing concern for Judah's obedience, if they had listened and obeyed (in Hebrew the same word means both listen and obey) as God spoke through a messenger, Jeremiah (Jer. 34:14, 17; 35:8, 10, 13, 14, 15, 16, 17, 18; 36:24; 37:2; 38:15, 20). These chapters, as we will expect, link Judah's failure to listen and obey with Jerusalem being burned.

There is a careful arrangement to these five chapters. They are introduced in Jeremiah 34:1–5, which recounts an encounter between Jeremiah and Judah's King Zedekiah when the Babylonian army is besieging Jerusalem. Jeremiah announces to Zedekiah, "I am going to give this city into the hand of the king of Babylon, and he shall burn it with fire" (34:2). The announcement sets the theme for the five chapters, the fiery destruction of Jerusalem that will occur because of Judah's failure to hear and obey God's word.

Jeremiah 34–35 is a pair of chapters that contrast the obedience of the Rechabites with the disobedience of Judah. Though Judah's leaders had made the decision to release slaves, an action that accorded with the stipulations of their covenant with God, they later reneged and took back their slaves. Judah's failure to honor its covenant with God draws harsh condemnation from Jeremiah and the warning that Jerusalem will be burned (34:22). By contrast, the Rechabites, despite their very difficult circumstances, continue to observe the strict terms of obedience to God commanded by their founder, Jonadab (see especially 35:12–17). Jeremiah 34–35 provides sharply contrasting examples of obedience by the Rechabites and disobedience by Judah.

Jeremiah 37–38 also is a pair of chapters that recount the imprisonment of the prophet Jeremiah during the siege of Jerusalem by the Babylonians. Jeremiah 37 begins with a summary of the situation in Judah in which neither Zedekiah "nor his servants not the people of the land listened to the words that he [the Lord] spoke" through the prophet Jeremiah. Jeremiah, even from prison, continues to threaten the fiery destruction of Jerusalem (37:8, 10; 38:17–18, 23), but Jeremiah's imprisonment signals that Judah is not willing to listen to or obey God. Judah's rejection of Jeremiah seals God's decision to destroy Jerusalem (37:17–18 especially). Thus, Jeremiah 34–35 and 37–38 have the same themes and make the same point: Judah has not listened to or obeyed God, so God will hand Jerusalem over to the Babylonians, who will burn Jerusalem with fire.

Connecting these two pairs of chapters is Jeremiah 36. This chapter presents an encounter between Jeremiah and King Jehoiakim (whom Zedekiah replaced as Judah's king when Jehoiakim was exiled by Babylon in 597 B.C.). Because Jeremiah is banned from the area of the Temple, he dictates his message and has his secretary Baruch read it at a Temple gate. The scroll is seized and eventually read to King Jehoiakim. As Jehoiakim listens to the scroll in his winter house, he cuts away sections of Jeremiah's scroll as it is read and burns it in the fire. The connection to the themes of the surrounding chapters is obvious. Judah has refused to listen to and obey God's word, and that refusal is dramatically portrayed when Jehoiakim burns the scroll containing the words of Jeremiah. Because Jehoiakim has burned God's word, God will burn Jerusalem.

These five chapters, and much of the material through Jeremiah 45, are presented as a biographical recounting of events in which Jeremiah participated. It may well be that Jeremiah did participate in the events that are recounted. However, as we have found repeatedly in the book of Jeremiah, the point of these chapters is not to offer an historically accurate account of exactly what occurred. The primary interest is, as throughout the book, theological. The concern is with what God was doing and why, and how

God's people were responding. So Jeremiah 34–38, while providing some basis for reconstructing the events near the time of the Babylonian invasion of Judah, mostly attempts to explain why God brought judgment against Judah and Jerusalem. Again we are invited to understand why God directed Judah's history toward captivity (1:3).

Jeremiah 34:1–7

34:1 **The word that came to Jeremiah from the LORD, when King Nebuchadrezzar of Babylon and all his army and all the kingdoms of the earth and all the peoples under his dominion were fighting against Jerusalem and all its cities:** 2 **"Thus says the LORD, the God of Israel: Go and speak to King Zedekiah of Judah and say to him: Thus says the LORD: I am going to give this city into the hand of the king of Babylon, and he shall burn it with fire.** 3 **And you yourself shall not escape from his hand, but shall surely be captured and handed over to him; you shall see the king of Babylon eye to eye and speak with him face to face; and you shall go to Babylon.** 4 **Yet hear the word of the LORD, O King Zedekiah of Judah! Thus says the LORD concerning you: You shall not die by the sword;** 5 **you shall die in peace. And as spices were burned for your ancestors, the earlier kings who preceded you, so they shall burn spices for you and lament for you, saying, "Alas, lord!" For I have spoken the word, says the LORD.**

6 **Then the prophet Jeremiah spoke all these words to Zedekiah king of Judah, in Jerusalem,** 7 **when the army of the king of Babylon was fighting against Jerusalem and against all the cities of Judah that were left, Lachish and Azekah; for these were the only fortified cities of Judah that remained.**

God instructs Jeremiah to deliver an oracle to King Zedekiah while the Babylonians are besieging Jerusalem in 588–587 B.C. (v. 1; compare 21:1–7 for another encounter between Zedekiah and Jeremiah). Further details of Judah's situation are provided in verse 7. The Babylonian siege of Jerusalem is far advanced. Siege warfare was common in the ancient Near East. A conquering army will besiege a capital city, cutting it off from military reinforcement, food, and, if possible, water. The conquering army will then systematically destroy outlying military strongholds so that the capital city was increasingly isolated. These verses suggest that the Babylonians had made considerable progress in Judah, so that only two fortified cities remained a part of Jerusalem (v. 7). Lachish and Azekah were located 23 and 18 miles southwest of Jerusalem, respectively. Among the remains at Lachish, archaeologists have found a letter written during the Babylonian siege of 588–587 B.C. from a military outpost between Lachish and Azekah . The outpost commander wrote:

And let my lord know that we are watching for the signals of Lachish according to all the indications which my lord has given, for we cannot see Azekah. (*ANET*, p. 329)

Azekah had apparently fallen to the Babylonians. One can sense that in Jeremiah 34 there is a good deal of historically useful information.

The report of Jerusalem's precarious situation introduces (v. 1) and concludes (vv. 6–7) these verses, but their main concern (in vv. 2–5) is the fate of Jerusalem and King Zedekiah's own fate at the hands of the Babylonians. The overwhelming force that Jerusalem faced is stressed by the repetition of the word "all." "All" of Nebuchadrezzar's army and "all the kingdoms of the earth and all peoples" under Nebuchadrezzar are fighting against "Jerusalem and all its cities" (v. 1). Because Jerusalem is so close to falling, an urgency surrounds all that is said and happens in these chapters. God has spoken a word of judgment, and that word is about to be fulfilled. King Zedekiah and all of Judah with him can no longer delay in responding to God.

Jeremiah's message to King Zedekiah is in two parts. In verses 2–3, Jeremiah announces that Jerusalem will fall to the Babylonians, who will burn it with fire (v. 2). This threat is a theme that will be evident through Jeremiah 38. The way these verses mix God's speech (in the first person, "I am going to give . . .") with description of what the king of Babylon will do (in the third person, "he shall burn it . . .") make clear that the Babylonian king will act as God's agent of judgment. With the inevitable fall of Jerusalem, Jeremiah also warns that King Zedekiah will meet the king of Babylon "eye to eye" and "face to face" (see 2 Kings 25:6–7 for a brief description of this encounter) and be exiled (v. 3). Zedekiah has been presented in the book of Jeremiah as reluctant to accept God's judgment and Judah's defeat (see 21:1–10). The prospects with which Jeremiah confronts Zedekiah, meeting the king of Babylon and being exiled, are quite bleak.

So, Jeremiah's more tempered word to Zedekiah (vv. 4–5) is quite surprising. In another encounter with Zedekiah, Jeremiah announces a much harsher judgment (21:7). Furthermore, the king's actual end is horrible; his sons are killed in front of him before his eyes are put out and he is taken to Babylon (39:5–9; 52:11). Zedekiah hardly dies "in peace" (v. 4). It has often been suggested that Jeremiah must be understood to be speaking conditionally to Zedekiah at this point; Jeremiah presents the best case scenario if Zedekiah will surrender to Babylon and accept God's judgment (see 21:9). In the book of Jeremiah, the prophet certainly is presented as speaking conditionally on some occasions. For instance, in Jeremiah

22:1–10, Jeremiah addresses the kings of Judah by offering a choice: "If you will obey this word . . . but if you will not heed these words . . ." (22:4–5, and also see 21:9 and 18:5–11). Understood in this way, Jeremiah may have been saying to Zedekiah, if you surrender, you will die in peace; however, if you continue to resist the Babylonians, it will be worse for you (for instance, the judgment threatened in Jeremiah 21).

As we continue through the book of Jeremiah, we encounter Zedekiah several more times (34:8–22; 37:1–21; 38:14–28). Reluctant to accept God's judgment and defeat by Babylon, Zedekiah is presented in the book of Jeremiah as a model of one to whom God spoke but who will not listen, to whom God called but will who not answer (35:17).

Jeremiah 34:8–22

34:8 The word that came to Jeremiah from the LORD, after King Zedekiah had made a covenant with all the people in Jerusalem to make a proclamation of liberty to them, 9 that all should set free their Hebrew slaves, male and female, so that no one should hold another Judean in slavery. 10 And they obeyed, all the officials and all the people who had entered into the covenant that all will set free their slaves, male or female, so that they will not be enslaved again; they obeyed and set them free. 11 But afterward they turned around and took back the male and female slaves they had set free, and brought them again into subjection as slaves. 12 The word of the LORD came to Jeremiah from the LORD: 13 Thus says the LORD, the God of Israel: I myself made a covenant with your ancestors when I brought them out of the land of Egypt, out of the house of slavery, saying, 14 "Every seventh year each of you must set free any Hebrews who have been sold to you and have served you six years; you must set them free from your service." But your ancestors did not listen to me or incline their ears to me. 15 You yourselves recently repented and did what was right in my sight by proclaiming liberty to one another, and you made a covenant before me in the house that is called by my name; 16 but then you turned around and profaned my name when each of you took back your male and female slaves, whom you had set free according to their desire, and you brought them again into subjection to be your slaves. 17 Therefore, thus says the LORD: You have not obeyed me by granting a release to your neighbors and friends; I am going to grant a release to you, says the LORD—a release to the sword, to pestilence, and to famine. I will make you a horror to all the kingdoms of the earth. 18 And those who transgressed my covenant and did not keep the terms of the covenant that they made before me, I will make like the calf when they cut it in two and passed between its parts: 19 the officials of Judah, the officials of Jerusalem, the eunuchs, the priests, and all the people of the land who passed between the parts of the calf 20 hall be handed over to their enemies and to those who seek their lives. Their corpses shall become food for the birds of the air and the wild animals of the earth. [21] And as for King Zedekiah of Judah and his officials, I will hand them over to their enemies and to those who seek their lives, to the army of the king of Babylon, which has withdrawn from you. [22] I am going to command, says the LORD, and will bring them back to this city; and they will fight against it, and take it, and burn it with fire. The towns of Judah I will make a desolation without inhabitant.

This story assumes the historical setting of the first verses of the chapter. It is about a release of slaves that is presumed to have occurred while Babylon was besieging Jerusalem in 588–587 B.C. There is little reason to question that something like what is remembered in these verses actually did occur. The event is recounted in two parts. First, we are told of a decision, involving King Zedekiah, to release slaves, and then of a subsequent decision to return them to slavery (vv. 8–11). Second, we are told what Jeremiah said on God's behalf to rebuke the decision to re-subjugate the slaves (vv. 12–22). This speech of Jeremiah consists of an accusation against Judah (vv. 12–16) that serves as the basis for an announcement of judgment (vv. 17–22).

Scholars have been able to use these verses to construct a likely sequence of events. It has been suggested that Zedekiah decided to make a covenant with the inhabitants of Jerusalem to release the slaves while the Babylonians were besieging the city (vv. 8–9). There is good logic for this proposal, inasmuch as during a siege, food and water become scarce. The release of slaves will have allowed slave owners to save valuable resources that slaves will have consumed. Then, with the approach of an Egyptian army (see 37:5), the Babylonians temporarily withdrew their siege and King Zedekiah and others in Jerusalem reconsidered their decision. Without the pressure of the siege, the release of slaves probably was not considered so necessary, and the decision was made to bring the slaves back into subjection (v. 11). This scenario is at least a plausible historical reconstruction of what may have occurred.

However, in recounting these events, our text is not interested in merely reporting what occurred. Rather, the story as we have it is most interested in what the event indicated about Judah's relationship with God. The story remembers how King Zedekiah took initiative to establish a "covenant" with the inhabitants of Jerusalem, which provided for the release of Hebrew slaves. Those to be released were Judeans held as slaves by other Judeans (vv. 8–9), probably because of unpaid debt (see below). Of course, we know that God took the initiative to establish a covenant with Israel. However, the "covenant" Zedekiah established should not be confused with the covenant at Sinai. The "covenant" initiated by Zedekiah was an agreement among the inhabitants of Judah to release slaves. This initiative of King Zedekiah to establish a "covenant" may also be intended to remind us of King Josiah, who led Judah to enter a covenant with God when he undertook the great reform of Judah several decades earlier (2 Kings 23:1–3; see Introduction).

While Zedekiah's covenant calling for the release of slaves was not the Sinai covenant, legal traditions rooted in the Sinai covenant did make provision for the release of Hebrew slaves held by other Hebrews. Jeremiah appeals to these legal and covenantal traditions as he responds to the "covenant" established by Zedekiah (v. 14) by referring to legal provisions in Deuteronomy 15 (also see Exodus 21:1–11):

> Every seventh year you shall grant a remission of debts. And this is the manner of the remission: every creditor shall remit the claim that is held against a neighbor, not exacting it of a neighbor who is a member of the community, because the LORD'S remission has been proclaimed. (Deut. 15:1)

> If a member of your community, where a Hebrew man or a Hebrew woman, is sold to you and works for you six years, in the seventh year you shall set that person free. (Deut. 15:12)

The release of Hebrew slaves in the time of Zedekiah, whatever motivated it, was at least consistent with the Sinai covenant as it had come to be understood. So the report of the release of slaves concludes on a positive note as Jeremiah affirms the obedience of the king and the inhabitants of Jerusalem (v. 10).

Verse 11 is pivotal in this story. It reports that the slave owners "turned around" and took back the slaves that had been set free. Throughout the book of Jeremiah we have heard Jeremiah call to Judah to "turn" from their evil or "return" to God (for instance, 3:14, 22; 4:1; 18:8; 26:3), though there is little to indicate they responded. Ironically, verse 11 reports that Judah finally did "turn back," but their turning was away from the covenantal obedience of releasing Hebrew slaves. The remainder of the chapter concerns God's response through Jeremiah to Judah's turning from obedience to disobedience.

That response places the release of slaves in historical and covenantal perspective. The covenant that commanded that slaves be released every seventh year was rooted in God's deliverance of Israel when they were slaves in Egypt (v. 14) and the Lord of Israel sided with them against their oppressive masters. Covenantal law required that Israel and Judah be communities in which God's concern for the marginal and oppressed be enacted concretely. So, those who became slaves due to their economic circumstances were not to be held in slavery forever. The covenant stipulations provided for a periodic social and economic adjustment when Hebrew slaves were to be released (again, see Exod. 21:1–11 and Deuteronomy 15). Those stipulations provided the ground for God to affirm the decision of those in Jerusalem to release their slaves. At last, God was able to see that Judah had "recently repented and did what was right in my sight" (vv. 14–15). Regretfully, God's affirmation of Judah has to be tempered by a "but" for which verse 11 has prepared us. The "but" is that Judah, after repenting and doing what was right in God's sight, "turned around and profaned my name" by bringing their slaves into subjection once more. Having repented and turned to God, Judah quickly turned from God again. Any hope that Judah might at last embrace the covenant is dashed. Judah remains disobedient.

In verses 12–16, God as a prosecutor presents charges and develops a case against Judah. Verses 17–22 announce the consequences of Judah's covenantal disobedience in three parts:

a. God's sentence is announced first by a play on the word "release" (v. 17). Judah has sinned in the matter of the "release" of slaves, so God announces a punishment of "release," God's release of covenant curse. The accusation against Judah makes specific reference to the legal tradition of the book of Deuteronomy (Deut. 15:12–18); the curse of Judah becoming a "horror" echoes the covenant curses of the book of Deuteronomy (Deut. 28:37).

b. Verses 18–20 refer to a ritual of covenant-making that is also referred to in Genesis 15:7–11 and 17. In this ritual, an animal is cut in half, and those entering the covenant walk between the halves of the carcass. The implication is that should the covenant be broken, the offending party will suffer the same fate, death, as the sacrificial animal (v. 18). The description of the ritual is used to introduce an account of concrete, historical enactment of covenant curse on Judah. God will hand the leaders of Judah over to their enemies, and they will be killed. The vivid image of corpses being devoured by birds and beasts is found among the covenant curses in Deuteronomy 28:26. With Babylon outside the walls of Jerusalem, the imagery of this curse will have been powerful.

c. Finally, King Zedekiah himself is sentenced by God. God had made a covenant with the people and kept it. Even King Josiah had made a covenant and sustained it so that Judah was again obedient (2 Kings 23). King Zedekiah is not like faithful Josiah, and his efforts to keep covenant are certainly nothing like the faithfulness of God. While Zedekiah and

Jerusalem turn toward covenantal obedience (v. 15), they quickly turn back to disobedience (vv. 11, 16). The judgment announced against Zedekiah is that God will "bring . . . back" against Jerusalem the Babylonian army that had withdrawn, and they will burn the city and make it a desolation (compare the covenant curse of Deut. 28:47ff.). Thus, the following sequence is suggested: Judah's repentance in releasing slaves has resulted in God's turning back the Babylonian army; however, Judah's turning back and re-subjecting their slaves will result in God bringing back the Babylonians to burn the city. The concluding threat that the Babylonians will burn Jerusalem (v. 22) is where this chapter begins (v. 2).

Jeremiah 34 is rooted in Israel's earliest memory of the Lord who freed slaves from the oppression of Egypt (v. 13). The God of the exodus made a covenant with Israel that provided specific ways for God's commitment to the marginalized and oppressed to be lived out in community. Hebrew slaves were not to be enslaved forever, but released every seventh year. Jeremiah 34 builds upon an understanding of who the Lord of the exodus is and what covenantal relationship demands. However, the chapter underscores the covenantal disobedience of Judah's leadership and the covenant curses that result.

The church is reminded by this story that God also calls the church to reflect in its life whom it has known God to be in Jesus Christ:

> Now by this we may be sure that we know him, if we obey his commandments. Whoever says, "I have come to know him," but does not obey his commandments, is a liar, and in such a person the truth does not exist; but whoever obeys his word, truly in this person the love of God has reached perfection. By this we may be sure that we are in him: whoever says, "I abide in him," ought to walk just as he walked.
>
> . . . Whoever says, "I am in the light," while hating a brother or sister, is still in the darkness. Whoever loves a brother or sister lives in the light, and in such a person there is no cause for stumbling. But whoever hates another believer is in the darkness, walks in the darkness, and does not know the way to go, because the darkness has brought on blindness. (1 John 2:3–6; 9–11)

Through Jesus Christ we have known God as the light of the world, and we are called to live in that light by how we relate to our brothers and sisters in the church.

Jeremiah 35:1–19

35:1 **The word that came to Jeremiah from the LORD in the days of King Jehoiakim son of Josiah of Judah: 2 Go to the house of the Rechabites, and** speak with them, and bring them to the house of the LORD, into one of the chambers; then offer them wine to drink. ³ So I took Jaazaniah son of Jeremiah son of Habazziniah, and his brothers, and all his sons, and the whole house of the Rechabites. ⁴ I brought them to the house of the LORD into the chamber of the sons of Hanan son of Igdaliah, the man of God, which was near the chamber of the officials, above the chamber of Maaseiah son of Shallum, keeper of the threshold. ⁵ Then I set before the Rechabites pitchers full of wine, and cups; and I said to them, "Have some wine." ⁶ But they answered, "We will drink no wine, for our ancestor Jonadab son of Rechab commanded us, 'You shall never drink wine, neither you nor your children; ⁷ nor shall you ever build a house, or sow seed; nor shall you plant a vineyard, or even own one; but you shall live in tents all your days, that you may live many days in the land where you reside.' ⁸ We have obeyed the charge of our ancestor Jonadab son of Rechab in all that he commanded us, to drink no wine all our days, ourselves, our wives, our sons, or our daughters, ⁹ and not to build houses to live in. We have no vineyard or field or seed; ¹⁰ but we have lived in tents, and have obeyed and done all that our ancestor Jonadab commanded us. ¹¹ But when King Nebuchadrezzar of Babylon came up against the land, we said, 'Come, and let us go to Jerusalem for fear of the army of the Chaldeans and the army of the Arameans.' That is why we are living in Jerusalem."

¹² Then the word of the LORD came to Jeremiah: ¹³ Thus says the LORD of hosts, the God of Israel: Go and say to the people of Judah and the inhabitants of Jerusalem, Can you not learn a lesson and obey my words? says the LORD. ¹⁴ The command has been carried out that Jonadab son of Rechab gave to his descendants to drink no wine; and they drink none to this day, for they have obeyed their ancestor's command. But I myself have spoken to you persistently, and you have not obeyed me. ¹⁵ I have sent to you all my servants the prophets, sending them persistently, saying, 'Turn now everyone of you from your evil way, and amend your doings, and do not go after other gods to serve them, and then you shall live in the land that I gave to you and your ancestors.' But you did not incline your ear or obey me. ¹⁶ The descendants of Jonadab son of Rechab have carried out the command that their ancestor gave them, but this people has not obeyed me. ¹⁷ Therefore, thus says the LORD, the God of hosts, the God of Israel: I am going to bring on Judah and on all the inhabitants of Jerusalem every disaster that I have pronounced against them; because I have spoken to them and they have not listened, I have called to them and they have not answered.

¹⁸ But to the house of the Rechabites Jeremiah said: Thus says the LORD of hosts, the God of Israel: Because you have obeyed the command of your ancestor Jonadab, and kept all his precepts, and done all that he commanded you, ¹⁹ therefore thus says the LORD of hosts, the God of Israel: Jonadab son of Rechab shall not lack a descendant to stand before me for all time.

Following Jeremiah 34, one would expect another event from the time of the Babylonian siege. However, Jeremiah 35 has its historical setting in the time of King Jehoiakim, who was king of Judah from 609–598 B.C. Undoubtedly this chapter is placed in this location in the book of Jeremiah to contrast the Rechabites with King Zedekiah and the inhabitants of Jerusalem as they are presented in Jeremiah 34. This chapter reports the visit of Jeremiah to the house of the Rechabites (vv. 1–11) and concludes with a comparison of the Rechabites to the inhabitants of Judah (vv. 12–19).

The Rechabites' origins can be traced to the time of King Jehu of Israel (842–815 B.C.). Their founder or "ancestor" was Jonadab (or Jehonadab in 2 Kings 10:15), son of Rechab (hence the name, Rechabites). The group was zealously devoted to God and staunchly opposed to baals and the fertility cults of Canaan. Their devotion had led them to participate with the soon-to-be king Jehu in the slaughter of a group of persons engaged in fertility worship and the destruction of their worship site (2 Kings 10:15–28). The Rechabites saw in Jehu a person who would restore the proper worship of God in the northern kingdom, Israel, at a time when the worship of the fertility gods posed a serious threat. The Rechabites played an important role in helping Jehu become king through a bloody revolution. We certainly need to be aware of the dangers of a group that would allow their religious zeal to lead to violence against others. The Rechabites represent a kind of religious fanaticism whose dangers we know well in our own time. Recognizing the problem, we also need to allow the text to use this potentially dangerous group to make a point.

Jeremiah's visit to the house of the Rechabites is commanded by God. Instructed to offer the Rechabites some wine, Jeremiah does so (vv. 2–5). However, the Rechabites' strong aversion to fertility cults had led them to reject many practices associated with these cults. When Jeremiah offers the Rechabites wine, they refuse by citing the commandments of their ancestor, Jonadab, which prohibited them from, among other things, drinking wine (vv. 6–7). The response of the Rechabites reveals their faithfulness to their ancestor Jonadab. Using almost identical words, verses 8 and 10 stress the Rechabites' obedience: "We have obeyed the charge of our ancestor Jonadab . . . in all that he commanded us" (v. 8); "we . . . have obeyed and done all that our ancestor Jonadab commanded us" (v. 10). The obedience of the Rechabites is the point to be understood from Jeremiah's visit to them.

Verses 12–19 are "the word of the Lord" spoken by Jeremiah contrasting the obedience of the Rechabites with the disobedience of Judah. From the obedience of the Rechabites, Judah is to learn a "lesson." The lesson assumes the narrative about Judah's disobedience in Jeremiah 34 and is presented in a carefully arranged four-part scheme that contrasts the Rechabites with the Judeans. An affirmation of the Rechabites' obedience begins and concludes the speech and surrounds two statements indicating Judah's guilt:

a. *Rechabites' obedience:* God observes that "the command has been carried out that Jonadab . . . gave to his descendants" (v. 14). The "lesson" begins by noting the Rechabites' obedience.

b. *Judah's disobedience:* God says of Judah, "But I myself have spoken to you persistently, and you have not obeyed me" (vv. 14–15). The Rechabites obeyed their long-deceased ancestor, but even though God spoke personally and persistently to Judah, they have not obeyed.

c. *Judah's disobedience:* Judah's disobedience is reinforced by a second statement of it: "I have sent . . . my prophets, sending them persistently, saying, 'Turn . . .' But you did not incline your ear or obey me" (v. 15; again, see 34:14, 17). By the use of the call to turn, we are reminded of the play on this word in Jeremiah 34: Judah finally does repent, only to turn back so that God will turn the Babylonians back on Jerusalem (34:11, 15, 16, 22).

d. *Rechabite obedience:* The "lesson" concludes with a statement that reaffirms that the Rechabites "carried out the command of their ancestor" but that Judah "had not obeyed me" (v. 16).

The contrast between the Rechabites' obedience of their ancestor and Judah's failure to listen to or obey God could hardly be made more forcefully. This text is not interested in debating the merits of the Rechabites' religious program or their fanaticism. Rather, the text wants to teach a "lesson" about obedience and disobedience. Whatever one may think of the theological ideas or religious zeal of the Rechabites, the point in Jeremiah 35 is that they obeyed their ancestor, and their obedience was in sharp contrast to Judah's disobedience of God.

The conclusion of Jeremiah 35 announces God's judgment on Judah (v. 17) but God's favorable intentions toward the Rechabites (vv. 18–19). Predictably, God will send disaster upon Judah "because I have spoken to them and they have not listened, I called to them and they have not answered." God's calls for Judah to return are in vain, and even when Judah finally does repent, it is short-lived and they soon turn back (34:11, 15, 16). Covenant curse, the Babylonian invasion, and loss of land are inevitable because Judah refuses to obey. Judah's failure in covenantal obedience will lead to plucking up and tearing down. Once more we are led to see why God directed Judah's history toward captivity (1:3).

By contrast, God promises the Rechabites that because of their obedience they will "not lack a descendant to stand before me for all time." The promise that they will have a descendant "to stand before God" suggests priestly service of some kind, though we know nothing of the Rechabites after 587 B.C. Whatever became of the Rechabites is not nearly so important as the "lesson" they offer about obedience. God had given Judah every opportunity to be an obedient community like the Rechabites by sending prophets who had called Judah persistently to "turn," but Judah mostly refused covenantal obedience; and, even when Judah did repent, they quickly turned again to disobedience (34:11, 15, 16). Had Judah been like the Rechabites, there would perhaps not be a book of Jeremiah concerned with God's plucking up and tearing down and God's building and planting beyond God's judgment of Judah.

Together, Jeremiah 34 and 35 present a contrast between one community, the Rechabites, that obeyed their ancestor, and another community, Judah, that disobeyed God's covenant. These chapters call us to look closely at the communities of faith of which we are a part to ask of their obedience. Obedience is carefully presented in these chapters as an appropriate response to the Lord's deliverance. The covenantal demand to release slaves was rooted in God's deliverance of slaves from Egypt. The question of obedience for those communities of God's people to which we belong is a question about the responsiveness of those communities to God. Because God had delivered Israel from Egypt, Judah was not free to do whatever it decided but was bound to God in covenant with its particular demands. So, too, the church is not free to do whatever we decide but is bound to the Lord of the church to witness to the good news of God's suffering love for the world. Frederick Buechner has written:

> But if good works are not the cause of salvation, they are nonetheless the mark and effect of it. If the forgiven man does not become forgiving, the loved man loving, then he is only deceiving himself. "You shall know them by their fruits," Jesus says, and here Gentle Jesus Meek and Mild becomes Christ the Tiger, becomes both at once, this stern and loving man. "Every tree that does not bear good fruit is cut down and thrown into the fire," he says, and Saint Paul is only echoing him when he writes to the Galatians, "The fruit of the Spirit is love, joy, peace, gentleness, self-control; against such there is no law.' ("Good Works," in *Listening to Your Life*, p. 260)

In Jesus Christ, God has called us to bear good fruit and awaits our response. The problem with Judah was that they had borne bad fruit with the result that God had to pluck them up and tear them down. God calls people in every time and place to bear good fruit—not as the cause of our salvation but as "the mark and effect of it."

Jeremiah 36:1–26

36:1 **In the fourth year of King Jehoiakim son of Josiah of Judah, this word came to Jeremiah from the LORD:** 2 **Take a scroll and write on it all the words that I have spoken to you against Israel and Judah and all the nations, from the day I spoke to you, from the days of Josiah until today.** 3 **It may be that when the house of Judah hears of all the disasters that I intend to do to them, all of them may turn from their evil ways, so that I may forgive their iniquity and their sin.**

4 **Then Jeremiah called Baruch son of Neriah, and Baruch wrote on a scroll at Jeremiah's dictation all the words of the LORD that he had spoken to him.** 5 **And Jeremiah ordered Baruch, saying, "I am prevented from entering the house of the LORD;** 6 **so you go yourself, and on a fast day in the hearing of the people in the LORD's house you shall read the words of the LORD from the scroll that you have written at my dictation. You shall read them also in the hearing of all the people of Judah who come up from their towns.** 7 **It may be that their plea will come before the LORD, and that all of them will turn from their evil ways, for great is the anger and wrath that the LORD has pronounced against this people."** 8 **And Baruch son of Neriah did all that the prophet Jeremiah ordered him about reading from the scroll the words of the LORD in the LORD's house.**

9 **In the fifth year of King Jehoiakim son of Josiah of Judah, in the ninth month, all the people in Jerusalem and all the people who came from the towns of Judah to Jerusalem proclaimed a fast before the LORD.** 10 **Then, in the hearing of all the people, Baruch read the words of Jeremiah from the scroll, in the house of the LORD, in the chamber of Gemariah son of Shaphan the secretary, which was in the upper court, at the entry of the New Gate of the LORD's house.**

11 **When Micaiah son of Gemariah son of Shaphan heard all the words of the LORD from the scroll,** 12 **he went down to the king's house, into the secretary's chamber; and all the officials were sitting there: Elishama the secretary, Delaiah son of Shemaiah, Elnathan son of Achbor, Gemariah son of Shaphan, Zedekiah son of Hananiah, and all the officials.** 13 **And Micaiah told them all the words that he had heard, when Baruch read the scroll in the hearing of the people.** 14 **Then all the officials sent Jehudi son of Nethaniah son of Shelemiah son of Cushi to say to Baruch, "Bring the scroll that you read in the hearing of the people, and come." So Baruch son of Neriah took the scroll in his hand and came to them.** 15 **And they said to him, "Sit down**

and read it to us." So Baruch read it to them. [16] When they heard all the words, they turned to one another in alarm, and said to Baruch, "We certainly must report all these words to the king." [17] Then they questioned Baruch, "Tell us now, how did you write all these words? is it at his dictation?" [18] Baruch answered them, "He dictated all these words to me, and I wrote them with ink on the scroll." [19] Then the officials said to Baruch, "Go and hide, you and Jeremiah, and let no one know where you are."

[20] Leaving the scroll in the chamber of Elishama the secretary, they went to the court of the king; and they reported all the words to the king. [21] Then the king sent Jehudi to get the scroll, and he took it from the chamber of Elishama the secretary; and Jehudi read it to the king and all the officials who stood beside the king. [22] Now the king was sitting in his winter apartment (it was the ninth month), and there was a fire burning in the brazier before him. [23] As Jehudi read three or four columns, the king would cut them off with a penknife and throw them into the fire in the brazier, until the entire scroll was consumed in the fire that was in the brazier. [24] Yet neither the king, nor any of his servants who heard all these words, was alarmed, nor did they tear their garments. [25] Even when Elnathan and Delaiah and Gemariah urged the king not to burn the scroll, he would not listen to them. [26] And the king commanded Jerahmeel the king's son and Seraiah son of Azriel and Shelemiah son of Abdeel to arrest the secretary Baruch and the prophet Jeremiah. But the LORD hid them.

Jeremiah 36 is about "the word of the Lord" that came to Judah through the words of Jeremiah. Just as importantly, this chapter is about Judah's response to that word announced by Jeremiah. The sheer number of occurrences of the term "word" or "words," sixteen times in the 32 verses of this chapter, suggests the emphasis of this chapter. However, the emphasis is not, as it has been through much of the book, on Jeremiah as God's spokesperson. In fact, Jeremiah does not speak much in Jeremiah 36, and when he does it is to his secretary, Baruch, and not as public address. Instead, God's word took written form as Jeremiah, banned from the Temple, dictates his message to Baruch. The written word is then read by Baruch, first to all the people of Judah as they gather for worship (vv. 9–10), then to a group of royal officials (vv. 11–19), and finally to the king himself (vv. 20–26).

Reflecting on the importance of the written word in this chapter, Robert Carroll comments in his commentary:

As the scroll is read out to the people thronging the temple to fast, and as it moves through the various echelons of Judean society on its way to the king, the nation's destiny is determined. When the king dismisses its claims by burning it, he seals the fate of himself and his people. The threats and curses in the scroll are not destroyed by the king's . . . act but released by it. . . . The king may burn the scroll, but he cannot prevents contents becoming operative. . . . Against Yahweh's word there is not effective power, not even that of a prophet-killing king. (*Jeremiah*, p. 663)

Or, to say the point of Jeremiah 36 in a slightly different manner, Jehoiakim might be able to ban the prophet from public speech and burn his scroll, but such actions only insure that the Babylonians will burn Jerusalem as God intends. God is shaping Judah's history, and King Jehoiakim is powerless to resist God's sovereign intentions announced through Jeremiah's spoken and written words.

The scroll Jeremiah dictated to Baruch was to contain "all the words" Jeremiah had spoken from the time of Josiah in the hope that when Judah heard the "disaster" God intended, they will "turn from their evil ways" so God could forgive them (vv. 2–3). The date of the events narrated in Jeremiah 36, if authentic or the addition of an editor, should be noted. The "fourth year of King Jehoiakim" marks the date when Babylon emerged as the political and military power in the ancient Near East. What God has threatened in vague terms, "the foe from the north" or "a boiling pot tilted away from the north" (1:11–14), has begun to take concrete historical form. The scroll is presented at the beginning of Jeremiah 36 as a last chance for Judah. The sense is that Judah, in hearing all of the words of the prophet at once, will understand the gravity of their crisis and "turn from their evil ways." One more time, God sets before Judah the chance to turn from evil and avoid evil.

The sense that God is offering Judah one last chance is reinforced in verses 4–10. "All the words" (v. 4) are to be read by Baruch on Jeremiah's behalf "in the hearing of all the people" (v. 6) in the hope that "all of them will turn from their evil ways" (v. 7). So, as "all the people in Jerusalem and all the people who came from the towns of Judah to Jerusalem" gather to observe a fast, Baruch reads the words of Jeremiah from the scroll "in the hearing of all the people" (vv. 9–10). There can be no excuse: All the people hear all the words about all the disasters God intends. The issue is, how will Judah respond?

We need to hear in two ways this call for all the people to respond to all of the prophets' words so they can all repent. One way we need to hear this plea is as part of the story that is unfolding in the book of Jeremiah. God has spoken through Jeremiah repeatedly to call Judah to "turn," but to no avail. Now, one last time all the words of the prophet are to be written and read so that all of Judah will have one last chance to "turn" from their evil or face the consequences. This story contributes to the unfolding plot of the book and invites us to read further to see how Judah did respond.

However, there is a second way we need to hear this story, and that is as a call to the community of God's people after the exile for whom the book of Jeremiah was originally intended. After all, we have in Jeremiah 36 the prophet's words in written form. The appeal of this chapter is directly to those who read (or heard read) the prophet's words written on the scroll. Of course, the book of Jeremiah was originally intended for persons during or just after the Babylonian exile. In a very real sense, however, we who are reading the book of Jeremiah today are also being addressed. The chapter calls for attention to God's word, awareness of God's sovereign freedom to bring judgment, but it also affirms God's desire for repentance and the willingness of God to forgive (vv. 3, 7). The scroll of Jeremiah anticipates the gospel of Jesus Christ and the good news that empowers us to confess our sin before God:

> If we say that we have no sin, we deceive ourselves, and the truth is not in us. If we confess our sins, he who is faithful and just will forgive us our sins and cleanse us from all unrighteousness. If we say that we have not sinned, we make him a liar, and his word is not in us. (1 John 1:8–10).

The question before Judah, before those exiled in 587 B.C., and before us is if we will trust God's forgiveness, confess our sin, and turn to God or if we will continue in our deceit.

In verses 11–19, the focus shifts from "all the people" (v. 6, 9, 10) to "all the officials" (v. 13). One of the royal officials has heard Baruch read the scroll at the gate of the Temple (v. 10) and brought word of it to a group of officials gathered at the king's house (vv. 11–13). The officials request that the scroll be brought to them. Baruch is summoned to read the scroll, and when he does the officials react with "alarm" and conclude that they "must report all these words to the king" (v. 16). There is a hint here about a response to Jeremiah's scroll, but only a hint. We cannot tell if the "alarm" of the officials signaled their recognition that they needed to "turn" (v. 3) to God or, as we have seen elsewhere in the book, their dismay with Jeremiah for his treasonous announcement of Judah's doom (compare Jeremiah 26). That the officials warn Baruch to hide along with Jeremiah suggests that they feared that the king will react very negatively. In any case, the officials "pass the buck," and the scroll is ordered taken to the king.

The decision to take Jeremiah's scroll to the king as well as the persons named in the list of officials serve as reminders of another occasion when a book or scroll found at the Jerusalem Temple (Jeremiah's scroll was read at a Temple gate) was taken to the king of Judah. 2 Kings 22–23 provide an account of the discovery of a book in the Temple when King Josiah was renovating it after a long period of Assyrian domination. The high priest gave that book to the royal secretary, Shaphan, who took it to King Josiah and read it to him. It is Shaphan's grandson, Micaiah, who heard Baruch read the scroll at the Temple and brought news of it to other royal officials (v. 11). When Shaphan read the scroll found in the Temple to King Josiah, Josiah's initial response was an act of penitence; he tore his clothes (2 Kings 22:11), sought God's guidance (2 Kings 22:13–20), and finally gathered all the people and made a covenant "to follow the Lord, keeping his commandments . . . with all his heart and all his soul, to perform the words . . . that were written in this book" (2 Kings 23:3). These reminders of King Josiah invite us as we read further in Jeremiah 36 to see if King Jehoiakim will respond to Jeremiah's scroll as his father, King Josiah, responded to the scroll found in the Temple in his time.

The scroll is finally taken to King Jehoiakim and read to him as he sits in his winter house before a fire (vv. 20–22). The text records three responses by King Jehoiakim to hearing the words of Jeremiah's scroll:

1. The story recounts that after several columns had been read, Jehoiakim cut them off with a knife and threw them into the fire until the entire scroll was burned (v. 23). Jehoiakim burned the scroll despite the urging of his advisors that he not do so (v. 25). Jehoiakim's decision to burn the scroll, as noted earlier, was quite ironic. Jeremiah had warned Jehoiakim that God would have the king of Babylon burn Jerusalem with fire (34:3, 22). The response of Judah's king was to burn the scroll on which was recorded God's words of judgment. One can hardly imagine a clearer signal that the king was unwilling to listen to Jeremiah, heed God's word, or "turn" to God and seek forgiveness (vv. 3, 7). This king would not heed his own advisors (v. 25), let alone God!

2. After reporting that Jehoiakim burned the scroll, the text notes carefully, "Yet neither the king, nor any of his servants who heard all these words, was alarmed, nor did they tear their garments" (v. 24). Jehoiakim's actions sharply contrasted with those of his father, King Josiah, when he heard the words of the book found in the Temple. King Josiah was "alarmed" (compare the reactions of the royal officials in v. 16 and the comment above), so alarmed that he tore his clothes and led all Judah to enter a covenant that committed them "to perform the words . . . that were written

in this book" (2 Kings 23:3). The text wants us to see how differently King Jehoiakim and King Josiah responded when confronted by God's word.

3. Finally, King Jehoiakim commanded that Jeremiah and Baruch be arrested (v. 26). The king, who would not listen to God's word, sought to punish God's messenger. As this story unfolds in Jeremiah 36, we are to understand that King Jehoiakim and all of Judah with him refused to listen to all of the words the Lord had spoken to Jeremiah (v. 4) and that King Jehoiakim and all of Judah with him ("all of them") refused to "turn from their evil ways" and seek God's forgiveness (v. 3).

In a way, Jeremiah 36 can be read as a contest between God and King Jehoiakim. God has Jeremiah write his words on a scroll so that Judah will hear (vv. 3, 6); Jehoiakim even refuses to listen to his advisors, so it is no surprise he will not listen to God (v. 25). God threatens to burn Jerusalem (34:2, 22); Jehoiakim responds by burning the scroll that threatens Judah's destruction (v. 23). God urges that Judah "turn" (v. 3); Jehoiakim hears God's word but refuses to repent (that is, he did not tear his garment, v. 24). Yet, as Jeremiah 36 concludes, it becomes clear that King Jehoiakim will not prevail against God. A clue to the futility of King Jehoiakim's efforts to resist God's intentions is found after Jehoiakim has ordered Jeremiah and Baruch arrested as the text notes, "But the Lord hid them" (the end of v. 26; we will hear more about Jeremiah's arrest in subsequent chapters). We have already been told that the royal officials warned Baruch to hide along with Jeremiah (v. 19). Yet, this text understands that what the officials advised was actually God's doing; "the Lord hid them" (v. 26). Even Jehoiakim's own advisors participate to accomplish God's ends. King Jehoiakim will not finally be able to resist God's intentions.

Jeremiah 36:27–32

36:27 **Now, after the king had burned the scroll with the words that Baruch wrote at Jeremiah's dictation, the word of the LORD came to Jeremiah:** 28 **Take another scroll and write on it all the former words that are in the first scroll, which King Jehoiakim of Judah has burned.** 29 **And concerning King Jehoiakim of Judah you shall say: Thus says the LORD, You have dared to burn this scroll, saying, Why have you written in it that the king of Babylon will certainly come and destroy this land, and will cut off from it human beings and animals?** 30 **Therefore thus says the LORD concerning King Jehoiakim of Judah: He shall have no one to sit upon the throne of David, and his dead body shall be cast out to the heat by day and the frost by night.** 31 **And I will punish him and his offspring and his servants for their iniquity; I will bring on them, and on the inhabitants of Jerusalem, and on the people of Judah, all the disasters with which I have threatened them—but they would not listen.**

³² **Then Jeremiah took another scroll and gave it to the secretary Baruch son of Neriah, who wrote on it at Jeremiah's dictation all the words of the scroll that King Jehoiakim of Judah had burned in the fire; and many similar words were added to them.**

What is hinted in verse 26 is made explicit in verses 27–32. King Jehoiakim will not be able to defeat God by burning a scroll. God orders Jeremiah to dictate another scroll that is to include all the words of the first scroll and to which "similar words" are added (vv. 28, 32). Among the additions to the first scroll is to be a fresh condemnation of Jehoiakim himself (v. 29). The king's resistance to God's word will result in judgment on the king but also on all of Judah. Regarding King Jehoiakim, he has burned the scroll by throwing it into the fire (v. 23); God announces that Jehoiakim will be "cast out" (the same Hebrew word translated *throw* in v. 23). Regarding Judah, God has Jeremiah dictate a scroll containing all his words recorded in the hope that when Judah hears "all the disasters" God intends, they will turn and seek forgiveness (v. 3). Through the newly dictated scroll, God warns Judah of "all the disasters with which I have threatened them" (v. 31). The logic is clear: Because King Jehoiakim burned the scroll, he sealed the fate of Jerusalem, which will be burned by the Babylonians. It could have been different if Judah had only listened and turned to God (vv. 3, 31).

Quite properly, scholars have used this material from Jeremiah 36 to attempt to reconstruct the steps by which the book of Jeremiah is handed down and preserved. Thus, it has been suggested that the first scroll may have concluded at Jeremiah 25:13:

> I will bring upon that land all the words that I have uttered against it, everything written in this book, which Jeremiah prophesied against all the nations.

The first scroll, then, would have included the material now found in Jeremiah 1:4 through Jeremiah 25:13. The second scroll and later additions would finally, after a lengthy process, have resulted in the book as we have it.

However, as interesting as it is to use the information from Jeremiah 36 to think about the process by which the book of Jeremiah developed, we should not miss a larger and more important point from Jeremiah's redictation of the scroll after King Jehoiakim burned the first. The larger point is that the new scroll signals God's enduring desire to be heard and for humankind to respond. God was not defeated by Jehoiakim's effort to burn one scroll. God's word would endure and what God intended would be accomplished (see Isa. 40:8; 55:10–13). We in the church affirm this about the persistence of God's word:

> In the beginning was the Word, and the Word was with God, and the Word is God. He was in the beginning with God. All things came into being through him, and without him not one thing came into being. What has come into being in him was life, and the life was the light of all people. The light shines in the darkness, and the darkness did not overcome it. (John 1:1–5)

Finally, not even the cross is able to frustrate God's word, the Word made flesh.

Jeremiah 37:1–10

37:1 **Zedekiah son of Josiah, whom King Nebuchadrezzar of Babylon made king in the land of Judah, succeeded Coniah son of Jehoiakim. ² But neither he nor his servants nor the people of the land listened to the words of the LORD that he spoke through the prophet Jeremiah.**

³ King Zedekiah sent Jehucal son of Shelemiah and the priest Zephaniah son of Maaseiah to the prophet Jeremiah saying, "Please pray for us to the LORD our God.' ⁴ Now Jeremiah was still going in and out among the people, for he had not yet been put in prison. ⁵ Meanwhile, the army of Pharaoh had come out of Egypt; and when the Chaldeans who were besieging Jerusalem heard news of them, they withdrew from Jerusalem.

⁶ Then the word of the LORD came to the prophet Jeremiah: ⁷ Thus says the LORD, God of Israel: This is what the two of you shall say to the king of Judah, who sent you to me to inquire of me, Pharaoh's army, which set out to help you, is going to return to its own land, to Egypt. ⁸ And the Chaldeans shall return and fight against this city; they shall take it and burn it with fire. ⁹ Thus says the LORD: Do not deceive yourselves, saying, "The Chaldeans will surely go away from us," for they will not go away. ¹⁰ Even if you defeated the whole army of Chaldeans who are fighting against you, and there remained of them only wounded men in their tents, they would rise up and burn this city with fire.

Jeremiah 37 and 38 are a pair of chapters held together by several features. Their most evident concern is the effort by the leaders of Judah to silence Jeremiah during Babylon's siege of Jerusalem. He was arrested as a traitor and treated quite harshly (37:11–16; 38:1–6), though finally rescued from a life-threatening situation (38:7–13; compare 37:19–21). Another feature of these two chapters is the relationship between Jeremiah and Zedekiah. Despite the rocky relationship between prophet and king presented earlier in the book (see Jeremiah 34, 21:1–10), and even despite Jeremiah's arrest and imprisonment, three times in these chapters King Zedekiah is presented seeking Jeremiah's counsel (37:6–10, 37:17–21, 38:14–26) in the hope that the fall of Jerusalem to the Babylonians can be prevented. Finally, Jeremiah's announcement of God's judgment of Judah continues in these chapters. The threat that Jerusalem will be burned is prominent and picks up this theme from Jeremiah 34 (37:8, 10; 38:17, 18, 23; see 34:2, 22). These chapters reinforce the claim that Judah's failure to listen to God or Jeremiah, vividly portrayed when Jehoiakim burns Jeremiah's scroll, insure that Jerusalem will be burned by the Babylonians as God's judgment.

Jeremiah 37:1–2 reads as if it is an introduction to King Zedekiah. It is possible that at one time in its development, the book of Jeremiah may have been arranged in an historical sequence and Jeremiah 37 began a section about King Zedekiah. Of course, we have already been introduced to King Zedekiah earlier in the book of Jeremiah, so we know that he did not listen "to the words of the Lord that he spoke through the prophet Jeremiah" (v. 2). Zedekiah appeals to Jeremiah that the prophet "pray for us to the Lord our God," a request that indicates he still has hope that Jerusalem could be spared (v. 3). The historical note in verse 5 suggests that Zedekiah has become optimistic when, during the Babylonian siege of Jerusalem, the approach of an Egyptian army causes the Babylonians to withdraw from the city temporarily. There is historical evidence that the Egyptians did send an army into the region in 588 B.C. and disrupt the Babylonian attack on Judah in process at that time. Jeremiah dashes quickly whatever optimism Zedekiah may have had. God's word is that the Egyptians will soon return to their land and the Babylonians will return; that, in fact, it is "deceptive" to think that the Babylonians will go away (v. 9). Jeremiah repeated the threat that the Babylonians will take Jerusalem and "burn it with fire" (v. 8). Verse 10 is particularly interesting. The lore that had long surrounded Jerusalem, even before David captured the city from the Jebusites and made it the capital city of Israel (later Judah), was that it could be protected from invaders even by the blind and lame (2 Sam. 5:5–6). Jeremiah turns the sense that Jerusalem was inviolable upside down and declares that if even a single wounded Babylonian soldier remains, he will accomplish God's intention to burn Jerusalem.

Jeremiah 37:11–21

37:11 **Now when the Chaldean army had withdrawn from Jerusalem at the approach of Pharaoh's army,** [12] **Jeremiah set out from Jerusalem to go to the land of Benjamin to receive his share of property among the people there.** [13] **When he reached the Benjamin Gate, a sentinel there named Irijah son of**

Shelemiah son of Hananiah arrested the prophet Jeremiah saying, "You are deserting to the Chaldeans." [14] And Jeremiah said, "That is a lie; I am not deserting to the Chaldeans." But Irijah would not listen to him, and arrested Jeremiah and brought him to the officials. [15] The officials were enraged at Jeremiah, and they beat him and imprisoned him in the house of the secretary Jonathan, for it had been made a prison. [16] Thus Jeremiah was put in the cistern house, in the cells, and remained there many days.

[17] Then King Zedekiah sent for him, and received him. The king questioned him secretly in his house, and said, "Is there any word from the LORD?" Jeremiah said, "There is!" Then he said, "You shall be handed over to the king of Babylon." [18] Jeremiah also said to King Zedekiah, "What wrong have I done to you or your servants or this people, that you have put me in prison? [19] Where are your prophets who prophesied to you, saying, 'The king of Babylon will not come against you and against this land'? [20] Now please hear me, my lord king: be good enough to listen to my plea, and do not send me back to the house of the secretary Jonathan to die there." [21] So King Zedekiah gave orders, and they committed Jeremiah to the court of the guard; and a loaf of bread was given him daily from the bakers' street, until all the bread of the city was gone. So Jeremiah remained in the court of the guard.

Jeremiah 37 concludes with an account of Jeremiah's arrest (vv. 11–16) and, while Jeremiah is in prison, another encounter between Zedekiah and Jeremiah (vv. 17–21).

During the siege of Babylon, Jeremiah attempts to leave Jerusalem to attend to some matter concerning family property (v. 12). While one is tempted to relate this departure to his redemption of family property at Anathoth (Jeremiah 32), this connection is not likely. When approached by his cousin about redeeming the family land at Anathoth, Jeremiah is already in prison (32:2); in these verses, Jeremiah has not been imprisoned (compare v. 4), but his attempted departure from Jerusalem results in his imprisonment. Jeremiah has lived under the accusation that he is a traitor for some time (see, for instance, Jer. 26) because he prophesied that Jerusalem would fall to the Babylonians and even urged surrender to Babylon (21:8–10). Jeremiah's effort to leave Jerusalem during the Babylonian siege will have easily been interpreted by persons loyal to Judah's leadership as another sign of Jeremiah's treasonous behavior. Jeremiah is arrested and accused of "deserting to the Chaldeans" (v. 13), a charge that Jeremiah denies as a "lie" (v. 14). Of course, the real "deception" is the optimistic idea held by the king that God will relent and turn back the Babylonians (v. 9). Just as the leadership of Judah has failed to listen to Jeremiah when he announced God's judgment, so they "would not listen" to his claim that he was not deserting (v. 14).

Upon arrest, Jeremiah is subject to brutal treatment by officials who are "enraged" with him. Undoubtedly, their rage has been brewing for a long time, and they finally have gotten hold of the prophet with an excuse to vent their anger. We are presented with police state brutality in an effort to silence Jeremiah for his harsh criticisms of Judah's leadership. Within the book of Jeremiah, the arrest and brutal treatment of the prophet needs to be read as another example, this one acted out through a violent assault, of Judah's failure to listen to God's word spoken by God's prophet. In Jeremiah 36, Jehoiakim had, in a sense, done violence to God's word by burning Jeremiah's scroll, and he had intended to have the prophet arrested. The assault reported in these verses is a rejection of God's word through a personal assault on God's messenger.

We should not be surprised by the brutal treatment of Jeremiah, for we have witnessed such treatment of persons who criticize establishment powers often in our world. For instance, during World War II, one of the prominent church leaders who resisted Hitler was a budding young theologian named Dietrich Bonhoeffer. He was finally arrested, imprisoned, and executed shortly before the end of the war. Bonhoeffer paid with his life for his Christian faith that led him to criticize the government of his country. More than fifty years after the war's end, efforts to clear Bonhoeffer's traitor status in Germany have still not been successful.

Surprisingly, when in prison Jeremiah is "secretly" approached by King Zedekiah who once more wants to know if there is "any word from the Lord" (v. 17). One can hardly imagine what might have led King Zedekiah to seek Jeremiah's counsel. Surely the king must have known not to expect good news from Jeremiah (compare vv. 3–10 and 21:1–7), though Zedekiah's question suggests that he remained optimistic that somehow God will relent. Perhaps it was desperation that drove Zedekiah back to Jeremiah as the siege of Jerusalem continued. Whatever brought Zedekiah to Jeremiah, the prophet feeds the king's optimism by replying to Zedekiah's question, "Is there any word from the Lord?" with the suggestive phrase, "There is!" (v. 17). Surely the king would have been encouraged, but only for the moment that Jeremiah might have allowed his response to hang in the air before reiterating, "You shall be handed over to the king of Babylon." Jeremiah's response underscores God's firm decision that Judah and Zedekiah will be plucked up and broken down. With Babylon outside the walls of Jerusalem, the inevitability of God's judgment should have been clear enough, but the king still could not hear.

With the king's agenda addressed, Jeremiah uses the occasion to plead his own cause in the form of a defense and a request. In his defense,

Jeremiah asks the king what wrong he has done to be put in prison. The Babylonian siege is proof enough that Jeremiah has not spoken "presumptuously" (compare Deut. 18:20–22, and see the discussion of the optimistic prophets in Jeremiah 28) but has spoken for the Lord. In fact, if Judah and Zedekiah have been deceived, it is by the prophets who announced that Babylon was no threat, but when the siege is in force, they were no where to be found (v. 19). Jeremiah has done no wrong. His defense leads him to a request that he not be returned to the prison where he has been kept and where his life is in danger. This encounter between Jeremiah and Zedekiah that began with the surprise of Zedekiah's inquiry of Jeremiah also ends in a surprising manner. The king changes the location of Jeremiah's imprisonment and orders a daily food ration for him, an extraordinary measure given the siege. It would seem that King Zedekiah has perhaps begun to realize that Jeremiah does indeed speak for God, whose sovereign intention to pluck up and tear down Judah will prevail. Though it is too late, the king, it seems, has finally begun to take God's prophet more seriously. Thus, Zedekiah begins to turn in a way that the community of God's people following the exile could observe and emulate.

Jeremiah 38:1–6

38:1 **Now Shephatiah son of Mattan, Gedaliah son of Pashhur, Jucal son of Shelemiah, and Pashhur son of Malchiah heard the words that Jeremiah was saying to all the people,** 2 **Thus says the LORD, Those who stay in this city shall die by the sword, by famine, and by pestilence; but those who go out to the Chaldeans shall live; they shall have their lives as a prize of war, and live.** 3 **Thus says the LORD, This city shall surely be handed over to the army of the king of Babylon and be taken.** 4 **Then the officials said to the king, "This man ought to be put to death, because he is discouraging the soldiers who are left in this city, and all the people, by speaking such words to them. For this man is not seeking the welfare of this people, but their harm."** 5 **King Zedekiah said, "Here he is; he is in your hands; for the king is powerless against you."** 6 **So they took Jeremiah and threw him into the cistern of Malchiah, the king's son, which was in the court of the guard, letting Jeremiah down by ropes. Now there was no water in the cistern, but only mud, and Jeremiah sank in the mud.**

Just when it seems that Judah's leadership might be ready to listen to Jeremiah, the prophet's situation takes a dangerous turn. A contingent of royal officials are particularly offended by Jeremiah's continued call for Judah to surrender to the Babylonians (vv. 2–3; compare 21:8–10, which is identified as from the time of Zedekiah and remembers the prophet's

words almost identically to the present text). For Jeremiah, who understands that God's intention is to pluck up and tear down Judah, surrender
to the Babylonians represents submission to God and will signal that, at
last, Judah is ready to listen and obey.

However, the logic of the court officials works in a different way. The
intervention of Egypt during the Babylonian siege (34:21; 37:5, 7) suggests
that the policy of Zedekiah's administration is to seek assistance from
Egypt to fend off the Babylonians. Obviously, if the court officials are optimistic that Egyptian intervention will save Judah, Jeremiah's counsel that
Judah surrender is quite dismaying. In a time of deep crisis, Jeremiah con-
tradicts the official government policy in a way that Judah's officials identify as dangerous to national security. He is "discouraging the soldiers . . .
and all the people." Jeremiah's counsel is interpreted as "harming" the
people rather than seeking their "welfare" (v. 4). Remember that Jeremiah's call for those exiled in 597 B.C. to seek the welfare of Babylon also
resulted in negative reaction (29:7, 25–28). Jeremiah risks a voice of dissent that is radically opposed to the official government policy, and as we
will see in the verses that follow, such public dissent is very dangerous. For
Judah's officials, Jeremiah is a traitor and deserves to die (v. 4).

We need to be aware of the depth of the issues that divided Jeremiah
and Judah's officials. More was at stake than differing assessments of the
proper political and military response to the Babylonian threat. More fundamentally, however, Jeremiah and Judah's officials understood who God
was and what God was about in very different ways. For an array of reasons that had to do with Judah's failure to obey God, Jeremiah understood
that Judah was to be captured by Babylon (37:8–10, 19) and the city was to
be burned by them (34:2, 22; 37:8, 10). Jeremiah understood that God was
sovereign over nations and kingdoms (1:10), and since God intended to
pluck up and tear down Judah, it only made sense to Jeremiah for Judah to
surrender to Babylon. For Jeremiah, surrender held the promise of "life"
(see 21:8–10). By contrast, Judah's officials were still convinced that God
was irrevocably committed to Judah's survival and thought that Judah
could be sustained by a political and military strategy that looked to Egypt.
So, for Judah's officials, surrender made no sense, and Jeremiah's call
undermined national morale and security. He was not only a traitor but—
probably worse—also a heretic who did not, from the perspective of
Judah's officials, understand God's commitment to Judah and Jerusalem.

Both Jeremiah and Judah's officials knew that human decisions had to
be made in a moment of extreme crisis in Judah's life. However, each urged
a very different course because each held a fundamentally different under-

standing of what God was about. The conflict between Jeremiah and Judah's officials is finally theological; it was about the different ways they thought about God. Too often in the church we fail to understand that beneath our conflicts about what we should do are conflicts about how we understand God. Persons who differ about issues—abortion, children at communion, prayer in public schools, which church school curriculum to use—probably differ about theology, about how they understand who God is and what God is about. More theological discussion in our churches may not resolve conflicts, but it would likely allow us to deal with conflicts nearer their source, in theology, in how we understand God.

The officials who think that Jeremiah deserves to die present their case to King Zedekiah. We have seen that the king seems to be developing some openness toward Jeremiah, some willingness to listen to the prophet. Zedekiah has been responsive to Jeremiah's request for a less severe imprisonment (37:21). However, when confronted by the officials' demands to deal harshly with Jeremiah, Zedekiah claims to be "powerless" (v. 5). The king turns Jeremiah over to the officials who think he should die, and they throw Jeremiah into a dry cistern where Jeremiah sinks in the mud (v. 6). King Jehoiakim tried to deal with God's word by burning it. Judah's officials try to deal with God's word by killing its spokesperson. Judah's failure to hear and obey continues.

Zedekiah's claim to be "powerless" is interesting. This may well reflect Zedekiah's political circumstance. He is made king by the Babylonians after their invasion of Judah in 597 B.C. Thus, Zedekiah is a political pawn of the Babylonians who replaced the legitimate king, Jehoiakim, exiled to Babylon. Further, the exile of Judah's key leaders by the Babylonians in 597 B.C. undoubtedly meant that the advisors with whom Zedekiah worked may not have been "the brightest and the best" but second-tier officials not deemed important enough by the Babylonians to deport. However, Zedekiah's real "powerlessness" was his wavering. He wavered about which course of action to follow, if he should risk Jeremiah's advice to surrender or stay the official course and see if Egyptian intervention would rescue Judah. Even more, Zedekiah wavered theologically, unsure whether he believed that God would protect Judah and Jerusalem "forever," as was commonly held; or if he was persuaded by Jeremiah's dissenting voice that God intended to pluck up and tear down Judah. At many levels, King Zedekiah is "powerless."

Meanwhile, Jeremiah was in a precarious position. Jeremiah's public dissent of the government's pro-Egyptian policy placed him in a life-threatening situation. However, it was finally not Jeremiah's politics that placed him in danger but his theology, the way he understood who God was and what God was about in his time and place. God promised Jeremiah, "I will deliver you out of the hand of the wicked, and redeem you from the grasp of the ruthless" (15:21; compare 1:8, 17–19). God's assurances to Jeremiah will be tested.

Jeremiah 38:7–13

38:7 **Ebed-melech the Ethiopian, a eunuch in the king's house, heard that they had put Jeremiah into the cistern. The king happened to be sitting at the Benjamin Gate,** [8] **So Ebed-melech left the king's house and spoke to the king,** [9] **"My lord king, these men have acted wickedly in all they did to the prophet Jeremiah by throwing him into the cistern to die there of hunger, for there is no bread left in the city."** [10] **Then the king commanded Ebed-melech the Ethiopian, "Take three men with you from here, and pull the prophet Jeremiah up from the cistern before he dies."** [11] **So Ebed-melech took the men with him and went to the house of the king, to a wardrobe of the storehouse, and took from there old rags and worn-out clothes, which he let down to Jeremiah in the cistern by ropes.** [12] **Then Ebed-melech the Ethiopian said to Jeremiah, "Just put the rags and clothes between your armpits and the ropes." Jeremiah did so.** [13] **Then they drew Jeremiah up by the ropes and pulled him out of the cistern. And Jeremiah remained in the court of the guard.**

Zedekiah's "powerless" wavering is again on display. The king is confronted by Ebed-melech (the name means "servant of the king"), who is identified as an Ethiopian and a eunuch. This man is not a Judean but a foreigner. Persons called "eunuchs" are found in positions in the king's court in the book of Jeremiah (29:2, where the Hebrew word for eunuchs is translated "court officials"; 34:19); the designation "eunuch" may not be about Ebed-melech's physical condition but may indicate that he is a court official or servant. Ebed-melech confronts Zedekiah to protest Jeremiah's treatment and is outspoken in his ethical judgment: "These men have acted wickedly in all that they did to the prophet Jeremiah" (v. 9). For an Ethiopian, an outsider, to confront the king about Jeremiah is an extraordinarily bold move and must have been quite risky. Jeremiah had been imprisoned by the decision of the highest officials in Judean government, officials whom this foreigner directly attacked. Ebed-melech must have risked being labeled a traitor by his concern for Jeremiah and must have known that he could well be thrown into the cistern with the prophet for his protest. During the McCarthy era in the 1950s, for instance, persons who defended those labeled as Communists by Joseph McCarthy themselves risked being called Communists or Communist sympathizers and subject to public scrutiny.

Ebed-melech's status as a foreigner is a significant feature of this story. One will not expect a person from outside the covenantal tradition of Israel and Judah to be very sympathetic to Jeremiah. Yet it is Ebed-melech, not some covenantal insider, who voices ethical concern for the actions taken against Jeremiah and names for the king the wickedness of the actions in which the king himself is at least complicit (v. 5). These inverted roles of "insiders" and "outsiders" remind us of this theme elsewhere in the Bible. For instance:

a. In the David and Bathsheba incident, there is an interesting contrast between David, Judah's king, and Uriah the Hittite, Bathsheba's husband and a foreigner (2 Samuel 11). David calls Uriah home from war and tries every way he can to entice Uriah to sleep with his wife. During times of war, the troops are not to have sexual relationships since they were, in ancient Israel's view of it, dedicated to God's service. If Uriah slept with Bathsheba, then her pregnancy would not any longer have been a problem for David. However, David, try as he might, cannot get Uriah to break his celibacy and sleep with Bathsheba. Uriah the Hittite, a foreigner and outsider to Judah, acts with integrity, something that escapes King David, an insider if there ever was one.

b. In Jesus' parable, it is a Samaritan, deemed a heretic and an outsider to the traditions of Israel, who knows who his neighbor is (Luke 10:25–37). The insiders, the priest and the Levite, pass by the beaten man on the other side of the road. The scandal of the parable is that the Samaritan, the outsider, is the one who recognizes who his neighbor is.

c. In Mark's Gospel, just before Jesus' crucifixion, the disciples are all offended when an unnamed woman anoints Jesus with costly perfume (Mark 14:3–9). Yet Jesus affirms the action by this outsider and rebukes his own disciples. It is a sign of her devotion and that she understands who Jesus is. The outsider, whose name is not even remembered in the gospel, understands what Jesus' disciples did not.

When confronted by Ebed-melech, King Zedekiah wavers once more and gives permission that Jeremiah be released from the cistern where his life is threatened (v. 10). It is another unexpected development in the story, and we are given no hint about why Ebed-melech risked speaking out in Jeremiah's defense or why the king would be moved by this foreigner to act against his inner circle of officials. For whatever the reasons, Jeremiah is saved from sure death and returned to the "court of the guard" where the king had placed him earlier after Jeremiah's appeal (v. 13; compare 37:21). When King Jehoiakim attempted to silence Jeremiah by burning his scroll, he failed; a second, even more extensive scroll, is dictated. Similarly, the efforts of the pro-Egyptian advisors of Zedekiah to silence Jeremiah also fail; the foreigner, Ebed-melech, risks his own life and amazingly succeeds in saving Jeremiah's life. God's spokesperson is not yet silenced.

Jeremiah 38:14–28

38:14 **King Zedekiah sent for the prophet Jeremiah and received him at the third entrance of the temple of the LORD. The king said to Jeremiah, "I have something to ask you; do not hide anything from me." [15] Jeremiah said to Zedekiah, "If I tell you, you will put me to death, will you not? And if I give you advice, you will not listen to me." [16] So King Zedekiah swore an oath in secret to Jeremiah, "As the LORD lives, who gave us our lives, I will not put you to death or hand you over to these men who seek your life."**

[17] **Then Jeremiah said to Zedekiah, "Thus says the LORD, the God of hosts, the God of Israel, If you will only surrender to the officials of the king of Babylon, then your life shall be spared, and this city shall not be burned with fire, and you and your house shall live. [18] But if you do not surrender to the officials of the king of Babylon, then this city shall be handed over to the Chaldeans, and they shall burn it with fire, and you yourself shall not escape from their hand." [19] King Zedekiah said to Jeremiah, "I am afraid of the Judeans who have deserted to the Chaldeans, for I might be handed over to them and they would abuse me." [20] Jeremiah said, "That will not happen. Just obey the voice of the LORD in what I say to you, and it shall go well with you, and your life shall be spared. [21] But if you are determined not to surrender, this is what the LORD has shown me— [22] a vision of all the women remaining in the house of the king of Judah being led out to the officials of the king of Babylon and saying,**

> **'Your trusted friends have seduced you**
> **and have overcome you;**
> > **Now that your feet are stuck in the mud,**
> > **they desert you.'**

[23]**All your wives and your children shall be led out to the Chaldeans, and you yourself shall not escape from their hand, but shall be seized by the king of Babylon; and this city shall be burned with fire."**

[24] **Then Zedekiah said to Jeremiah, "Do not let anyone else know of this conversation, or you will die. [25] If the officials should hear that I have spoken with you, and they should come and say to you, 'Just tell us what you said to the king; do not conceal it from us, or we will put you to death. What did the king say to you?' [26] then you shall say to them, 'I was presenting my plea to the king not to send me back to the house of Jonathan to die there.'" [27] All the officials did come to Jeremiah and questioned him; and he answered them in the very words the king had commanded. So they stopped questioning him, for the conversation had not been overheard. [28] And Jeremiah remained in the court of the guard until the day that Jerusalem was taken.**

With the Babylonian army outside Jerusalem, a power struggle goes on inside the city. On one side are Judah's officials with their pro-Egyptian policy and confidence that God will rescue Jerusalem. On the other side is Jeremiah, confident that God intends to pluck up and tear down Jerusalem, and who urges submission to God by surrender to Babylon. Wavering "powerless" between Judah's officials and God's prophet is King Zedekiah, unable to make up his mind whom to believe or which course to follow. Once more, Zedekiah sends for Jeremiah, and in these verses we hear their extended conversation.

Zedekiah wants Jeremiah to speak frankly with him, but Jeremiah, having had a close brush with death in the cistern, is reluctant to say too much for fear it will cost him his life (vv. 14–16). When Jeremiah spoke forthrightly with Zedekiah the last time (37:17–20), Judah's officials heard of it and Zedekiah capitulated, powerless to the officials' demands that Jeremiah be silenced (vv. 4–5). This conversation between the king and prophet begins cautiously, with Jeremiah extracting from the king the promise that he will not be handed over to those who seek his life (v. 16). Yet, that Jeremiah is able to get Zedekiah to make this promise suggests that increasingly the king is being persuaded by Jeremiah and, against Judah's officials, is open to hear God's word and entertains the option of surrender (compare the introduction to Jeremiah 37–38 in 37:1–2).

With assurance from Zedekiah that he will not be turned over again to the court officials who have sought his life, Jeremiah once more lays out the options open to the king (vv. 17–18). They concern whether the city will or will not be burned (a theme developed beginning at Jeremiah 34), and whether Zedekiah will live or die. The option that Jeremiah urges is surrender, which will mean that the city will not be burned, that Zedekiah's life will be spared, and that he and his house (that is, his line of succession) will live. The other option is not to surrender. In this case, Jeremiah warns, the Babylonians will capture the city, burn it, and take Zedekiah, too. Undoubtedly Zedekiah can imagine the counsel of his advisors that is exactly opposite of Jeremiah's: to surrender is death, to resist is life (see v. 4).

The conversation begins with Jeremiah cautious and fearful. Jeremiah's presentation of options to Zedekiah leaves the king cautious and fearful. Interestingly, Zedekiah fears not the Babylonians, as we might expect, but Judeans who have deserted to the Babylonians (v. 19). Zedekiah has assured Jeremiah to begin the conversation (v. 16); now it is Jeremiah who offers Zedekiah assurance, though conditionally. It will go well with Zedekiah and his life will be spared if he will "just obey the voice of the Lord in what I say to you" (v. 20). This, in summary, is what has been demanded of Judah all along, and it is demanded of Zedekiah in particular. The need for Judah and its kings to listen and obey has been an important theme of the most recent chapters of the book. If Zedekiah will listen and obey (see 34:10, 17; 35:8, 10, 14–16; 36:3, 24; 37:2), he will understand that God intends to pluck up and tear down Judah and he will surrender as Jeremiah urges. If Zedekiah fails to listen and obey, he will see his wives and children led out as captives. As they are led away, Jeremiah warns that they will say to Zedekiah, "Your trusted friends seduced you . . ." (v. 22). Zedekiah can trust his friends, Judah's officials, and continue to resist Babylon, but Jeremiah warns of the dire consequences of that choice; or Zedekiah can "obey the voice of the Lord in what I say," surrender to the Babylonians, spare the city from being burned, and save his own life and the lives of his wives and children.

The conversation between Jeremiah and Zedekiah concludes as the king has Jeremiah promise not to tell the court officials, the proponents of a pro-Egyptian policy, about their conversation (vv. 24–28). The tone of these verses suggests that at last Zedekiah is leaning toward Jeremiah's point of view. Zedekiah knows that the officials who favored an Egyptian policy seek to silence Jeremiah. So, Zedekiah tries to protect the prophet and keep confidential the counsel he has received from Jeremiah. Perhaps King Zedekiah has begun to listen, but if so, there is no indication that he acts. Babylon is outside Jerusalem. Judah has not listened or obeyed, so God intends to pluck up and tear down Judah. Judah has burned God's word and tried to kill God's prophet, so Babylon is ready to burn Jerusalem.

Reflecting on these chapters of the book of Jeremiah, Ronald Clements has very helpfully observed:

> The prophetic interpretation of the calamitous events which befell Jerusalem in 587 B.C. is thereby strongly pointed to indicate the reality of human freedom and the validity and efficacious nature of human choices. It affirms the openness of human history to the will and purpose of God. Within that purpose catastrophes can and do occur, but they are not enacted as the unreasoned whim of an all-encompassing superior power. Rather, catastrophe is viewed as the consequence of bad decisions, brought about in continued and repeated defiance of the divine warnings that had been given to Israel and Judah. (*Jeremiah*, pp. 222–23)

Zedekiah and Jehoiakim, Judah's officials and the Rechabites, Jeremiah and Ebed-melech all engage in difficult conversations about hard choices as real participants with responsibility to shape the moment of history God left open to them. As creatures made in the image of God, we should expect the same difficult conversations, hard choices, and real responsibilities as God leaves open how we might shape our moment of history.

"I Am Going to Fulfill My Words against This City"
Jeremiah 39–45

God has threatened to destroy Judah and Jerusalem. Jeremiah 39–45 recounts the fulfillment of God's word of judgment. In Jeremiah 40 it is the captain of the Babylonian guard who gives voice to the meaning of Jerusalem's destruction in the book of Jeremiah: "The Lord your God threatened this place with disaster; and now the Lord have brought it about" (40:2–3). God has threatened the destruction of Jerusalem and accomplished it; God's word will be fulfilled.

The material in these chapters divides into several sections: Jeremiah 39:1–40:6 narrates the fall of Jerusalem and its aftermath especially for King Zedekiah and Jeremiah; Jeremiah 40:7–41:18 concerns Gedaliah, who is appointed governor of Judah by the Babylonians after the fall of Jerusalem; Jeremiah 42:1–43:7 relates Jeremiah's conflict with a group of Judeans who want to flee to Egypt against Jeremiah's counsel; Jeremiah 43:8–44:30 tells about Jeremiah and the Judeans in Egypt; and, Jeremiah 45 is Jeremiah's final word to his secretary, Baruch.

THE FALL OF JERUSALEM
Jeremiah 39:1–40:6

Jeremiah 39:1–10

39:1 **In the ninth year of King Zedekiah of Judah, in the tenth month, King Nebuchadrezzar of Babylon and all his army came against Jerusalem and besieged it;** 2 **in the eleventh year of Zedekiah, in the fourth month, on the ninth day of the month, a breach is made in the city.** 3 **When Jerusalem is taken, all the officials of the king of Babylon came and sat in the middle gate: Nergal-sharezer, Samgar-nebo, Sarsechim the Rabsaris, Nergal-sharezer the Rabmag, with all the rest of the officials of the king of Babylon.** 4 **When King Zedekiah of Judah and all the soldiers saw them, they fled, going out of the**

city at night by way of the king's garden through the gate between the two walls; and they went toward the Arabah. ⁵ But the army of the Chaldeans pursued them, and overtook Zedekiah in the plains of Jericho; and when they had taken him, they brought him up to King Nebuchadrezzar of Babylon, at Riblah, in the land of Hamath; and he passed sentence on him. ⁶ The king of Babylon slaughtered the sons of Zedekiah at Riblah before his eyes; also the king of Babylon slaughtered all the nobles of Judah. ⁷ He put out the eyes of Zedekiah, and bound him in fetters to take him to Babylon. ⁸ The Chaldeans burned the king's house and the houses of the people, and broke down the walls of Jerusalem. ⁹ Then Nebuzaradan the captain of the guard exiled to Babylon the rest of the people who were left in the city, those who had deserted to him, and the people who remained. ¹⁰ Nebuzaradan the captain of the guard left in the land of Judah some of the poor people who owned nothing, and gave them vineyards and fields at the same time.

What was announced by Jeremiah as God's word or intention finally occurs. The siege of Jerusalem lasted approximately 18 months, from December 589 B.C./January 588 B.C. until June/July 587 B.C., when the Babylonians breached Jerusalem's wall and entered the city (other biblical accounts of the fall of Jerusalem can be found in 2 Kings 25 and Jer. 52:4–16). Jeremiah declared that "all the tribes of the kingdom of the north . . . shall come and all of them shall set their thrones at the entrance of the gates of Jerusalem" (1:15), and that is what happened: "When Jerusalem was taken, all the officials of the king of Babylon came and sat in the middle gate" (v. 3). Jeremiah spoke God's word, and it has been fulfilled.

With the Babylonians inside Jerusalem, King Zedekiah attempts to flee. He goes toward Arabah, that is, the region of the Jordan River valley, but is caught by the Babylonians near Jericho and brought before the Babylonian king who "passed sentence on him" (vv. 4–5). Zedekiah, as Jeremiah warned, meets the king of Babylon "eye to eye" and "face to face" (34:3). Zedekiah had been appointed to govern Judah by the Babylonians after their attack on Judah in 597 B.C. (see 2 Kings 24:13–17), so he is a puppet of Babylonians who has caused them a great deal of difficulty. The harsh sentence imposed on Zedekiah was predictable, though still shocking in its brutality! Zedekiah's sons are executed before his eyes; then, with the vision of his sons' death lingering, he is blinded and taken to Babylon in exile (vv. 6–7; he died in exile, see 52:11). However, the point of these gruesome details about Zedekiah's punishment is not the brutality of the Babylonians but the fulfillment of God's word. Jeremiah offered King Zedekiah an option to spare his life and also to spare Jerusalem from being burned by surrendering to the Babylonians (38:17). Zedekiah wavered, waited too long, and finally, as Jeremiah warned, was "not able to escape from their hand" (38:18). In Zedekiah's punishment, God's word is fulfilled.

The fulfillment of God's word of judgment is also emphasized in the conclusion of these verses. The execution of Judah's nobles by the Babylonians (v. 6) fulfills Jeremiah's warning about death by "famine, pestilence, and sword" (see 14:12; 15:2; 18:21; 19:6–7; 21:7; 24:10; 27:8). Further, Jeremiah announced that Jerusalem will be burned if Judah did not surrender (21:10; 38:17–18), and verse 8 reports the fulfillment of that word. The accounts of the fall of Jerusalem in 2 Kings and Jeremiah 52 report that in addition to the king's house, the Temple is also burned. One senses that this text in Jeremiah 39 wants to stress the responsibility of Zedekiah and Judah's kings for the exile. The report that both deserters and those who remained in the city were exiled is somewhat puzzling. Jeremiah had distinguished the fates of those who surrendered from those who remained in the city (for instance, 21:9); here they are all exiled.

Despite some discrepancies, the overall intention of these verse is to stress that God's word of judgment announced by Jeremiah was fulfilled. The disaster that God has threatened finally occurred.

Jeremiah 39:11–14

39:11 **King Nebuchadrezzar of Babylon gave command concerning Jeremiah through Nebuzaradan, the captain of the guard, saying,** 12 **"Take him, look after him well and do him no harm, but deal with him as he may ask you."** 13 **So Nebuzaradan the captain of the guard, Nebushazban the Rabsaris, Nergal-sharezer the Rabmag, and all the chief officers of the king of Babylon sent** 14 **and took Jeremiah from the court of the guard. They entrusted him to Gedaliah son of Ahikam son of Shaphan to be brought home. So he stayed with his own people.**

King Zedekiah refused to listen to God's word, and the judgment that had been threatened is fulfilled. The word of the Lord concerning Jeremiah is also fulfilled. God promised Jeremiah that those who opposed him would "not prevail" and that he would be saved and delivered (1:19; 15:20–21). After the fall of Jerusalem, King Nebuchadrezzar of Babylon gives orders about Jeremiah that the captain of the Babylonian guard should "take him, look after him well and do him no harm" (v. 12; a somewhat different account of Jeremiah's situation after the fall of Jerusalem follows in 40:1–6). Judah's officials considered Jeremiah a traitor, beat him, imprisoned him, and sought to kill him (38:4). However, this text wants to make clear that Judah's officials did "not prevail" against Jeremiah. Instead, the Babylonians deliver him from the court of the guard where he is in prison and save him from death at the hands of his own people. Jeremiah is released to Gedaliah, about whom we will hear more shortly (Jer. 40:7–41:18).

The note at the end of verse 14 that Jeremiah "stayed with his own people" is important. Jeremiah was arrested as a traitor when he attempted to leave Jerusalem (37:11–16), and the charge against Jeremiah was that he was "discouraging" the soldiers and all the people (38:4). In other words, the leadership of Judah had accused Jeremiah of deserting his own people. With the fall of Jerusalem, it is King Zedekiah who attempts to flee Jerusalem in an effort to escape whatever the Babylonians intended for the people of Judah. The king and the Judean officials who flee with him were the ones who desert their people. By contrast, Jeremiah chooses to stay "with his own people." Jeremiah is here remembered as faithful to the people of Judah and to the Lord.

Jeremiah 39:15–18

39:15 **The word of the LORD came to Jeremiah while he was confined in the court of the guard:** [16] **Go and say to Ebed-melech the Ethiopian: Thus says the LORD of hosts, the God of Israel: I am going to fulfill my words against this city for evil and not for good, and they shall be accomplished in your presence on that day.** [17] **But I will save you on that day, says the LORD, and you shall not be handed over to those whom you dread.** [18] **For I will surely save you, and you shall not fall by the sword; but you shall have your life as a prize of war, because you have trusted in me, says the LORD.**

With the Babylonian victory over Judah, most of the residents of Judah and Jerusalem faced harsh treatment. They had rejected God's word, and as a consequence judgment was fulfilled against them (the people's houses were burned, and many were exiled, vv. 8–9). However, there were some who escaped God's harshest judgments, Jeremiah being most notable. The final verses of Jeremiah 39 concern another person who is to be spared judgment, Ebed-melech, who had boldly defended Jeremiah before King Zedekiah and rescued the prophet from sure death in the cistern into which he had been thrown (38:7–13).

God instructs Jeremiah to deliver a message to Ebed-melech. Predictably, one part of the message interprets what happened to Jerusalem as the fulfillment of the word of the Lord: "I am going to fulfill my words against this city for evil . . ." (v. 16). We have seen how this chapter has emphasized that with the fall of Jerusalem, God was fulfilling the word of judgment. In contrast to the evil God intended against Jerusalem and its officials who would not listen to Jeremiah, God promises to save Ebed-melech. He has bluntly criticized Judah's officials for their treatment of Jeremiah ("these men have acted wickedly in all that they did to the prophet Jeremiah," 38:9). While Judah's nobles are killed by the Babylonians (v. 6), Ebed-melech is assured by God that he will "not fall by the sword" (v. 18) but will have his life "as a prize of war" because he "trusted in me" (v. 18). One cannot miss the ironic twist that Ebed-melech is promised his life as a prize of war, while the officials of Judah whom he opposed become Babylon's prizes of war.

God's affirmation of Ebed-melech's "trust" in God is significant. Judah trusted in everything but God. They trusted in their fortified cities to protect them from the nation whom God is sending against them (5:17). They trusted in "deceptive words" that indicated God is unconditionally committed to Jerusalem, its Temple and the Davidic monarchy (7:4). Further, Judah failed to heed Jeremiah's admonition to trust the Lord and shun trust in mere mortals (17:5, 7). Even with the siege of Jerusalem underway, Judah's leaders trusted in "mere mortals," in Egypt's ability to turn back the Babylonians (37:6–10). By contrast, Ebed-melech, a foreigner and outsider to the covenantal traditions of Israel and Judah, trusted God enough to risk speaking out against the injustice done Jeremiah and to rescue Jeremiah from certain death in his cistern prison (38:7–13). In trusting God, Ebed-melech found the courage to risk his life; for his trust in God, God saved Ebed-melech's life.

The story of Ebed-melech, the outsider, serves as a reminder to all of us church insiders of the trust to which God calls us. The Thirty Years' War brought great suffering to parts of Europe; it inspired the German poet Georg Neumark to pen lines based on Psalm 55:22, which called persons suffering much to continue to trust in God. Sung as a hymn in many churches, Neumark's poem expresses the bold trust in God found in the the covenantal outsider, Ebed-melech, trust for which we insiders might well pray:

> If you but trust in God to guide you,
> with hopeful heart through all your ways,
> you will find strength, with God beside you,
> to bear the worst of evil days;
> For those who trust God's changeless love
> build on the rock that will not move.
>
> Sing, pray, and keep God's ways unswerving;
> offer your service faithfully,
> and trust God's word, through undeserving,
> there find the trust to set you free;
> God will not fail to guide and bless
> those who embrace God's faithfulness.
> (*The New Century Hymnal*, no. 410, vv. 1, 3)

Jeremiah 40:1–6

40:1 **The word that came to Jeremiah from the LORD after Nebuzaradan the captain of the guard had let him go from Ramah, when he took him bound in fetters along with all the captives of Jerusalem and Judah who were being exiled to Babylon.** [2] **The captain of the guard took Jeremiah and said to him, "The LORD your God threatened this place with this disaster;** [3] **and now the LORD has brought it about, and has done as he said, because all of you sinned against the LORD and did not obey his voice. Therefore this thing has come upon you.** [4] **Now look, I have just released you today from the fetters on your hands. If you wish to come with me to Babylon, come, and I will take good care of you; but if you do not wish to come with me to Babylon, you need not come. See, the whole land is before you; go wherever you think it good and right to go.** [5] **If you remain, then return to Gedaliah son of Ahikam son of Shaphan, whom the king of Babylon appointed governor of the towns of Judah, and stay with him among the people; or go wherever you think it right to go." So the captain of the guard gave him an allowance of food and a present, and let him go.** [6] **Then Jeremiah went to Gedaliah son of Ahikam at Mizpah, and stayed with him among the people who were left in the land.**

These verses provide a second account of Jeremiah's release by the Babylonians after the fall of Jerusalem (see 39:11–14). The details of the two accounts differ, though some have suggested that they should be read in sequence. King Nebuchadrezzar intended Jeremiah to be released and well treated (39:11–14). However, Jeremiah ends up among those who are to be exiled to Babylon and is taken bound to Ramah. At Ramah, a town a few miles north of Jerusalem where arrangements were made to deport captives from Judah to Babylon, Jeremiah is set free and given a choice to go to Babylon or to remain in Judah. Jeremiah chooses to stay in Judah, and, as indicated in Jeremiah 39, he goes to Gedaliah who is (or is soon to be) the Babylonian appointed governor of Judah. Opinions differ as to whether Jeremiah 39 and 40 reflect a single event that occurred in two stages or two accounts of the same event told in slightly different ways.

The words of the captain of the Babylonian guard are the most important feature of this story. Obviously, the Babylonian guard is an outsider like Ebed-melech. There would be no reason to expect that he would understand anything about the God of Israel and Judah or what the Lord intended (again, like Ebed-melech, who would not be expected to have the ethical sensitivity to perceive the injustice done to Jeremiah, 38:9). Yet, the Babylonian captain of the guard voices what the leaders and people of Judah has failed to perceive:

The Lord your God threatened this place with this disaster; and now the Lord has brought it about, and has done as he said, because all of you sinned against the Lord and did not obey his voice. (vv. 2–3)

Cynically, one could claim that the words of the Babylonian served well Babylonian self-interest and propaganda. As a matter of historical fact, that may be so. However, the book of Jeremiah has as its primary concern a theological understanding of the exile (1:3). The Babylonian guard may have voiced the empire's propaganda, but he also gives expression to what the writers of the book of Jeremiah came to understand about the Babylonian captivity. The exile fulfilled God's word of judgment when Judah failed to obey the Lord's voice. From the beginning of Jeremiah 39, the point that is made again and again is that the fall of Jerusalem to Babylon and all that surrounded that terrible event fulfilled the word spoken by God's prophet, Jeremiah.

This story of the Babylonian guard who expressed the meaning of Judah's fall connects to the story of Ebed-melech. Both of these outsiders perceived what Judah's leaders, insiders, should have perceived. The perception of the Babylonian military official in this story is reminiscent of the confession made by the Roman centurion at the cross (Matt. 27:54; Mark 15:39; Luke 23:47). Jesus on the cross was surrounded by all of those who should have known who he was and what God was about through him— his family, his disciples, the leaders of God's people. Yet it was the Roman centurion who at Jesus' death confessed what all the insiders should have known, "Truly, this man was God's Son" (Mark and Matthew; Luke: ". . . this man was innocent"). Ebed-melech, the Babylonian captain of the guard, and the Roman centurion are all persons who, despite standing outside the covenantal traditions of God's people, understood what God was about. By these stories, we are all called to be both humble about what we claim to know about God and to be alert to the new and surprising things God might be about.

The other details of these verses closely parallel the first story of Jeremiah's release: the Babylonian's intention that Jeremiah be well cared for; the prophet's choice to remain in Judah; Jeremiah's association with Gedaliah. The story concludes by affirming Jeremiah's commitment to the people of Judah, noting that Jeremiah stayed "among the people who were left in the land" (v. 6; 39:14 says "with his own people"). This concluding note about Jeremiah's decision to stay with "the people who were left in the land" anticipates the material to follow and a conflict between Jeremiah and a group of Judeans about staying in Judah or fleeing to Egypt.

GEDALIAH
Jeremiah 40:7–41:18

Following the fall of Judah to Babylon, the Babylonians appointed Gedaliah as governor in their new Judean territory. We have been introduced
to Gedaliah in the preceding material (39:14; 40:5). The remainder of
Jeremiah 40 and Jeremiah 41 focus on Gedaliah and his efforts to establish
order in Judah after the Babylonian victory of 587 B.C. Gedaliah's tenure
as governor was short and ended violently. There are no clear indications
of how long after the fall of Judah the events narrated in these chapters
occurred. Some have suggested that it was just a few months, others as long
as two or three years. Still, most scholars believe that these chapters provide a fairly accurate historical account of events in Judah sometime
around 587 B.C. At the same time, this material does reveal a theological
perspective compatible with that found throughout the book of Jeremiah.
The prophet Jeremiah is not mentioned in this material; he is reintroduced
in Jeremiah 42.

Jeremiah 40:7–12

40:7 **When all the leaders of the forces in the open country and their troops
heard that the king of Babylon had appointed Gedaliah son of Ahikam governor in the land, and had committed to him men, women, and children,
those of the poorest of the land who had not been taken into exile to Babylon,** [8] **they went to Gedaliah at Mizpah—Ishmael son of Nethaniah, Johanan
son of Kareah, Seraiah son of Tanhumeth, the sons of Ephai the Netophathite,
Jezaniah son of the Maacathite, they and their troops.** [9] **Gedaliah son of
Ahikam son of Shaphan swore to them and their troops, saying, "Do not be
afraid to serve the Chaldeans. Stay in the land and serve the king of Babylon, and it shall go well with you.** [10] **As for me, I am staying at Mizpah to represent you before the Chaldeans who come to us; but as for you, gather wine
and summer fruits and oil, and store them in your vessels, and live in the
towns that you have taken over."** [11] **Likewise, when all the Judeans who were
in Moab and among the Ammonites and in Edom and in other lands heard
that the king of Babylon had left a remnant in Judah and had appointed
Gedaliah son of Ahikam son of Shaphan as governor over them,** [12] **then all
the Judeans returned from all the places to which they had been scattered
and came to the land of Judah, to Gedaliah at Mizpah; and they gathered
wine and summer fruits in great abundance.**

Gedaliah came from a family whom we have encountered before in the
book of Jeremiah. This family supported King Josiah's reform efforts
and also supported the prophet Jeremiah. Gedaliah's grandfather was

Shaphan, the secretary of King Josiah, who brought the book found during the Temple renovations to King Josiah and read it to him (2 Kings 22). This book, thought to be part of the book of Deuteronomy, spurred on King Josiah's reform efforts. Gedaliah's father, Ahikam, helped rescue Jeremiah from the officials of Judah when they arrested Jeremiah and placed him on trial after he spoke at the Temple (26:24). Gedaliah thus came from a family that supported reform in Judah and whose theological and political perspective was compatible with that of Jeremiah. Though no mention is made of this family during Judah's last years before the Babylonian victory in 587 B.C., it is likely they would have continued to support Jeremiah, for instance, in his call for surrender to Babylon. Given what we know from the book of Jeremiah, it also seems likely that Gedaliah would have been perceived by the Babylonians as a Judean with whom they could work.

Those who remained in Judah or who has fled to nearby areas after 587 B.C. are portrayed in these verses as rallying around Gedaliah (vv. 7–8, 11–12). Among those who come to Gedaliah are not only some "of the poorest of the land who had not been taken into exile to Babylon" (v. 7) but also persons of more prominence whose names are recorded (for instance, Ishmael is later identified as part of the royal family, 41:1) and who commanded troops (vv. 8, 12). Gedaliah had established a base at Mizpah, about eight miles north of Jerusalem. He was probably not able to use Jerusalem as a headquarters because of the Babylonian destruction of the city.

To help those who come to him deal with their situation, Gedaliah offers a two-pronged approach. First, he encourages those gathered at Mizpah to remain in the land and to submit to the Babylonians. This approach is consistent with the policy of surrender that Jeremiah had urged prior to 587 B.C. Behind this policy was, for Jeremiah, the theological assumption that God intended Judah to submit to Babylon. Gedaliah himself takes responsibility to "represent" the Judeans before the Chaldeans. Although Gedaliah knows submission is necessary, his offer to "represent" the Judeans to the Chaldeans suggests that he intends more than capitulation; it is some kind of cooperative relationship that he will broker.

Second, Gedaliah encourages those who remain in Judah to reestablish themselves agriculturally and economically (v. 10; compare v. 12). Because some of those connected with Gedaliah were commanders of troops (v. 8), Gedaliah seems to have urged that these troops give up any armed resistance to the Babylonians and resume their agricultural activities. Thus Gedaliah proposes to deal with the Babylonian reality while at the same time encouraging those who remain in Judah after 587 B.C. to resume their lives and reestablish themselves economically.

Although there is no reason to doubt that we can discern in these verses some of what was occurring in Judah in the months (or maybe years) after 587 B.C., this text also portrays God's restoration of Judah and Israel in a way that reflects the vision of Jeremiah 30–33. For instance, the indication in verse 12 of the abundance of a harvest is hardly consistent with a land recently devastated and pillaged by an invading army. Instead, this picture of abundance reflects sections of the book of Jeremiah that present God's restoration as a time of renewed blessing and abundance (see 31:5, 12–14 particularly). The image of people gathering around Gedaliah may also be influenced by the vision that God's restoration would involve a return to the promised land (see 31:8–9, 10, 21, 24; 33:12–13). Even the reference to Mizpah, while having a well-established connection with Gedaliah in Jeremiah 40–41, may anticipate God's deliverance of Judah. In an earlier time, Mizpah was associated with Samuel and the deliverance of Israel from a menacing foreign threat, the Philistines (1 Samuel 7). While reflecting historical events, it also seems that these verses have been influenced by a theological perspective that looked beneath what was occurring and saw in those events signs of God's restoration, building and planting after plucking up and tearing down.

Jeremiah 40:13–41:3

40:13 **Now Johanan son of Kareah and all the leaders of the forces in the open country came to Gedaliah at Mizpah** 14 **and said to him, "Are you at all aware that Baalis king of the Ammonites has sent Ishmael son of Nethaniah to take your life?" But Gedaliah son of Ahikam would not believe them.** 15 **Then Johanan son of Kareah spoke secretly to Gedaliah at Mizpah, "Please let me go and kill Ishmael son of Nethaniah, and no one else will know. Why should he take your life, so that all the Judeans who are gathered around you would be scattered, and the remnant of Judah would perish?"** 16 **But Gedaliah son of Ahikam said to Johanan son of Kareah, "Do not do such a thing, for you are telling a lie about Ishmael."**

41:1 **In the seventh month, Ishmael son of Nethaniah son of Elishama, of the royal family, one of the chief officers of the king, came with ten men to Gedaliah son of Ahikam, at Mizpah. As they ate bread together there at Mizpah,** 2 **Ishmael son of Nethaniah and the ten men with him got up and struck down Gedaliah son of Ahikam son of Shaphan with the sword and killed him, because the king of Babylon had appointed him governor in the land.** 3 **Ishmael also killed all the Judeans who were with Gedaliah at Mizpah, and the Chaldean soldiers who happened to be there.**

The tranquillity and resurgence of Judah under Gedaliah are short-lived. Johanan, son of Kareah, tells Gedaliah that the king of the Ammonites, Baalis, intends to have him killed (v. 13; see v. 8). Ammon was a territory practically due east of Mizpah across the Jordan. That the king of Ammon instigates a plot to assassinate Gedaliah suggests that Babylon had not defeated the Ammonites, who still enjoyed political independence. However, the Ammonites must have seen Gedaliah's cooperation with the Babylonians as a significant threat.

The king of Ammon is able to enlist in his assassination plot Ishmael, son of Nethaniah, who with Johanan was among those who gathered with his troops around Gedaliah at Mizpah. We are not told immediately why a Judean who had joined Gedaliah would turn on him, but a clue is given in Jeremiah 41:1. Ishmael was "of the royal family, one of the chief officers of the king." Thus, the plot against Gedaliah is initiated in Ammon out of resentment of his cooperation with Babylon but finds a sympathetic participant in a member of the Judean royal family who evidently still hopes to resist the Babylonians. The issues, theological and political, raised by Jeremiah prior to 587 B.C. about resistance or surrender (21:1–10; 38:17–18) are unresolved, and the conflict is about to be acted out between Gedaliah, who embraces surrender (and was moving Judah toward restoration), and Ishmael, who still favors resistance.

For reasons that are not clear, Gedaliah refuses to allow Johanan to intercept the plot and deal with Ishmael (v. 16). Ishmael arrives in Mizpah and shares a meal with Gedaliah (41:1). Again, why Gedaliah chooses to host the person that he has been warned seeks his life is not clear. Gedaliah's hospitality is betrayed, and Ishmael kills Gedaliah during the meal (41:2). Then the violence escalates, and Judeans with Gedaliah are killed along with some Babylonian troops (v. 3). The hope of Gedaliah that it would go "well" for those who remained in Judah (40:9) is shattered. There is the awful spectacle of Judeans killing Judeans and the threat that the Babylonians will respond harshly to the attack on their troops.

Jeremiah 41:4–10

41:4 **On the day after the murder of Gedaliah, before anyone knew of it, 5 eighty men arrived from Shechem and Shiloh and Samaria, with their beards shaved and their clothes torn, and their bodies gashed, bringing grain offerings and incense to present at the temple of the LORD. 6 And Ishmael son of Nethaniah came out from Mizpah to meet them, weeping as he came. As he met them, he said to them, "Come to Gedaliah son of Ahikam." 7 When they**

reached the middle of the city, Ishmael son of Nethaniah and the men with him slaughtered them, and threw them into a cistern. [8] But there were ten men among them who said to Ishmael, "Do not kill us, for we have stores of wheat, barley, oil, and honey hidden in the fields." So he refrained, and did not kill them along with their companions.

[9] Now the cistern into which Ishmael had thrown all the bodies of the men whom he had struck down was the large cistern that King Asa had made for defense against King Baasha of Israel; Ishmael son of Nethaniah filled that cistern with those whom he had killed. [10] Then Ishmael took captive all the rest of the people who were in Mizpah, the king's daughters and all the people who were left at Mizpah, whom Nebuzaradan, the captain of the guard, had committed to Gedaliah son of Ahikam. Ishmael son of Nethaniah took them captive and set out to cross over to the Ammonites.

Ishmael's violent outburst does not end with the murder of Gedaliah and those with him at Mizpah. The next day, a group of eighty religious pilgrims arrives in the vicinity of Mizpah from cities to the north. The purpose of these pilgrims is to offer sacrifices in Jerusalem, several miles south of Mizpah. The shaved beards and torn clothing of these pilgrims (v. 5) suggest they are going to participate in some rite of mourning for the fallen city of Jerusalem. As these pilgrims approach Mizpah, Ishmael, as a ruse, comes out to greet them, weeping to convey his sympathy with their cause, and invites the party into Mizpah to meet Gedaliah (v. 6). The pilgrims do not know what we readers do, that Ishmael has already killed Gedaliah. Once in the city, Ishmael slaughters the pilgrims as he had Gedaliah and the others at Mizpah the day before, and then he throws their bodies into a cistern. Ten men are spared who indicate to Ishmael that they have food hidden in the fields (v. 8). The massacre over, Ishmael seizes hostages from those who remain in Mizpah and seeks refuge back in Ammon, which had sponsored his mission to kill Gedaliah (v. 10).

Ishmael's murder of Gedaliah can at least be explained as a plot devised between a king of a neighboring state frightened by Gedaliah's cooperation with Babylon, and Ishmael, a Judean patriot who saw Gedaliah as a traitor. Ishmael's murder of these pilgrims is very difficult to understand. Why Ishmael lured pilgrims who were mourning Jerusalem into Mizpah to slaughter them is inexplicable. One will think that a Judean patriot would have had sympathy with the cause of pilgrims mourning Jerusalem's destruction. Ishmael's willingness to spare the lives of ten men with hidden food suggests that his actions were not entirely motivated by some cause or principle but also by an unexplained rage from which he could be distracted by the promise of something good to eat.

Without a clear motive for Ishmael's barbarism, it is difficult to know all that these verses mean to convey. Certainly they suggest the breakdown of civil order in Judah after 587 B.C. In the best light, Ishmael can be understood as a misguided patriot. However, from what we hear about him in these verses, he appears less a patriot and more a psychopath. The headmaster of a Scottish school at which 16 children were murdered by a gunman one morning caught the horror of the Ishmaels of the world when he said, "Evil visited us yesterday and we don't know why. We don't understand it and never will" (*Newsweek*, March 25, 1996, p. 26). The brutal rampage of Ishmael is difficult to understand and frightening because we know there are persons like him in our world, persons whose rage leads to inexplicable brutality.

Jeremiah 41:11–18

41:11 **But when Johanan son of Kareah and all the leaders of the forces with him heard of all the crimes that Ishmael son of Nethaniah had done, 12 they took all their men and went to fight against Ishmael son of Nethaniah. They came upon him at the great pool that is in Gibeon. 13 And when all the people who were with Ishmael saw Johanan son of Kareah and all the leaders of the forces with him, they were glad. 14 So all the people whom Ishmael had carried away captive from Mizpah turned around and came back, and went to Johanan son of Kareah. 15 But Ishmael son of Nethaniah escaped from Johanan with eight men, and went to the Ammonites. 16 Then Johanan son of Kareah and all the leaders of the forces with him took all the rest of the people whom Ishmael son of Nethaniah had carried away captive from Mizpah after he had slain Gedaliah son of Ahikam—soldiers, women, children, and eunuchs, whom Johanan brought back from Gibeon. 17 And they set out, and stopped at Geruth Chimham near Bethlehem, intending to go to Egypt 18 because of the Chaldeans; for they were afraid of them, because Ishmael son of Nethaniah had killed Gedaliah son of Ahikam, whom the king of Babylon had made governor over the land.**

Johanan, who had warned Gedaliah of Ishmael's plot to kill him (40:8, 15), when he hears of Ishmael's crimes, pursues him with his troops and intercepts Ishmael at Gibeon. There has been considerable debate about this location, which is usually associated with a site southwest of Mizpah. If Ishmael were fleeing to Ammon, he would have traveled east from Mizpah, not southwest. Earlier in Israel's history, David defeated the son of Saul at Gideon to take control of Israel, but it is not clear that we are meant to connect the events of this text with David's victory at Gideon.

In any case, Johanan defeats Ishmael's troops, though Ishmael himself escapes and goes on to Ammon. The captives whom Ishmael has taken from Mizpah (v. 10) are freed and go with Johanan. However, at this point the story takes an unexpected turn, because Johanan, rather than returning to Mizpah as we might expect, turns south "intending to go to Egypt" (v. 17). He decides to go to Egypt because he fears Babylonian reprisals in response to the murder of Gedaliah. While Johanan has been a loyal supporter of Gedaliah, Johanan seems to fear that Babylon might not discriminate about which Judean commander it was that had killed their appointee. Johanan may have been correct in fearing Babylonian reprisals, for there was a third deportation to Babylon (in addition to 597 and 587 B.C.) in 582 B.C. (see Jer. 52:30).

As we have read about Gedaliah, we can recognize that the events of 587 B.C. did not resolve tensions about what it meant to be God's people or how to live as such. Though Jeremiah is not mentioned in these stories about Gedaliah, Ishmael, and Johanan, we can see reflected in this material pre-587 B.C. theological assumptions and political strategies but in a post-587 B.C. setting:

a. Gedaliah urged that those not deported stay in the land and work with the Babylonians. This was like the position that Jeremiah had held prior to 587 B.C. Theologically, Jeremiah understood that this position honored God's intention that Judah submit to Babylon and undergirded the political option favored by Jeremiah: surrender to the Babylonians (38:17–18).

b. Ishmael is a patriot who fiercely sought Judean independence, a position that is most like that held by Judah's kings prior to 587 B.C. They assumed God's enduring commitment to Judah and the Davidic monarchy, an assumption that undergirded a political policy that resisted surrender in the confidence that God would not allow Babylon to prevail against Judah.

c. Johanan, who wanted to seek refuge in Egypt, took a position that seems to have been favored by some Jerusalem officials (and maybe King Zedekiah) during the last days of Judah. These officials looked for Judah to be rescued from Babylon by a pro-Egyptian policy. Their position assumed that God's role is minimal; they could make their own arrangements to be secure. Johanan's decision to seek refuge in Egypt sets the stage for the next section of the book of Jeremiah, a confrontation between Jeremiah and Johanan and his supporters (42:1–43:7).

We should not particularly be surprised that theological and political issues from before Judah's defeat lingered despite the Babylonian defeat of Judah in 587 B.C. Enduring human issues and tendencies confront persons, societies, and the church generation after generation. For instance, earlier in the book of Jeremiah, we reflected on the issue of idolatry and the enduring human temptation to seek security apart from God by our own cleverness (so, perhaps, Johanan in our current text). In our century, we have witnessed the horror of the Holocaust, but anti-Semitism still endures. In the United States, slavery was abolished long ago, and eventually laws were passed to insure the civil rights of all citizens. Yet racism persists. Dramatic events may occur, but humans beings change slowly and must surely test God's patience.

"REMAIN IN THIS LAND"
Jeremiah 42:1–43:7

It is not clear how Johanan and those on their way to Egypt came into contact with the prophet Jeremiah, but they did. This section of the book of Jeremiah, which extends into Jeremiah 43, concerns the conflict between Jeremiah and those Judeans with Johanan, who intended to go to Egypt to escape the Babylonians from whom they feared reprisal because of Gedaliah's murder. This section of the book has three sections: (a) those who intend to go to Egypt inquire of Jeremiah what God would have them do (42:1–6); (b) Jeremiah responds at length to this inquiry (42:7–22); (c) against Jeremiah's counsel, Johanan and those with him decide to go to Egypt anyway (43:1–7).

Jeremiah 42:1–6

42:1 **Then all the commanders of the forces, and Johanan son of Kareah and Azariah son of Hoshaiah, and all the people from the least to the greatest, approached** [2] **the prophet Jeremiah and said, "Be good enough to listen to our plea, and pray to the LORD your God for us—for all this remnant. For there are only a few of us left out of many, as your eyes can see.** [3] **Let the LORD your God show us where we should go and what we should do."** [4] **The prophet Jeremiah said to them, "Very well: I am going to pray to the LORD your God as you request, and whatever the LORD answers you I will tell you; I will keep nothing back from you."** [5] **They in their turn said to Jeremiah, "May the LORD be a true and faithful witness against us if we do not act according to everything that the LORD your God sends us through you.** [6] **Whether it is good or bad, we will obey the voice of the LORD our God to whom we are sending you, in order that it may go well with us when we obey the voice of the LORD our God."**

Johanan and those with him are on their way to Egypt to escape the reprisals they fear from the Babylonians because of Gedaliah's murder, and they have gotten as far as Bethlehem, south of Jerusalem (41:17–18). Though the story does not make clear how this group met Jeremiah, they approach the prophet and ask him to pray to the Lord about "where we should go and what we should do" (v. 3).

Their inquiry of the prophet is reminiscent of the occasions when King Zedekiah approached Jeremiah (see Jeremiah 21 and the several instances in Jeremiah 37–38), though with a difference. The stories about Zedekiah make it seem that he came to Jeremiah with a preconceived notion of how he will respond. For instance, Jeremiah had told King Zedekiah on numerous occasions that God intended the Babylonians to capture Jerusalem, but the king was not deterred. During the siege of Jerusalem, Zedekiah again approached Jeremiah with almost the same request as we find in our present text. "Please pray to the Lord our God" (37:3; compare v. 2). We are led to believe that Zedekiah wanted to hear only one response from Jeremiah, that God's mind had changed and Jerusalem would be saved.

The inquiry from those with Johanan has a different tone that suggests they sincerely want the prophet's guidance. The tone is evident in their initial approach to Jeremiah, "Be good enough to listen to our plea . . ." (v. 2), and even more so in their response after Jeremiah agrees to pray for them. They swear an oath that holds them accountable before God if they fail to "act according to everything that the Lord . . . sends us through you [Jeremiah]" (v. 5) and then reinforce their oath by pledging to Jeremiah that "Whether it is good or bad, we will obey the voice of the Lord our God" (v. 6). Those who approach Jeremiah about going to Egypt at least indicate their willingness to heed the prophet's words and obey God.

The exile occurred, of course, because in Judah there were too many persons like King Zedekiah who failed to listen to God's prophet. Those who approach Jeremiah present themselves as willing to listen and ready to obey God. However, Jeremiah's own response to this inquiry is guarded. Jeremiah indicates only that he will pray to God as requested and will hold nothing back when he responds: the truth, the whole truth, and nothing but the truth.

Jeremiah 42:7–22

42:7 **At the end of ten days the word of the LORD came to Jeremiah. 8 Then he summoned Johanan son of Kareah and all the commanders of the forces who were with him, and all the people from the least to the greatest, 9 and said to them, "Thus says the LORD, the God of Israel, to whom you sent me** to present your plea before him: ^{10} If you will only remain in this land, then I will build you up and not pull you down; I will plant you, and not pluck you up; for I am sorry for the disaster that I have brought upon you. ^{11} Do not be afraid of the king of Babylon, as you have been; do not be afraid of him, says the LORD, for I am with you, to save you and to rescue you from his hand. ^{12} I will grant you mercy, and he will have mercy on you and restore you to your native soil. ^{13} But if you continue to say, 'We will not stay in this land,' thus disobeying the voice of the LORD your God ^{14} and saying, 'No, we will go to the land of Egypt, where we shall not see war, or hear the sound of the trumpet, or be hungry for bread, and there we will stay,' ^{15} then hear the word of the LORD, O remnant of Judah. Thus says the LORD of hosts, the God of Israel: If you are determined to enter Egypt and go to settle there, ^{16} then the sword that you fear shall overtake you there, in the land of Egypt; and the famine that you dread shall follow close after you into Egypt; and there you shall die. ^{17} All the people who have determined to go to Egypt to settle there shall die by the sword, by famine, and by pestilence; they shall have no remnant or survivor from the disaster that I am bringing upon them.

^{18} "For thus says the LORD of hosts, the God of Israel: Just as my anger and my wrath were poured out on the inhabitants of Jerusalem, so my wrath will be poured out on you when you go to Egypt. You shall become an object of execration and horror, of cursing and ridicule. You shall see this place no more. ^{19} The LORD has said to you, O remnant of Judah, Do not go to Egypt. Be well aware that I have warned you today ^{20} that you have made a fatal mistake. For you yourselves sent me to the LORD your God, saying, 'Pray for us to the LORD our God, and whatever the LORD our God says, tell us and we will do it.' ^{21} So I have told you today, but you have not obeyed the voice of the LORD your God in anything that he sent me to tell you. ^{22} Be well aware, then, that you shall die by the sword, by famine, and by pestilence in the place where you desire to go and settle."

Jeremiah's response to the inquiry from those who intended to go to Egypt comes after ten days (v. 7). It is a lengthy response, in two parts. The first part of Jeremiah's response (vv. 7–17) indicates both the positive consequences of obeying God and the negative consequences of disobedience. The second part of Jeremiah's response (vv. 18–22) stresses only the negative consequences of disobedience, and so underscores the negative aspects of the first part of the prophet's response. On the whole, the prophet's response stresses much more the harsh consequences of disobedience than the possibilities that come with obedience.

The first part of Jeremiah's response is expressed conditionally (if . . . then) and indicates the consequences of both obeying (vv. 10–12) and disobeying (vv. 13–17) God:

a. Obedience to God, Jeremiah indicates, means to "remain in this land" (v. 10). This is, of course, not the option to which those with Johanan were inclined, since they are already on their way to Egypt when they inquire of Jeremiah. At the same time, they have expressed their willingness to obey God no matter what God's response. Jeremiah expresses the consequences of remaining in the land using the language from his call to be a prophet (1:10). Remaining in the land means that God will "build you up and not pull you down" or that God will "plant you and not pluck you up" (v. 10). Prior to his assassination, Gedaliah had focused on remaining in the land, and we should probably read the account of Gedaliah's governorship (40:7–12) as a portrayal of the building and planting and planting promised in these verses by God.

God's promise to build and plant the remnant of Judah if they remain in the land is supported by a series of divine assurances:

1. God is "sorry" for the disaster brought upon Judah (v. 10). The same Hebrew word here translated "sorry" is used elsewhere in the book to indicate God's changed mind (or heart: 18:8, 10; 26:3). The sense here is not that God has made a mistake in destroying Judah but regrets what has happened (even though Judah gave God no other options) and is eager for something different. God has plucked up and torn down, but, that accomplished, the Lord is ready to build and plant.
2. God will "save," "rescue," and have "mercy" on the remnant of Judah (vv. 11–12; compare 30:8, 9 11; 31:7, 20). These assurances are all linked to Babylon. Judah is no longer to fear Babylon (v. 11) because God has a new function for Babylon in relation to Judah. God has used Babylon to express anger and judgment through the exile of 587 B.C., so there has been reason to fear Babylon (or at least how God would use Babylon). Following 587 B.C., Babylon will have a different role as the agent of God's saving, rescue, and mercy. Verse 12 summarizes the point: "I [God] will grant you mercy, and he [Babylon] will have mercy on you, and restore you to your native soil."

The Judeans want to flee to Egypt because they fear the Babylonians (41:17–18), but following 587 B.C., the Babylonians are to be the agents of God's mercy. It is possible, even necessary, to remain in the land.

b. Disobedience of God, Jeremiah indicates, means refusing to remain in the land and instead going to the land of Egypt where the remnant think they can escape war and famine (vv. 13–14). The brutality of Ishmael and the murder of Gedaliah certainly must have made Judah an uninviting place. However, God warns that Egypt will not provide an escape from war and famine. The futility of flight to Egypt is reinforced as Jeremiah threatens that those who go to Egypt will "die by sword, by famine, by pestilence; they shall have no remnant or survivor from the disaster I am bringing upon them" (v. 17). If the remnant remains in the land, God is ready to move beyond the disaster to build and plant (v. 10); if the remnant flees to Egypt, their troubles will intensify.

The second part of Jeremiah's response to Johanan and those with him (vv. 18–22) reinforces God's judgment upon those who might flee to Egypt. Jeremiah equates God's anger that resulted in the destruction of Jerusalem with God's anger with those who might flee to Egypt (v. 18). Prior to 587 B.C., Jeremiah has defined obedience/disobedience and their consequences concretely in relationship to the situation Judah faced: obedience=surrender to Babylon=life; disobedience=resist Babylon=death. After 587 B.C., Jeremiah again defines obedience/disobedience and their consequences concretely in relationship to the situation Judah faces: obedience=remain in the land=life; disobedience=flee to Egypt=death. The threats against those who might flee to Egypt articulated in verse 18 are common covenantal curses that we have encountered often in the book of Jeremiah. However, the main thrust of this part of Jeremiah's response is that if the remnant of Judah live or die, receive blessing or curse, is built again or further uprooted, depends upon the decisions they make (vv. 19–22).

One would think that after the fall of Jerusalem to the Babylonians, it would have been abundantly clear that Judah's decisions mattered in what God did. Johanan and those who intended to go to Egypt have indicated to Jeremiah that whatever God said, they will do (v. 21). God has indicated they are to remain in the land. If they obey, God intends to build them up and not pull them down (v. 10), but if they do not obey, they are choosing death (v. 22). Surely with the fall of Jerusalem such a fresh memory, God's people will obey.

Jeremiah 43:1–7

43:1 **When Jeremiah finished speaking to all the people all these words of the LORD their God, with which the LORD their God has sent him to them,** [2] **Azariah son of Hoshaiah and Johanan son of Kareah and all the other insolent men said to Jeremiah, "You are telling a lie. The LORD our God did not send you to say, 'Do not go to Egypt to settle there';** [3] **but Baruch son of Neriah is inciting you against us, to hand us over to the Chaldeans, in order that**

they may kill us or take us into exile in Babylon." ⁴ So Johanan son of Kareah and all the commanders of the forces and all the people did not obey the voice of the LORD, to stay in the land of Judah. ⁵ But Johanan son of Kareah and all the commanders of the forces took all the remnant of Judah who had returned to settle in the land of Judah from all the nations to which they had been driven— ⁶ the men, the women, the children, the princesses, and everyone whom Nebuzaradan the captain of the guard had left with Gedaliah son of Ahikam son of Shaphan; also the prophet Jeremiah and Baruch son of Neriah. ⁷ And they came into the land of Egypt, for they did not obey the voice of the LORD. And they arrived at Tahpanhes.

The people who have pledged to "obey the voice of the Lord" (42:5–6) choose instead to go their own way. It is difficult to tell, in reflection, if remaining in the land was ever a real consideration. When they inquired of Jeremiah where they should go and what they should do (42:3), they were already on their way to Egypt (41:17–18). Maybe that was all they ever intended, and their consultation with Jeremiah was a formality. Yet, Johanan and his followers had at least indicated their intention to listen to and obey God. Having made such a show of good intention, they find it necessary to make excuses about why they were choosing to disregard the prophet's counsel.

Jeremiah's warning not to go to Egypt is dismissed as a "lie" (v. 2). In the book of Jeremiah, it is the prophet who identifies the deceptions, lies, and deceit of the community: the deceptive words of the Temple liturgy (7:3–4); deceptive social practices supported by falsification of the Torah by scribes (8:8–12); the lies of Judah's prophets supporting social injustice (23:14) and imagining that the Babylonian threat will quickly pass (27:10; 28:15; 29:21). Those determined to go to Egypt turn the charge back on Jeremiah; his counsel not to go to Egypt is identified as the "lie," though they are careful not quite to accuse the prophet directly. They lay the problem on Baruch, the prophet's secretary, whom they charge is in league with the Babylonians in a plot to have Johanan and his followers killed or exiled (v. 3) The suspicion that the prophet and his scribe are Babylonian sympathizers lingers in Judah from before the Babylonian victory (see 38:2–4).

There are clues in the text to suggest we are not to take the charges against Jeremiah and Baruch too seriously. Preceding the accusation that Jeremiah and Baruch are presenting a "lie," Johanan and his followers are called "insolent" men (v. 2). That is, they are audacious and bold and claim to know more than God and the prophet. Following the charge that Jeremiah and Baruch have lied, the text notes that these men "did not obey the voice of the Lord" (v. 4). Judah's failure to obey God's word has resulted in the defeat of Judah by Babylon in 587 B.C.; it had led to plucking up and tearing down. God has offered Johanan and his followers to "build you up and not pull you down" if they remained on the land. They choose instead to go to Egypt. We can only expect God's judgment to continue against the remnant of Judah, which has learned little from the catastrophe of 587 B.C.

This section of the book concludes as Johanan and his followers go to Egypt, taking Jeremiah with them. Why they took Jeremiah is unclear. What does seem clear is that Johanan has always intended to reach Tahpanhes in Egypt, and there is never an intention to take Jeremiah's counsel seriously if it contradicted what is intended in the first place.

The events that led the remnant of Judah to go to Egypt are presented from a perspective consistent with the whole of the book of Jeremiah. It is a perspective that sees God's future connected with those exiled to Babylon (Jeremiah 24, 29) and those willing to remain in the land after the exile and work with the Babylonians (Jeremiah 42). From this perspective, Johanan and his followers are "insolent men" who did "not obey." However, we need to be aware that Johanan and his followers faced a difficult situation. They lived in a very complex and troubling circumstance, and in the midst of their confusing moment in history, they had to decide to do one thing or another: endure the chaos of Judah or seek security in Egypt; cooperate with the Babylonians or live as refugees among the Egyptians; heed Jeremiah's counsel or conclude that Jeremiah had lied. While the text calls Johanan and his followers "insolent," they surely thought they were being sensible.

Is the book of Jeremiah being fair when it labels Johanan and his followers "disobedient"? One way to look at this issue is to recognize that the book of Jeremiah has the advantage of hindsight. Those who finally edited the book knew of both the fall of Jerusalem to the Babylonians and the eventual dominant role played by the Babylonian exiles in sustaining God's people after 587 B.C. The book of Jeremiah reflects the perspective of those that finally won out and had a major role in shaping the community of God's people. From this perspective, Johanan and his followers were on the losing side.

Yet, the perspective taken by the book of Jeremiah about Johanan and his followers is not totally satisfying. Most of us live our lives where Johanan and his followers found themselves, in the midst of very complex and confusing events where we must choose to do one thing or another: join one church or another, give financial support to one organization or another, take employment at one firm or another, vote for one candidate or another. As we attempt to be obedient, we do not have the advantage of hindsight. We must make decisions today and tomorrow the best we can.

So, besides the long-term historical judgment about Johanan, we must ask if there are other features about the decision to go to Egypt that justify the judgment of the book of Jeremiah that Johanan and his followers were insolent and disobedient. There may be. In choosing to go to Egypt, Johanan and his followers were acting out of self-interest. Egypt was safe, away from the trouble in Judah, a place that promised security and comfort (see 42:14). To stay in Judah was risky and difficult. Rebuilding the community of God's people in Judah would have required hardships: difficult living conditions, an unsettled social climate, the need to cooperate with the dreaded Babylonians. Given these choices, these texts about Johanan and those intending to go with him to Egypt suggest that God expected Johanan and his followers to choose risky obedience over calculated security. The Lord intended to rebuild a community of God's people in Judah and expected Johanan and his followers to participate in that risky enterprise.

In the same way, Jesus has called his disciples to take up their cross and follow him, to choose risky obedience over calculated security in the service of God's reign. We, too, live where we must make choices that are not often easy or obvious, and in circumstances where life is messy and history is complex. However, it may be that by reading carefully and praying long over a book like the book of Jeremiah, we will come to understand the risky obedience God expects.

JEREMIAH IN EGYPT
Jeremiah 43:8–44:30

Jeremiah was taken by Johanan and his followers to Egypt. Obviously, Jeremiah, who had condemned the idea of going to Egypt and urged the Judeans with Johanan to remain in the land, did not want to go to Egypt himself. In this section of the book of Jeremiah, Jeremiah is in Egypt, and a series of texts tells of the prophet's condemnation of the Judeans in Egypt and of God's intentions to destroy Egypt. In particular, Jeremiah condemns the idolatry of the Judeans in Egypt, who were sacrificing to gods and goddesses they thought would bring them security and comfort.

Jeremiah 43:8–13

43:8 **Then the word of the** LORD **came to Jeremiah in Tahpanhes:** ⁹ **Take some large stones in your hands, and bury them in the clay pavement that is at the entrance to Pharaoh's palace in Tahpanhes. Let the Judeans see you do it,** ¹⁰ **and say to them, Thus says the** LORD **of hosts, the God of Israel: I am going to send and take my servant King Nebuchadrezzar of Babylon, and he will set his throne above these stones that I have buried, and he will spread his royal canopy over them.** ¹¹ **He shall come and ravage the land of Egypt, giving**

> **those who are destined for pestilence, to pestilence,**
> **and those who are destined for captivity, to captivity,**
> **and those who are destined for the sword, to the sword.**

¹² **He shall kindle a fire in the temples of the gods of Egypt; and he shall burn them and carry them away captive; and he shall pick clean the land of Egypt, as a shepherd picks his cloak clean of vermin; and he shall depart from there safely.** ¹³ **He shall break the obelisks of Heliopolis, which is in the land of Egypt; and the temples of the gods of Egypt he shall burn with fire.**

Several times the book of Jeremiah has remembered that the prophet undertook an action to give vivid expression to his message. These have been something like object lessons. For instance, Jeremiah buries a loincloth in a stream and when he retrieves the ruined loincloth, uses it to express his message that God's people had become, like the loincloth, good for nothing (Jeremiah 13). On another occasion, Jeremiah places yoke bars across his shoulders to signify that God intends that Judah and its neighbors submit to Babylon (Jeremiah 27; chapter 28, Hananiah breaks the yoke bars off Jeremiah as a way of saying he does not think God will allow Babylon to defeat Judah). In this first text about Jeremiah in Egypt, the prophet again is instructed by God to perform a symbolic act.

Jeremiah is to take some stones and bury them under the pavement that is outside the palace of the king of Egypt (the Pharaoh), which was located in Tahpanhes, the Egyptian city where the Judeans had come (v. 9). Jeremiah is then to announce that it is God's intention for the Babylonians to overtake Egypt and for the king of Babylon to set up his throne above the stones that Jeremiah had buried (v. 10). The Judeans who had gone to Egypt did so in part to escape the Babylonians whom they feared (41:18). The prophet Jeremiah is to announce that God is still using the Babylonians. God even calls the king of Babylon "my servant" (v. 10). Judah resisted God and resisted submission to the Babylonians before 587 B.C. The Judeans resisted the Babylonians in the land of Judah after 587 B.C. and fled to Egypt to escape them. Jeremiah declares that there will be no escape from God or from God's agent, the Babylonians. The Judeans can flee to Egypt, but they cannot escape God, the Sovereign who plucks up and tears down nations and kingdoms (1:10).

Many of the specific judgments mentioned in these verses match judgments threatened against Judah earlier in the book. For instance, God threatened that a kingdom from the north would set up a throne at the gates of Jerusalem (1:15), and they did (39:3). With some Judeans in Egypt, God threatened that the king of Babylon would set up a throne in front of the palace of the Pharaoh in Tahpanhes. The threat against Egypt expressed in verse 11 (pestilence, captivity, and sword) is almost identical to the threat once spoken against Judah in Jeremiah 15:2 (pestilence, sword, famine, captivity). God threatens to burn the temples of the gods of Egypt and carry off captives (vv. 12–13) just as God threatened to burn Jerusalem and exile its inhabitants. And did!

The Judeans who fled to Egypt hoped to escape the Babylonians, but the king of Babylon was the Lord's servant. What the Judeans were attempting to escape by their flight to Egypt was not the Babylonians, but God. Judah, despite the disaster of 587 B.C., was not yet willing to listen to and obey God. They will not surrender to the Babylonians before 587 B.C. as God had commanded. After 587 B.C. they refuse to live in the land with the Babylonians as God commanded. However, Jeremiah announces that the Judeans cannot escape the Sovereign of the nations in Egypt either. God will use the Babylonians to pluck up and tear down Egypt in the same way God used the Babylonians to pluck up and tear down Judah.

Jeremiah 44:1–14

44:1 **The word that came to Jeremiah for all the Judeans living in the land of Egypt, at Migdol, at Tahpanhes, at Memphis, and in the land of Pathros,** 2 **Thus says the LORD of hosts, the God of Israel: You yourselves have seen all the disaster that I have brought on Jerusalem and on all the towns of Judah. Look at them; today they are a desolation, without an inhabitant in them,** 3 **because of the wickedness that they committed, provoking me to anger, in that they went to make offerings and serve other gods that they had not known, neither they, nor you, nor your ancestors.** 4 **Yet I persistently sent to you all my servants the prophets, saying, "I beg you not to do this abominable thing that I hate!"** 5 **But they did not listen or incline their ear, to turn from their wickedness and make no offerings to other gods.** 6 **So my wrath and my anger were poured out and kindled in the towns of Judah and in the streets of Jerusalem; and they became a waste and a desolation, as they still are today.** 7 **And now thus says the LORD God of hosts, the God of Israel: Why are you doing such great harm to yourselves, to cut off man and woman, child and infant, from** the midst of Judah, leaving yourselves without a remnant? [8] Why do you provoke me to anger with the works of your hands, making offerings to other gods in the land of Egypt where you have come to settle? Will you be cut off and become an object of cursing and ridicule among all the nations of the earth? [9] Have you forgotten the crimes of your ancestors, of the kings of Judah, of their wives, your own crimes and those of your wives, which they committed in the land of Judah and in the streets of Jerusalem? [10] They have shown no contrition or fear to this day, nor have they walked in my law and my statutes that I set before you and before your ancestors.

[11] Therefore thus says the LORD of hosts, the God of Israel: I am determined to bring disaster on you, to bring all Judah to an end. [12] I will take the remnant of Judah who are determined to come to the land of Egypt to settle, and they shall perish, everyone; in the land of Egypt they shall fall; by the sword and by famine they shall perish; from the least to the greatest, they shall die by the sword and by famine; and they shall become an object of execration and horror, of cursing and ridicule. [13] I will punish those who live in the land of Egypt, as I have punished Jerusalem, with the sword, with famine, and with pestilence, [14] so that none of the remnant of Judah who have come to settle in the land of Egypt shall escape or survive or return to the land of Judah. Although they long to go back to live there, they shall not go back, except some fugitives.

This is a judgment speech by Jeremiah that has two parts: Jeremiah brings accusations against the Judeans in Egypt (vv. 1–10) and then he announces God's judgment upon them (vv. 11–14).

The accusations that Jeremiah brings against the Judeans who had fled to Egypt begin with a rehearsal of how the destruction of Jerusalem and the defeat of Judah occurred (vv. 2–7). The themes are all familiar. Judah's destruction is not an accident but the result of God's intention and action (vv. 2, 7). God acted not arbitrarily but in response to Judah's idolatry (vv. 3–4). God tried to persuade Judah to turn from its idolatry through prophets "persistently sent," but those in Judah "did not listen or incline their ear, to turn from their wickedness" (vv. 4–5). The Judeans in Egypt lived through the Babylonian victory of 587 B.C., saw Jerusalem in ruins, saw Judah as a desolation. Jeremiah reminds his audience in Egypt of that which they should have known: idolatry and the failure to listen to God's prophets are a formula for disaster.

At verse 8 the focus shifts from the Judeans responsible for the disaster of 587 B.C. ("they" in vv. 2–7) to Jeremiah's current audience, the Judeans who fled to Egypt ("you" in vv. 8–10). Those Judeans who fled to Egypt, Jeremiah charges, are just like those Judeans who were responsible for the disaster of 587 B.C. The Judeans in Egypt continue in idolatry, "making offerings to other gods in the land of Egypt" (v. 8). Although their residence has shifted from Judah to Egypt, their behavior and relationship to God has not changed at all. The situation is as tragic as it is inexplicable. The Judeans in Egypt seem to have "forgotten the crimes" of their ancestors" (v. 9) and show "no contrition or fear to this day" (v. 10). Despite God's judgment, despite being plucked up and pulled down, the Judeans in Egypt continue in the ways of their ancestors, who caused the disaster of 587 B.C. by their idolatry.

So it is not at all surprising that Jeremiah announces on God's behalf that the time of judgment has not yet passed, that the Judeans in Egypt will continue to experience God's plucking up and tearing down (vv. 11–14). Again, the judgments announced are familiar and parallel the judgments God previously announced and enacted against Judah: "they shall perish . . . fall . . . by the sword and by famine they shall perish . . . they shall die by the sword . . . become an object of execration and horror, of cursing and ridicule" (v. 12). Just as God "punished Jerusalem," so, too, will God punish the "remnant of Judah," who, except for some fugitives, will never return to their land again (vv. 13–14).

We read in the book of Jeremiah that God intends building and planting after plucking up and tearing down. However, this harsh judgment speech makes quite clear that there is nothing automatic about the succession of judgment and restoration but that the time for building and planting waits for God's decision. God intends restoration, yet for those Judeans who flee to Egypt and continue in idolatry, God's plucking up and tearing down will continue. Of course, restoration depends upon God's mercy and forgiveness (30:18; 31:20, 34; 33:26; 42:12). At the same time, the book of Jeremiah understands that God expects the people to turn and repent, especially after they have experienced the consequences of their rebellion against God. There is no easy formula about the relationship of God's judgment and restoration in the book of Jeremiah. Both God's forgiveness and mercy and Judah's repentance play a part in the building and planting God intends.

The apostle Paul also thought about how God's grace and human repentance were related. Paul wrote about this issue in Romans as the relationship of sin and grace:

Should we continue to sin in order that grace may abound? By no means! How can we who died to sin go on living in it? Do you not know that all of us who have been baptized into Christ Jesus were baptized into his death? Therefore we have been buried with him by baptism into death, so that, just as Christ was raised from the dead by the glory of the Father, so we too might walk in newness of life. (Rom. 6:1–4)

We might say that through the destruction of Jerusalem, Judah was "baptized into . . . death" (plucking up and tearing down), though what God intended was "newness of life" (building and planting). Judah refused God's offer, refused to repent, refused the newness God had in mind. In the church, we affirm that we receive "newness of life" through God's grace; but having experienced God's grace, we are not to continue living in sin but instead are to "walk in newness of life."

Jeremiah 44:15–19

44:15 **Then all the men who were aware that their wives had been making offerings to other gods, and all the women who stood by, a great assembly, all the people who lived in Pathros in the land of Egypt, answered Jeremiah:** [16] **"As for the word that you have spoken to us in the name of the LORD, we are not going to listen to you.** [17] **Instead, we will do everything that we have vowed, make offerings to the queen of heaven and pour out libations to her, just as we and our ancestors, our kings and our officials, used to do in the towns of Judah and in the streets of Jerusalem. We used to have plenty of food, and prospered, and saw no misfortune.** [18] **But from the time we stopped making offerings to the queen of heaven and pouring out libations to her, we have lacked everything and have perished by the sword and by famine."** [19] **And the women said, "Indeed we will go on making offerings to the queen of heaven and pouring out libations to her; do you think that we made cakes for her, marked with her image, and poured out libations to her without our husbands' being involved?"**

Jeremiah's words are met with total defiance, at least from one group of Judeans who reside in southern Egypt at Pathros. We are able to discern in this material the sharp conflicts that developed among various factions of those who survived the disaster of 587 B.C. The group who is presented in these verses must have been held in particular contempt by those who preserved the traditions about the prophet Jeremiah.

Those who answer Jeremiah are men who are aware that their wives are making sacrifices to "the queen of heaven," as well as other women who observe the practice. "The queen of heaven" is mentioned in Jeremiah 7:18 and was the Assyrian and Babylonian goddess Ishtar, associated with war and fertility. The defiance of this group to Jeremiah is blatant and forthright. They do not intend to listen to the prophet. Furthermore, they think they can justify their actions. They tell Jeremiah that when Judah made sacrifices to the queen of heaven, they had "plenty of food, and prospered, and saw no misfortune" (v. 17); however, when these sacrifices stopped, they "lacked everything and have perished by the sword and by famine" (v. 18).

Historically, one can hear in this response the impact of the reform efforts of King Josiah (640–609 B.C.) after the long period of Assyrian domination of Judah. Josiah's efforts to refurbish the Temple in Jerusalem and the "covenant" he enacted when a scroll was found during the Temple renovation (2 Kings 22–23) were efforts to rid Judah of idolatrous practices that had become prominent during the years of Assyrian domination of Judah. It is very likely that King Josiah ended, as best he could, sacrifices to Ishtar, the queen of heaven. The prophet Jeremiah is often identified with Josiah's reform efforts (at least as supportive of them), and we have seen that persons in Judah who supported Jeremiah had connections with Josiah (especially the family of Shaphan, which included Ahikam and Gedaliah; see 2 Kings 22:8ff.; Jer. 26:24; 40:7). Thus, through this group in Egypt that challenged Jeremiah, we hear what must have been a long-standing conflict within Judah between those who supported King Josiah's reforms and those who resisted them.

Within the book of Jeremiah, there are two issues raised by these verses. First, this group is quite open in their reasons for continuing to make sacrifices to the queen of heaven. In the perception of this group, the sacrifices were an effective means of securing themselves. When they made the sacrifices, they perceived that they were well off; when the sacrifices ceased, they perceived that they suffered. So they have come to entrust themselves to the queen of heaven, and they have every intention of continuing their sacrifices (v. 19). For the group of Judeans in this text, the queen of heaven obviously has become their god. Luther said:

> A god is that to which we look for all good and where we resort for help in every time of need; to have a god is simply to trust and believe in one with our whole heart. . . . Now, I say, whatever your heart clings to and confides in, that is really your God. (Luther, *Large Catechism*, 44)

However, for Judah and Israel, God is the One who brought them out of Egypt and gave them the Promised Land. Jeremiah speaks for the God of Israel who demands that Israel and Judah not cling to or entrust themselves to any other gods. In a direct way, the Judeans, who in this text confront Jeremiah, have made an intentional choice that the queen of heaven will be their god. For the church, God is not only the One who brought Israel out of Egypt, but the One whom Jesus called "Father" and who raised Jesus from the dead. We in the church do well to ask if we trust the One whom we confess to be our God and the God of Jesus Christ, or if we, with perhaps less direct awareness than the Judeans of this text, have come to entrust ourselves to others—our accomplishments, our wealth, our national identity, for instance—because they seem to promise us "eternal good."

A second issue is raised by this text through the radically different assessments made by Jeremiah and those who worshiped the queen of heaven. Those who worshiped the queen of heaven were confident that Judah's well-being and their own could be traced to the sacrifices offered this goddess or the cessation of such sacrifices (vv. 17–18). Jeremiah, by contrast, was confident that the disaster that befell Judah was a result of idolatry, including the worship of the queen of heaven (v. 3); and, Jeremiah claimed, the same kind of idolatry would lead to God's judgment upon the remnant of Judah in Egypt (vv. 9–10). Both Jeremiah and the Judeans who challenged him worked with the same events before them but understood them in different ways. Undoubtedly, the different perceptions had to do with the "trust" (or faith) that each placed in their God. Trusting Yahweh, the God of Israel, led Jeremiah to see one way; trusting Ishtar, the queen of heaven, led the Judeans in Egypt to see another way. If we are honest, there is no rational way to judge between these claims anymore, perhaps, than to explain why we fall in love and have a deeply committed relationship with one person and not another. Jeremiah could not refute the claims of the Judeans worshiping the queen of heaven, but he knew that trusting the God of Israel made all the difference for him. Likewise, we in the church have no way to prove that Jesus is the servant Lord who deserves our trust and commitment, but having come to trust Jesus makes all the difference for us in what we see and understand and how we live our lives in God's world.

Jeremiah 44:20–30

44:20 Then Jeremiah said to all the people, men and women, all the people who were giving him this answer: [21] "As for the offerings that you made in the towns of Judah and in the streets of Jerusalem, you and your ancestors, your kings and your officials, and the people of the land, did not the LORD remember them? Did it not come into his mind? [22] The LORD could no longer bear the sight of your evil doings, the abominations that you committed; therefore your land became a desolation and a waste and a curse, without inhabitant, as it is to this day. [23] It is because you burned offerings, and because you sinned against the LORD and did not obey the voice of the LORD or walk in his law and in his statutes and in his decrees, that this disaster has befallen you, as is still evident today."

[24] Jeremiah said to all the people and all the women, "Hear the word of the LORD, all you Judeans who are in the land of Egypt, [25] Thus says the LORD

of hosts, the God of Israel: You and your wives have accomplished in deeds what you declared in words, saying, 'We are determined to perform the vows that we have made, to make offerings to the queen of heaven and to pour out libations to her.' By all means, keep your vows and make your libations! [26] Therefore hear the word of the LORD, all you Judeans who live in the land of Egypt: Lo, I swear by my great name, says the LORD, that my name shall no longer be pronounced on the lips of any of the people of Judah in all the land of Egypt, saying, 'As the LORD God lives.' [27] I am going to watch over them for harm and not for good; all the people of Judah who are in the land of Egypt shall perish by the sword and by famine, until not one is left. [28] And those who escape the sword shall return from the land of Egypt to the land of Judah, few in number; and all the remnant of Judah, who have come to the land of Egypt to settle, shall know whose words will stand, mine or theirs! [29] This shall be the sign to you, says the LORD, that I am going to punish you in this place, in order that you may know that my words against you will surely be carried out: [30] Thus says the LORD, I am going to give Pharaoh Hophra, king of Egypt, into the hands of his enemies, those who seek his life, just as I gave King Zedekiah of Judah into the hand of King Nebuchadrezzar of Babylon, his enemy who sought his life."

The dispute between Jeremiah and the Judeans who worshiped the queen of heaven is concluded in these verses. There is a twofold organization to this address:

a. First, Jeremiah recounts Judah's idolatry that led to the disaster of 587 B.C. (vv. 20–23). The ground of these arguments is familiar to us by now and does not require long reflection. The disaster befell Judah and Jerusalem because God's people made burnt offerings to other gods and would not listen to God or obey God's law.

b. Second, Jeremiah indicates what God will do to those Judeans in Egypt who continue to engage in the kind of idolatry that caused Judah and Jerusalem to be destroyed (vv. 24–30). The familiar "therefore," connected with speeches in which prophets announced God's judgment, occurs in verse 26. Jeremiah warns that God is watching the people "for harm and not for good" (v. 27). At the very beginning of the book of Jeremiah, the Lord declares, "I am watching over my word to perform it" (1:13). Throughout the book, we have seen how God fulfills this word, most dramatically in the destruction of Judah and Jerusalem. God's words are matched by actions. What God says, God does. Those Judeans in Egypt after 587 B.C. should have had no doubt that God's word would be fulfilled, so the threat that the Lord intends them harm and not good is ominous. The harm intended is that but few will survive the sojourn in Egypt (v. 28).

There is good reason that God's name will "no longer be pronounced on the lips of any of the people of Judah in all the land of Egypt" (v. 26), and it is that the Lord intends the Judeans in Egypt to perish (v. 27).

Verse 28 is particularly important and a key to the dispute between Jeremiah and the Judeans with him in Egypt. Jeremiah cannot refute the claims of those who insist that Judah is better off with the queen of heaven than the God of Israel. However, Jeremiah does insist that in time, it will be obvious who is the sovereign of history. Thus, when only a small remnant of Judeans returns from Egypt to Judah, it will be clear whose words stand, "mine or theirs." The dispute in Jeremiah 44 is much like the dispute between Jeremiah and the optimistic prophets from earlier in the book; only the fall of Judah to the Babylonians and the long exile finally was able to resolve the conflict. So, too, the conflict between those who claimed that Judah's well-being depended upon sacrifices to the queen of heaven, on the one hand, and Jeremiah, who claimed that such sacrifices brought death for Judah, will only be adjudicated in time as the course of history unfolds.

Meanwhile, Jeremiah indicates that a sign of God's judgment will be the assassination of Pharaoh Hophra (vv. 29–30). This pharaoh was murdered in approximately 570 B.C. It seems that Jeremiah, or at least those who finally edited the book of Jeremiah, used this event of which they were aware as a "sign" (v. 29) to indicate that once again, the word of the Lord spoken through the words of the prophet Jeremiah were being and would be fulfilled.

This speech of Jeremiah is the last direct word of the prophet to Judah. The story of Jeremiah and the people ends where it began, with an affirmation about God's sovereignty and certainty that the Lord is directing the course of Judah's history. Yet, as through much of the book, this claim by Jeremiah is disputed. Earlier in the book, for instance, the Jerusalem leadership disputed Jeremiah's perception that the Lord was directing Judah's history toward defeat by Babylon and captivity. At the end of the book, the claim of Jeremiah that God will judge Egypt and the Judeans who fled there is disputed by those who claim that the queen of heaven directed Judah's history toward well-being when proper sacrifices were made.

The community of the synagogue and of the church have preserved the memory of the prophet Jeremiah in the book that bears his name to witness to the truth of Jeremiah's claims. The very existence of the book of Jeremiah within the canon of Jewish and Christian scripture says that the communities of God's people gathered in the synagogue and the church have been convinced that in the disputes between Jeremiah and the leaders of Judah, between Jeremiah and the optimistic prophets, between

Jeremiah and the worshipers of the queen of heaven, Jeremiah has it right and was a faithful witness to God. Jeremiah was the spokesperson for the God who was sovereign over history, who brought Israel out of Egypt, and then who brought Judah to captivity in Babylon (1:3). The synagogue and church have judged that in the dispute between whose words will stand, "mine or theirs" (v. 28), Jeremiah's have stood.

Yet such a judgment is never easy and always involves a fundamental decision about whom and what we will trust (44:15–19). In deciding about which word we believe will stand, there is never enough evidence, never certainty, never a clear choice. The church believes that God's word has become flesh and that the Lord's reign has been seen through one who kept company with sinners and tax-collectors who touched lepers and talked to women, who preached that the meek would inherit the earth, and who was killed on a cross as a common criminal. Other voices find such claims incredible, but we still believe, like Jeremiah, what we cannot possibly prove.

Jeremiah 45:1–5

45:1 **The word that the prophet Jeremiah spoke to Baruch son of Neriah, when he wrote these words in a scroll at the dictation of Jeremiah, in the fourth year of King Jehoiakim son of Josiah of Judah:** 2 **Thus says the LORD, the God of Israel, to you, O Baruch:** 3 **You said, "Woe is me! The LORD has added sorrow to my pain; I am weary with my groaning, and I find no rest."** 4 **Thus you shall say to him, "Thus says the LORD: I am going to break down what I have built, and pluck up what I have planted—that is, the whole land.** 5 **And you, do you seek great things for yourself? Do not seek them; for I am going to bring disaster upon all flesh, says the LORD; but I will give you your life as a prize of war in every place to which you may go."**

Jeremiah 45 concerns Jeremiah's secretary Baruch and is dated in the fourth year of King Jehoiakim. This date is when Baruch wrote down all the words of Jeremiah and read them at the Temple (Jeremiah 36). Thus, the chapter is not related historically to the events in Egypt, which have been the concern of the preceding chapters. Rather, Jeremiah 45 serves as a conclusion to the book of Jeremiah up to this point. In the next chapter, the book takes a different direction with a series of oracles against the nations (Jeremiah 46–51), and the book as a whole concludes in Jeremiah 52. As we examine this chapter, we need to be attentive to the ways it functions as a conclusion to the story of God's decision to pluck up and tear down Judah, and to the ways the chapter may point beyond plucking up and tearing down toward God's promised building and planting.

The chapter remembers a complaint of Baruch (vv. 1–3) and God's response to Baruch through Jeremiah (vv. 4–5). Baruch's complaint is that God "added sorrow to my pain" and that Baruch has found no "rest" (v. 3). Like the complaints of Jeremiah himself (especially in chapters 11–20), the language of Baruch's complaint is quite general and impossible to relate specifically to the circumstances of the scribe's life. What was the pain and sorrow he experienced? How had he found no rest? We cannot know. We do know that Baruch was closely associated with Jeremiah, so we should not be surprised that he suffered the same rejection and ostracism as the prophet. Baruch wrote and read the prophet's words of judgment at the Temple; when King Jehoiakim burned the original scroll, Baruch rewrote the scroll and added to it (Jeremiah 36). Baruch assisted Jeremiah with his purchase of the family field in Anathoth (Jeremiah 32). Most telling, just prior to taking him to Egypt, the Judeans who rejected Jeremiah's warning not to go to Egypt accused Baruch (and not, for a change, Jeremiah) of plotting to have the Judeans who remained in the land after 587 B.C. either killed by the Babylonians or exiled to Babylon. We have seen throughout the book that Jeremiah as God's spokesperson is rejected and so suffered. Baruch, Jeremiah's close associate, suffered similarly and like Jeremiah, voiced complaint about his situation.

God's response to Baruch's complaint is in three parts:

a. God's intention to "break down" and "pluck up" Judah is reinforced (v. 4). God's judgment is once again expressed with the verbs from the call of Jeremiah (1:10). The use of this language further connects Baruch with Jeremiah. God's intention to pluck up and break down Judah are voiced by Jeremiah but written by Baruch (Jeremiah 36). God's judgment is associated not just with Jeremiah but also with the prophet's secretary. We readers know that after the Babylonian victory over Judah, the survivors suspected Baruch, even more than Jeremiah, of plotting ill against them with the Babylonians (43:3). Baruch had been involved by God as a participant in breaking down and plucking up Judah.

b. God rebukes Baruch. The question of verse 5 does not serve as an invitation for Baruch to respond to God but for God to denounce Baruch. In the midst of God's judgment of Judah and "all flesh" (v. 5; this reference to "all flesh" anticipates Jeremiah 46–51, oracles against the nations), Baruch is accused of seeking "rest" (v. 3) and "great things" for himself (v. 5). Whatever Baruch may have had in mind (we cannot know specifically), God's rebuke suggests that his expectations were unrealistic. In a situation in which many were suffering terribly (or would), Baruch had grandiose hopes, which God judged inappropriate. Perhaps Baruch may be compared to a person who in the midst of an economic downturn wants a big raise so to have new house, a new car, and an extended vacation. A more modest vision, having a job at all, may be much more appropriate. The Babylonian threat made Baruch's expectations unrealistic.

c.) God's response to Baruch concludes with a promise, but it is a promise much more modest than "great things" or even the "rest" wished for by Baruch. God promises Baruch that he will have his "life as a prize of war." This same promise is made to Ebed-melech, who rescued Jeremiah from death in the cistern just before the fall of Jerusalem (39:18). In a situation in which many will lose their lives, God promises Baruch that which many in Judah will have been only too glad to have, his life. Many will perish, but Baruch will live. God does not promise Baruch as much as he may have hoped, but it is a gracious promise given the circumstances.

We can read this story as simply tying up a loose end in the book of Jeremiah and resolving what will happen to Baruch, who has appeared from time to time. Sometimes movies conclude with all the main characters appearing on the screen behind a brief synopsis of what became of them: "Joe married Suzanne, they had two children and lived happily ever after." However, it seems that Jeremiah 45 intends to do more than bring closure to Baruch, and that it functions to conclude the book of Jeremiah to this point.

One way to understand Jeremiah 45 is as a signal that God's future is with Baruch, Jeremiah, and that small remnant of Judah who saw that God's future is with the Babylonian option. Jeremiah announced that God's building and planting will be with the "good figs" exiled to Babylon (Jeremiah 24). He urged surrender to the Babylonians as the option for life, and resistance to the Babylonians as the way of death (Jeremiah 21; 38:17–18). He counseled that cooperation with the Babylonians rather than flight to Egypt was the option for life (42:7–17). Baruch himself was identified with the pro-Babylonian option of Jeremiah, and he was rejected for it (43:3). Then, in Jeremiah 45, it is Baruch who is promised life after God's plucking up and tearing down. The promise is surely more than a personal word to Baruch; it is a claim about where God's future is to be: with Baruch, with Jeremiah, with all of those who submitted to God's intentions for plucking up and tearing down, risked the Babylonian option, and with whom God will in the future build and plant (Jeremiah 24).

A second way to understand Jeremiah 45 as the counterpart to Jeremiah 1. In Jeremiah 1, the prophet Jeremiah is introduced as God's spokesperson, charged to be faithful to God (1:17), and promised God's protection even in the midst of adversity (1:18–19). In Jeremiah 45, near the conclusion of the book of Jeremiah, the scribe who is responsible for writing the words of Jeremiah (Jeremiah 36), is given a similar charge and promise.

Baruch cannot expect "rest" and "great things," but as the one who recorded the Lord's word of plucking up and tearing down, he is promised at least his life by God. Thus, Jeremiah and Baruch, the messengers of God's word, pained and weary from the assaults of those who resisted this word and rejected its messengers, are promised God's protection. Their enemies who rejected their message will not prevail (1:18–19) against them. They will have their lives (45:5), and as a sign of God's faithfulness to God's word, we have their book!

"Concerning the Nations"
Jeremiah 46–51

Most of the book of Jeremiah concerns God's dealings with Israel and especially with Judah. Throughout Jeremiah 1–45, Babylon is the agent of God's judgment, the nation called to pluck up and tear down Judah. In Jeremiah 46–51, the focus shifts, and these chapters are "the word of the Lord that came to the prophet Jeremiah concerning the nations" (46:1). Several nations are addressed in these chapters (in order): Egypt, the Philistines, Moab, Ammon, Edom, Damascus (Syria), Kedar, Hazor, Elam, and finally Babylon. Before considering these chapters in detail, some general comments may help our reading:

1. It is not likely that the prophet Jeremiah spoke or dictated many of the oracles against the nations found in Jeremiah 46–51. He may well have been responsible for some of the oracles against Egypt, especially, for we have seen that the prophet was clearly anti-Egypt in his understanding of what God intended for Judah. However, many of the oracles against the nations may have been added to the book by later editors who were attempting to understand the exile of 587 B.C. as part of a wider scheme of God's activity. Another clue that the oracles against the nations came from later editors of the book is that there are references to events that probably occurred after Jeremiah's lifetime.

2. Jeremiah 46–51 contains what are called "oracles against the nations," a common feature of Old Testament prophetic books (see, for instance, Amos 1:3–2:16; Isa. 13:1–23:18; Ezek. 25:1–32:32; Joel 3). We do not know much about how these oracles came to be part of various prophetic books. A few have suggested that these oracles reflect a worship ritual that affirmed God as the ruler of the nations. Support for this idea comes from the presence of the theme that God is the ruler of the nations in the book of Psalms (for instance, see Psalms 2; 66:24–35; also Psalms 76, 82, 83, and especially 96–99) which was used in worship in the Temple in Jerusalem.

3. Within the book of Jeremiah, the prophet is appointed by the Lord to be a prophet "over nations and kingdoms" (1:10), and the oracles against the nations fill out the concern of the book for the wide range of God's dominion. The book of Jeremiah up to this point has been primarily concerned with Judah and Babylon and, to a lesser extent in the latter chapters, Egypt. Obviously, God ruled over Israel and Judah, a claim central to the whole book of Jeremiah. Yet, that was not the extent of God's reign. The book of Jeremiah has presented the Lord's rule as universal, extending to Babylon and beyond, so that God held the whole created order accountable (for example, see Jer. 5:22; 8:7; 10:12–13). The inclusion of these chapters underscores the claim of the book that God's concern was not simply with Judah and Babylon as the agent of Judah's judgment but also God's rule over all nations and the whole of creation.

4. In the prophetic books of the Old Testament, the reason given for God's judgment of the nations is their pride or unrestrained brutality. While the nations may have once served the Lord's intentions to bring judgment on Judah or Israel, the oracles against the nations typically indicate the ways these nations exceeded the bounds God set for them and are called to account. Thus, for instance, in the book of Amos the Ammonites are threatened with judgment because of their harsh brutality that served only "to enlarge their territory" (1:13); or, in Isaiah, it is Moab's pride that leads to God's judgment (Isa. 16:6–7).

In the book of Jeremiah, some of the oracles against the nations are quite clear about the reasons for God's judgment. This is true of the oracles against Moab, for instance, and especially those concerning Babylon. However, in reading the oracles against the nations in Jeremiah, we will note that they do not treat all the nations in the same manner. In some cases, the book of Jeremiah reflects a mood of awe and mystery, unclear, for instance, why God may have used Babylon as an agent of judgment against some nation or another. In the book, God's judgment of a nation is not always directly attributed to that nation's pride or brutality.

5. Often in the prophetic books, God's judgment of the nations functions to reassure Israel and Judah that the Lord intended their restoration. God's judgment of nations that had attacked Judah or Israel, even if as agents of the Lord's judgment, signaled the beginning of restoration. So, scattered among the oracles against the nations in the prophetic books, including Jeremiah, are reassurances that God's judgment of the nations foreshadowed restoration and well-being for Judah and Israel (for

example, Isa. 14:1–2, 32; 16:5; Ezek. 28:24–26; Joel 3:18–21; and Jer. 46:27–28, 50:17–20).

Yet, in the book of Jeremiah, there is a connection between God's judgment of the nations and restoration of Judah even beyond the claims expressed directly in Jeremiah 46–51. In Jeremiah 30–33, God's promised restoration of Judah is connected with judgment of the nations (30:11, 16, 20). We have seen in reading the book of Jeremiah how the destruction of Judah and Jerusalem (Jeremiah 39) needs to be understood as the fulfillment of God's threat to pluck up and tear down. In the same way, the oracles against the nations, which imagine the judgment of Judah's enemies and oppressors, especially Babylon, need to be read as pointing toward the fulfillment of God's promise of building and planting.

A further clue that the oracles against the nations foreshadow Judah's restoration can be found at the beginning of the book of Jeremiah. The relationship between God and the people is imagined to be such that the Lord will bring disaster upon any nation that harms Israel:

> Israel was holy to the Lord,
>   the first fruits of his harvest.
> All who ate of it became guilty;
>   disaster came upon them,
>   says the LORD.
>   (2:3)

The oracles against the nations, which indicate the Lord will bring disaster upon Judah's enemies, remind us of God's earlier relationship with Israel and signal the restoration of relationship between God and the people.

6. Finally, before we read the oracles against the nations, we need to note two connections between Jeremiah 46–51 and Jeremiah 45. First, in responding to Baruch in Jeremiah 45, God threatens to bring "disaster upon all flesh" (45:5). This threat is realized in Jeremiah 46–51 with God's judgment against the nations, that is, against "all flesh" (interestingly, the phrase "all flesh" is used at the beginning and end of the story of the flood—Gen. 6:13; 9:17—God's judgment on "all flesh"). Second, Jeremiah 45 concerns Baruch, Jeremiah's scribe. In Jeremiah 51, we are introduced to Seraiah, Baruch's brother, about whom it is reported that Jeremiah dictated the oracles against the nations. We will need to examine what it means that Baruch's brother was the scribe who recorded the oracles against the nations.

AGAINST EGYPT
Jeremiah 46:1–28

In the latter chapters of the book, Egypt plays a significant role. King Zedekiah and his officials looked to Egypt to save Jerusalem and Judah from Babylon (37:6–10); and a group of Judeans fled to Egypt after the Babylonian victory of 587 B.C. against Jeremiah's counsel, taking the prophet with them (Jeremiah 43). In both cases, the book understands that Judah's relationship with Egypt worked against God's purposes. So, the oracles against the nations begin with Egypt, but they conclude with Babylon. Babylon is the nation that throughout the book has been the agent of God's judgment and was at the time the book of Jeremiah was written the dominant power in the ancient Near Eastern world. If God was sovereign over nations and kingdoms, then Egypt and Babylon were the primary test cases.

Jeremiah 46:1–12

46:1 The word of the LORD that came to the prophet Jeremiah concerning the nations.

²Concerning Egypt, about the army of Pharaoh Neco, king of Egypt, which was by the river Euphrates at Carchemish and which King Nebuchadrezzar of Babylon defeated in the fourth year of King Jehoiakim son of Josiah of Judah:

3   Prepare buckler and shield,
      and advance for battle!
4   Harness the horses;
      mount the steeds!
      Take your stations with your helmets,
      whet your lances,
      put on your coats of mail!
5   Why do I see them terrified?
      They have fallen back;
      their warriors are beaten down,
      and have fled in haste.
      They do not look back—
      terror is all around!
      says the LORD.
6   The swift cannot flee away,
      nor can the warrior escape;
      in the north by the river Euphrates
      they have stumbled and fallen.
7   Who is this, rising like the Nile,

       like rivers whose waters surge?
8 Egypt rises like the Nile,
    like rivers whose waters surge.
    It said, Let me rise, let me cover the earth,
    let me destroy cities and their inhabitants.
9 Advance, O horses,
    and dash madly, O chariots!
    Let the warriors go forth:
    Ethiopia and Put who carry the shield,
    the Ludim, who draw the bow.
10 That day is the day of the LORD GOD of hosts,
    a day of retribution,
    to gain vindication from his foes.
    The sword shall devour and be sated,
    and drink its fill of their blood.
    For the LORD GOD of hosts holds a sacrifice
    in the land of the north by the river Euphrates.
11 Go up to Gilead, and take balm,
    O virgin daughter Egypt!
    In vain you have used many medicines;
    there is no healing for you.
12 The nations have heard of your shame,
    and the earth is full of your cry;
    for warrior has stumbled against warrior;
    both have fallen together.

The immediately preceding chapters of the book of Jeremiah have been concerned with Egypt, so it is not surprising that the oracles against the nations begin with Egypt. It may also be that Egypt comes first because a powerful memory for Judah and Israel was God's deliverance of the Hebrew people from slavery in Egypt. However, with Judah's defeat by the Babylonians, all claims about God's sovereignty over the nations were called into question. Since Israel and Judah had their beginning with God's triumph over Pharaoh (Exodus 1–15), Egypt was an important test of the claim that God had dominion "over nations and over kingdoms" (1:10). The Lord's continuing dominion over Egypt is affirmed in Jeremiah 46 when it is asserted that the course of Egypt's history is being directed toward defeat by Babylon in the same way that God has directed Judah's history toward that same end.

The claim that God was directing the course of history in the events that surrounded Judah's exile is asserted from the very beginning of the book. Jeremiah 1:1–3 affirms that God has directed the course of Judah's history toward the captivity (1:3). However, this claim is not easy for modern people; we are used to thinking about history being shaped by factors we can readily study and analyze: economics, military strategies, diplomatic initiatives, the schemes of national leaders. The persistent claim of the book of Jeremiah is that it is God who directs the course of history, and that claim in Jeremiah 46–51 is extended from Judah to other nations and kingdoms like Egypt.

The oracles against Egypt begin with reference to Babylon's defeat of Egypt in 605 B.C. at Carchemish, a location on the Euphrates River approximately 60 miles west of Haran, the capital city of Assyria (vv. 2–3). In 605 B.C., Assyria was an empire in decline. Assyria had destroyed the northern kingdom of Israel in 722 B.C. and had also dominated Judah. However, by about 630 B.C., Assyria was too weak to have any influence on Judah, and King Josiah was able to initiate reforms in Judah. With the decline of Assyria, there was a struggle for dominance in the ancient Near Eastern world between Egypt and the new emerging power, Babylon. As one episode in this struggle, Judah's King Josiah was killed in 609 B.C. when he attempted to stop an Egyptian army from advancing through his territory to attempt to prop up Assyria against Babylon. Egypt was beaten back by Babylon in 609 B.C. but was not defeated. From 609 B.C. until 605 B.C., Judah was a vassal state of Egypt's. However, in 605 B.C., Egypt and Babylon again confronted one another in battle, and this time Egypt was soundly defeated. Judah became a vassal state of Babylon.

This brief recollection of the Babylonian defeat of Egypt is used to introduce the prophetic oracle of verses 4–12, which make the claim that God intended a Babylonian victory. Even as God directed the course of Judah's history toward captivity (1:3), so God directed the course of Egypt's history toward domination by Babylon. God was "over nations and over kingdoms" (1:10), and that included Egypt as well as Judah. The language and images of verses 4–12 used to describe the defeat of Egypt by Babylon are similar to those used to describe the defeat of Judah by Babylon earlier in the book. The point is to affirm that "the Lord God of hosts" was ultimately responsible for the Babylonian victory (v. 10). This oracle builds to and then flows from the assertion of verse 10 that Egypt's defeat was God's doing.

This oracle begins with a scene that portrays Egypt preparing for battle (vv. 3–4). Commanders give orders for the troops to put on their battle gear and prepare the war chariots. However, the impressively equipped army is inexplicably defeated and is described in full retreat (vv. 5–6). The mighty Egyptian army is stricken by the same "terror" from the north that had afflicted Judah (again, vv. 5–6; see 6:22–25, where similar language is used).

At verse 7, the imagery shifts. Egypt is compared to the Nile River with its famous floods, intending to "surge" over and destroy the earth. Egypt is quoted in verse 8 as saying, "Let me rise, let me cover the earth, let me destroy cities and their inhabitants." This sounds very much like a verse from Moses' victory song after the exodus in which Pharaoh is quoted as boasting:

> I will pursue, I will overtake,
>   I will divide the spoil, my desire shall have its fill of them.
> I will draw my sword, my hand shall destroy them.
>   (Exod. 15:9)

At the exodus, God easily overcame the pretentious boasting of Pharaoh, and Israel went free. It seems likely that God's exodus victory over Pharaoh is being remembered in these verses. Despite the intention of Egypt to be like the Nile (vv. 7–9), this oracle affirms that the Lord directed what happened to Egypt. The day in which Egypt hoped to demonstrate its might was instead "the day of the Lord God of hosts" when God got "retribution . . . vindication from his foes" (v. 10). So, Egypt was "devoured" by the sword (remember God's judgment on Judah to destroy by the sword) as God's sacrifice (v. 10). As at the exodus, Egypt's might and pretense were no match for the Lord's intentions. "The land of the north" became a sacrificial altar upon which God offered up Egypt for slaughter.

The oracle concludes by reflecting upon the impact of God's "sacrifice" of Egypt. God calls Egypt a "virgin daughter," a term that affirmed a special relationship which made the daughter's rebellion and judgment all the more poignant to God (see 14:17; 18:13; 31:4, 13). For Egypt, like Judah, there was "no healing" (v. 11; see 8:22; 30:12–15) but only "shame" before the nations (v. 11; compare 3:24–25; 13:26; 14:3). Egypt may have intended to direct the course of history by surging like the Nile, but God is finally sovereign over even Egypt. In case anyone doubted it, what was true at the beginning of Israel's life at the exodus remains true even after 587 B.C.

Jeremiah 46:13–26

46:13 **The word that the LORD spoke to the prophet Jeremiah about the coming of King Nebuchadrezzar of Babylon to attack the land of Egypt:**

^14 **Declare in Egypt, and proclaim in Migdol;**
   proclaim in Memphis and Tahpanhes;

Say, "Take your stations and be ready,
for the sword shall devour those around you."
15 Why has Apis fled?
Why did your bull not stand?
—because the LORD thrust him down.
16 Your multitude stumbled and fell,
and one said to another,
"Come, let us go back to our own people
and to the land of our birth,
because of the destroying sword."
17 Give Pharaoh, king of Egypt, the name
"Braggart who missed his chance."
18 As I live, says the King,
whose name is the LORD of hosts,
one is coming
like Tabor among the mountains,
and like Carmel by the sea.
19 Pack your bags for exile,
sheltered daughter Egypt!
For Memphis shall become a waste,
a ruin, without inhabitant.
20 A beautiful heifer is Egypt—
a gadfly from the north lights upon her.
21 Even her mercenaries in her midst
are like fatted calves;
they too have turned and fled together,
they did not stand;
for the day of their calamity has come upon them,
the time of their punishment.
22 She makes a sound like a snake gliding away;
for her enemies march in force,
and come against her with axes,
like those who fell trees.
23 They shall cut down her forest,
 says the LORD,
though it is impenetrable,
because they are more numerous
than locusts;
they are without number.
24 Daughter Egypt shall be put to shame;
she shall be handed over to a people from the north.
25 The LORD of hosts, the God of Israel, said: See, I am bringing punishment upon Amon of Thebes, and Pharaoh, and Egypt and her gods and

her kings, upon Pharaoh and those who trust in him. [26] **I will hand them over to those who seek their life, to King Nebuchadrezzar of Babylon and his officers. Afterward Egypt shall be inhabited as in the days of old, says the LORD.**

This second oracle against Egypt also begins with a brief historical reference, though it is not clear to what event verse 13 refers. There has been speculation that this verse has in mind the intervention of Egypt when Babylon was besieging Jerusalem in 588/87 B.C. However, there was also a decisive Babylonian invasion and victory over Egypt in 568 B.C., and those who edited the book of Jeremiah after 587 B.C. may well have been referring to this later event.

In any case, the point of this oracle is that "the Lord of hosts" is giving Egypt over to Babylon. Again, this oracle speaks of the destruction of Egypt by Babylon in terms almost identical to the ways that the book of Jeremiah has described Judah's destruction by Babylon. For instance, this oracle begins with a call for Egypt to prepare for the approach of an enemy: "Declare in Egypt . . ." (v. 14). This cry to prepare for the advance of an enemy is much like that heard in Jeremiah 4:5, "Declare in Judah (compare, too, 4:15). Egypt, like Judah, is to be devoured by the "sword" (vv. 14, 16, and pervasively in the book of Jeremiah). Memphis, like Jerusalem, is to become a "waste, ruin, without inhabitant" (v. 19; see 4:7; 9:11; 26:9; 34:22). The destruction of the Jerusalem Temple and king's residence are spoken of as the destruction of Judah's "forest" (21:14; the figure of speech reflects the fine wood used to build these structures); this oracle imagines that Babylon will cut down Egypt's forest (v. 23). Judah has been exiled, and Egypt will also be exiled (v. 19 and pervasively in the rest of the book regarding Judah). This vision of Babylonian supremacy is consistent with the position of the prophet Jeremiah that God intended Babylonian victory that Judah was powerless to resist. Just as Judah was given over to Babylon, so the Lord will give Egypt over to Babylon, and Egypt will not be able to resist or frustrate God's intentions.

In the first oracle against Egypt, there is a hint that Egypt's defeat occurred in part because of Egypt's pride (especially in verse 8, where Egypt seemed to brag about its intentions). In this second oracle against Egypt, God's decision to allow Babylon to triumph over Egypt is more explicitly presented as a punishment for Egypt's pride and bragging (v. 21). Further, there is a direct and pointed contrast between the king of Egypt (v. 17, the pharaoh) and "the King, whose name is the Lord of hosts" (v. 18). Pharaoh's name is to be "Braggart who missed his chance," but the Lord of hosts will send Egypt into exile and leave Memphis, the Egyptian capital, "a waste . . . without habitation" (vv. 18–19). Connected to the bragging of Pharaoh in this oracle are references to Apis, the bull god of Egypt (v. 15), that will not be able to stand before the power of the Lord who effects Egypt's defeat by Babylon. Pharaoh brags of his power and that with Egypt's god, Apis, they can do as they wish. The counter claims of this oracle are that "the Lord of hosts" will treat Egypt as a heifer (v. 20, a castrated bull) that cannot withstand attack, and that Egypt will be like a snake having to flee before woodsmen come to destroy a forest (v. 22). The Lord will punish Pharaoh for his pride and bring Egypt to shame (v. 24).

Verses 25–26 are a summary of Jeremiah 46, likely added at some late point in the development of the book of Jeremiah. However, at the end of verse 26 is a brief note of hope or promise for Egypt. God intends the restoration of Judah and Israel (Jeremiah 30–33), and also, after God's judgment upon Egypt, God even intends to restore Egypt so that it will "be inhabited as in the days of old" (v. 26). The Lord ultimately intends the well-being of the whole creation and of "all flesh" (45:5), even the longest standing enemy of Israel, Egypt. We are reminded of the flood story in Genesis in which God's judgment of "all flesh" (6:17) finally is spent, and God promises that "all flesh" will never again be cut off. So in the church we remember how at Pentecost, with representatives from the nations gathered, God poured out the Spirit "upon all flesh" (Acts 2:17) who were to be made new in Jesus Christ. God's intention is ultimately the well-being of all nations and of the whole creation.

Jeremiah 46:27–28

27 **But as for you, have no fear, my servant Jacob,**
   and do not be dismayed, O Israel;
   for I am going to save you from far away,
   and your offspring from the land of their captivity.
   Jacob shall return and have quiet and ease,
   and no one shall make him afraid.
28 **As for you, have no fear, my servant Jacob,**
   says the LORD,
   for I am with you.
   I will make an end of all the nations
   among which I have banished you,
   but I will not make an end of you!
   I will chastise you in just measure,
   and I will by no means leave you unpunished.

In sharp contrast to the harsh judgment of Egypt, these verses offer strong assurance to Judah. God will act on Judah's behalf: "I am going to save you" (v. 27). God will rescue Judah, so Judah is told to "have no fear," an encouragement that appears in both verses (along with the assurance at the end of v. 27, "no one shall make him afraid"). Egypt is to be judged, but Judah is to be restored.

These verses are also found in Jeremiah 30:10–11, where they contribute to the theme that God will eventually "restore the fortunes" (30:3) of Judah by reversing the effects of judgment. Most notably, God promises that those taken captive will be returned to the land, where they will have "quiet and ease" (v. 27; 30:10). The repetition of this passage among the oracles against the nations changes where the emphasis of the passage falls. Reading these verses alongside the oracles against Egypt, the promise that dominates is, "I will make an end of all the nations among which I have banished you" (v. 28). God's judgment of the nations is significant for Judah because it foreshadows God's restoration. Certainly by this point in the book of Jeremiah there can be no doubt that God will punish Judah (so the end of v. 28, "I will by no means leave you unpunished"). However, the Lord intends restoration, and the restoration is signaled by God's judgment of the nations among which Judah has been banished.

In the early chapters of the book of Jeremiah, the word of the Lord dominantly announces judgment against Judah, and eventually, that word is fulfilled when Jerusalem is sacked by the Babylonians (Jeremiah 39). Scattered throughout the book, however, are passages that promise restoration, and in Jeremiah 30–33, promises of restoration dominate. This word of promise includes the assurance that the Lord will judge the nations that were used to punish Judah. With the oracles against the nations and the announcement of judgment upon Egypt, there is a clue that the Lord's word of promise, like the word of judgment, will be fulfilled. Yet, we cannot forget, though it is but briefly mentioned in verse 26, that God finally intends the restoration of Egypt as well. Finally in the reign of God, even old enemies like Israel and Egypt will find well-being together.

In the New Testament, an important claim of the apostle Paul is that through Jesus Christ God has brought peace to the human family so that even old enemies can live together as members of God's household. In Paul's world, the apostle saw the old enemies as Jews and Gentiles, people who lived apart and alienated because of the social customs and taboos of the first-century world. Paul understood that through Jesus Christ these old enemies were reconciled:

So then you are no longer strangers and aliens, but you are citizens with the saints and also members of the household of God, built upon the foundation of the apostles and prophets, with Christ Jesus himself as the cornerstone. (Eph. 2:19–20)

In our world we often perceive the deep divisions among peoples: among races, among social classes, among peoples of different nations, political parties, people who support conflicting causes (environmental protection and economic progress), who hold different values. This oracle, which imagines the well-being God intends even for Egypt, reminds us of the gospel of Jesus Christ, which breaks down the dividing walls that divide us so that strangers and aliens can live together in peace.

AGAINST THE PHILISTINES
Jeremiah 47:1–7

Contrary to popular assumptions, the Philistines, though defeated by King David as he became king of Israel (approximately 960 B.C.), remained in control of the Mediterranean coast of Palestine and were still in place during Judah's last days. To be sure, the Philistines were not a military power and threat like Egypt or Babylon, but they were a group who were a long-standing enemy of Judah and Israel. Enemy or not, the harshness of what happened to the Philistines at the hands of the Babylonians is pondered toward the conclusion of this oracle.

Jeremiah 47:1–7

47:1 **The word of the LORD that came to the prophet Jeremiah concerning the Philistines, before Pharaoh attacked Gaza:**
  2 **Thus says the LORD:**
  See, waters are rising out of the north
  and shall become an overflowing torrent;
  they shall overflow the land and all that fills it,
  the city and those who live in it.
  People shall cry out,
  and all the inhabitants of the land shall wail.
  3 **At the noise of the stamping of the hoofs of his stallions,**
  at the clatter of his chariots, at the rumbling of their wheels,
  parents do not turn back for children,
  so feeble are their hands,
  4 **because of the day that is coming**

to destroy all the Philistines,
to cut off from Tyre and Sidon
every helper that remains.
For the LORD is destroying the Philistines,
the remnant of the coastland of Caphtor.
5 Baldness has come upon Gaza,
Ashkelon is silenced.
O remnant of their power!
How long will you gash yourselves?
6 Ah, sword of the LORD!
How long until you are quiet?
Put yourself into your scabbard,
rest and be still!
7 How can it be quiet,
when the LORD has given it an order?
Against Ashkelon and against the seashore—
there he has appointed it.

The first verse of the chapter suggests an attack by Pharaoh on the Philistines from the south. The remainder of the verses describe an attack on the Philistines from the north by Babylon. Some have suggested that the poem reflects Babylon's destruction of Ashkelon in 604 B.C., though there is not enough information given to be clear what historical events might have given rise to the oracle. Similarly, whether Jeremiah or a later editor was responsible for this poem is difficult to determine.

The oracle against the Philistines begins in verse 2, and the water imagery reminds us of the initial oracle against Egypt (46:7). Egypt may have intended to be like mighty waters that would surge over the land, but the rising waters actually came out of the north, from Babylon, with destructive and irresistible force. In the ancient world, water was associated with chaos. God's ordering of the waters was crucial to the creation (Genesis 1); God's judgment of "all flesh" (45:5) was by a flood; and, in the exodus, God delivered the Hebrew slaves through the water, that is, chaos and death. The Philistines are threatened with the rising waters out of the north, and though Babylon is not named explicitly in this oracle, there can be no doubt that it is the Babylonian army that overflows the Philistines. The symbolic expression of the threat faced by the Philistines is made concrete in verse 3 through the portrayal of a well-equipped army whose advance leaves people so paralyzed with fear that they flee without their children (remember the descriptions of Judah's panic before an advancing army earlier in the book, for instance, see 4:5–8, 29–31; 6:1–8).

In verse 4, the poem develops further, and we are told that the Philistines are threatened "because of the day that is coming." This is the same day with which the Egyptians had to contend, "the day of the Lord" when God gains vindication and retribution "from his foes" (46:10). Babylon may have been the agent of judgment, but the cause of the Philistines' judgment is God (v. 4). Tyre and Sidon seem to be included in this oracle because they were allies of the Philistines (both were located along the Mediterranean coast) who might have provided assistance.

With the assertion that God is destroying the Philistines, this oracle reaches its climax. The Philistines are humiliated and reduced to expressions of shame and grief; their heads are shaved and they gash themselves (v. 5; see 16:6 and 41:5, where similar acts of contrition are reported). Verses 6–7 are more difficult. It is not even clear who is supposed to be speaking these words or to whom they are addressed. The concern of these verses is the "sword of the Lord" and its harsh way with the Philistines. Of course, this oracle has affirmed that it was God's intention for the Babylonians to destroy the Philistines, so the Babylonians need to be understood as the "sword of the Lord." Were one to summarize these two verses, the cry seems to be an emphatic "Stop!" Perhaps this is the cry of the Philistines themselves, or maybe it is the musing of whoever composed this poem (Jeremiah or a later editor) about the harsh fate of the Philistines at the hands of the Babylonians and God's role in the Philistines' brutal treatment. The conclusion is likely a disturbing one for us, an affirmation that the "sword of the Lord"—that is, the Babylonians—is not out of control, as verse 6 suggests, but is acting as God intends: "the Lord has given it [the sword] an order" (v. 7).

The intention of verses 6–7 seems to have been to make sense out of the Babylonian military sweep of the Palestinian region. The defeat of Judah was attributed to Judah's rebellion against God; Egypt, to the extent that they were boastful, also deserved God's judgment at the hand of the Babylonians (46:20–21). No clear reasons are given why the Philistines deserved to be destroyed. This oracle affirms that God was surely responsible for what befell the Philistines; there is certainty that the Lord is sovereign "over nations and over kingdoms" (1:10). But, this oracle is not able to explain the logic of God's sovereignty in the case of the Philistines. Confidence that the Lord directs the course of history is not pressed in this oracle in an effort to explain too much about God's motives, purposes, or intentions. The writer of these verses has left us to ponder a troubling mystery about what seemed the harsh destruction of the Philistines by the Babylonians.

AGAINST MOAB
Jeremiah 48:1–47

The oracles against Moab are quite extensive, surprisingly so since none of the other smaller nations that surrounded Judah—the Philistines in Jeremiah 47, or the Ammonites, Edom, Kedar, Hazor, Elam, and Damascus in Jeremiah 49—are given nearly the attention that Moab receives in this chapter. Why Moab received such extensive attention is difficult to know.

Moab was a nation to the east of Judah, across the Jordan River (the region is called the Transjordan). Conflict between Israel and Judah and Moab was long-standing, and it is remembered in the Bible as preceding Joshua (see Numbers 21; Judges 3, 11). During the time of Jeremiah, the tensions between Judah and Moab continued. For instance, when King Jehoiakim of Judah rebelled against Babylon shortly after 600 B.C. and Babylon finally retaliated, the Moabites participated with Babylon in raids against Judah (2 Kings 24:1–2). Later, Moab joined Judah under King Zedekiah in a rebellion against Babylon usually dated to 595/94 B.C (see Jeremiah 27:1–11). This rebellion ultimately resulted in the Babylonian destruction of several rebellious states, including Judah and likely Moab. Regretfully, it is not possible to relate the oracles in this chapter to exact dates and events in Moab's history. Even the locations named in this chapter are not all readily identifiable.

This chapter contains the most extensive treatment of Moab in the Bible, though other prophetic books also contain oracles against Moab (Isa. 15–16; Amos 2:1–3; Ezek. 25:8–11; Zeph. 2:8–11). It appears that some material in this chapter is related to (often, it is claimed to have been borrowed from) other Old Testament texts concerned with Moab: verse 5 from Isaiah 15:5; verses 43–44 from Isaiah 24:17–18; verses 45–46 from Numbers 21:28–29; and verses 29–39 resemble various sections of Isaiah 15–16. These similarities between texts concerned with Moab may suggest that by the time of the Babylonian exile, there had developed some standard ways in which Moab, a long-standing enemy of Judah, was regarded to have been held accountable by God.

There are several divisions in this chapter, though it is often difficult to determine with certainty where one section ends and another begins. A comparison of how several commentaries on the book of Jeremiah divide this chapter will quickly reveal the difficulty. It is likely that these oracles against Moab were developed and expanded over a long time, and many editors had a hand in bringing Jeremiah 48 to its present arrangement.

Jeremiah 48:1–10

48:1 Concerning Moab.
Thus says the LORD of hosts, the God of Israel:
> Alas for Nebo, it is laid waste!
> Kiriathaim is put to shame, it is taken;
> the fortress is put to shame and broken down;
> 2 the renown of Moab is no more.
> In Heshbon they planned evil against her:
> "Come, let us cut her off from being a nation!"
> You also, O Madmen, shall be brought to silence;
> the sword shall pursue you.
> 3 Hark! a cry from Horonaim,
> "Desolation and great destruction!"
> 4 "Moab is destroyed!"
> her little ones cry out.
> 5 For at the ascent of Luhith
> they go up weeping bitterly;
> for at the descent of Horonaim
> they have heard the distressing cry of anguish.
> 6 Flee! Save yourselves!
> Be like a wild ass in the desert!
> 7 Surely, because you trusted in your strongholds and your treasures,
> you also shall be taken;
> Chemosh shall go out into exile,
> with his priests and his attendants.
> 8 The destroyer shall come upon every town,
> and no town shall escape;
> the valley shall perish,
> and the plain shall be destroyed,
> as the LORD has spoken.
> 9 Set aside salt for Moab,
> for she will surely fall;
> her towns shall become a desolation,
> with no inhabitant in them.
> 10 Accursed is the one who is slack in doing the work of the LORD; and
> accursed is the one who keeps back the sword from bloodshed.

Through this oracle, God announces destruction such that "the renown of Moab" will be no more and Moab will be "cut . . . off from being a nation" (v. 2). An enemy, unnamed at this point in these oracles, "planned evil" (v. 2) against Moab, and this enemy's invasion will cause weeping and cries of anguish among the Moabites (v. 5; this verse seems to be a repetition of Isa. 15:5, which is also about Moab). So the cry goes up, "Flee! Save yourselves" (v. 6; compare 4:6; 6:1 where Judah had received a similar warning). The vocabulary used in the first six verses, typical of the book of Jeremiah, leaves little doubt that Moab is to experience God's judgment and its consequences: shame, desolation, destruction, weeping, and anguish.

These same themes occur in verses 8–9, which announce that an again unnamed "destroyer" will attack the towns of Moab "as the Lord had spoken" (v. 8). Moab's destruction is no more accidental than Judah's. The Lord intends it. Verse 7, which links the initial and latter expressions of judgment in this oracle, provides the reason for God's judgment of Moab. Moab trusted in "strongholds and . . . treasures"; further, they relied on their god, Chemosh. The perspective of the book of Jeremiah is clear, that trust in the God of Israel alone results in life and blessing; to place one's trust in "mere mortals" will result in curse and death (17:5–8). Moab is to be punished for its misplaced trust; Moab chose death and will be destroyed.

Verse 10, usually thought to be a later addition to the text, pronounces a curse on anyone "who is slack in doing the work of the Lord . . . who keeps back the sword . . ." Moab's destroyer (v. 8) works under the threat of divine curse to finish the assigned task. The verse underscores that Moab's destruction is God's intention and that Moab will not be able to escape.

Jeremiah 48: 11–13

48:11 **Moab has been at ease from his youth,**
          settled like wine on its dregs;
          he has not been emptied from vessel to vessel,
          nor has he gone into exile;
          therefore his flavor has remained
          and his aroma is unspoiled.
      12 **Therefore, the time is surely coming, says the LORD, when I shall send to him decanters to decant him, and empty his vessels, and break his jars in pieces.** 13 **Then Moab shall be ashamed of Chemosh, as the house of Israel was ashamed of Bethel, their confidence.**

Fine wines are produced by allowing them to set undisturbed so the sediment ("dregs," v. 11) settles out and does not contaminate the wine. Wine that is decanted, poured into containers, too soon or too often is of lesser quality because the dregs mix into the wine. These verses compare Moab to a fine wine that has not been decanted in that Moab has escaped any attack resulting in exile (v. 11). Moab had been fortunate to have remained "unspoiled" for so long ("at ease from his youth"). It is not hard to imagine in verse 11 a certain envy from Judeans at their neighbors' good fortune. However, Moab's "unspoiled" state is about to change. God announces that Moab will soon be decanted, that is, exiled; or worse, Moab's vessels will be broken and the rich wine spilled (v. 12), that is, totally destroyed. These clever images of ruined or spilled wine are a colorful way to describe the same reality as verses 1–10. God intends to destroy Moab.

The Moabites trust in their god, Chemosh, who is identified as the cause for Moab's ruin. When destroyed, Moab will be "ashamed" of the confidence they placed in Chemosh (v. 13) even as the northern kingdom of Israel was ashamed of the idols they had worshipped at Bethel. Bethel, of course, was one of the worship centers of Israel where King Jeroboam had erected a calf (1 Kings 12:28–29). The prophet Amos harshly condemned the worship practices at Bethel, which he saw to be idolatrous (Amos 5:5; 7:10–17). When Israel was finally destroyed and exiled by the Assyrians in 722 B.C., the confidence placed by the Israelites in the idols they had worshiped at Bethel was understood to be largely responsible. Thus, this oracle claims that when the Moabites were finally exiled, they would be ashamed of the "confidence" they had placed in their idol, Chemosh.

This oracle can be helpful to us in the church if we heed its warning to examine in which idols we ourselves may have placed our confidence. For instance, we might find that we place a false "confidence" in our nationality, or our racial background, or our economic status. We might believe that, or at least live as if we believed that, one or more of these give us value, worth, and security. In fact, none do or can, but only our relationship to God through Jesus Christ. Less helpful is to use this oracle as an excuse to condemn or belittle the religious practices of others in our world who may be Hindu, Muslim, or Buddhist. Dialogue with persons of different religious traditions is a complex matter requiring great humility and patience by all involved. This oracle can be heard to work against the kind of caring and humble interfaith dialogue that is so important to the well-being of our world.

Jeremiah 48:14–28

48:14 **How can you say, "We are heroes**
and mighty warriors"?
15 **The destroyer of Moab and his towns has come up,**
and the choicest of his young men have gone down to slaughter,

says the King, whose name is the LORD of hosts.

16 The calamity of Moab is near at hand
and his doom approaches swiftly.

17 Mourn over him, all you his neighbors,
and all who know his name;
say, "How the mighty scepter is broken,
the glorious staff!"

18 Come down from glory,
and sit on the parched ground,
enthroned daughter Dibon!
For the destroyer of Moab has come up against you;
he has destroyed your strongholds.

19 Stand by the road and watch,
you inhabitant of Aroer!
Ask the man fleeing and the woman escaping;
say, "What has happened?"

20 Moab is put to shame, for it is broken down;
wail and cry!
Tell it by the Arnon,
that Moab is laid waste.

21 Judgment has come upon the tableland, upon Holon, and Jahzah, and
Mephaath, 22 and Dibon, and Nebo, and Beth-diblathaim, 23 and Kiriathaim,
and Beth-gamul, and Beth-meon, 24 and Kerioth, and Bozrah, and all the
towns of the land of Moab, far and near. 25 The horn of Moab is cut off, and
his arm is broken, says the LORD.

26 Make him drunk, because he magnified himself against the LORD; let
Moab wallow in his vomit; he too shall become a laughingstock. 27 Israel was
a laughingstock for you, though he was not caught among thieves; but when-
ever you spoke of him you shook your head!

28 Leave the towns, and live on the rock,
O inhabitants of Moab!
Be like the dove that nests
on the sides of the mouth of a gorge.

Verses 14–20 develop from the boast of the Moabites that they are
"heroes and mighty warriors" (v. 14). Given the centuries of conflict
between Judah and Moab, Judeans certainly must have experienced the
military prowess of the Moabites, heard their boasts, and perhaps even
believed them. The claim of this oracle is that the "heroes and mighty warriors" of Moab are about to confront an even stronger adversary, "the
King, whose name is the Lord of hosts" (v. 15). This text pits the powerful Moabites against the God of Israel. With the crisis of exile, an issue that
the people of Israel and Judah confronted again and again was whether the

Lord was sovereign, whether the God of Israel directed the course of history, or whether there was another, maybe the god of the Moabites or the Babylonians. The clear affirmation of this text is that "the King, whose name is the Lord of hosts," is "the destroyer of Moab" (vv. 15, 18) who will break Moab's power ("mighty scepter" and "glorious staff") and lay Moab to waste. God directs the course of history, even Moab's history.

The remaining verses of this section of Jeremiah 48 also affirm that God is sovereign over Moab, though different images are used to make the point. Citing locations that are assumed to encompass the whole of Moab, verses 21–25 announce that Moab has been judged and Moab's power (in these verses "horn" and "arm") broken. Further, Moab, which has "magnified himself against the Lord" (compare the boast of v. 14) and treated Judah as a "laughingstock," is itself to become a "laughingstock" when God makes Moab become drunk and vomit (vv. 26–27). Though the imagery of these verses is repulsive, it affirms God's power to dominate Moab and reflects a similar scene from Jeremiah 25 in which God makes the nations drink from a cup of wrath. Overpowered by God the destroyer, the Moabites will have little left to do but flee to caves and hide (v. 28).

Jeremiah 48:29–33

48:29 **We have heard of the pride of Moab—**
  he is very proud—
  of his loftiness, his pride, and his arrogance,
  and the haughtiness of his heart.
30 **I myself know his insolence, says the LORD;**
  his boasts are false,
  his deeds are false.
31 **Therefore I wail for Moab;**
  I cry out for all Moab;
  for the people of Kir-heres I mourn.
32 **More than for Jazer I weep for you,**
  O vine of Sibmah!
  Your branches crossed over the sea,
  reached as far as Jazer
  upon your summer fruits and your vintage
  the destroyer has fallen.
33 **Gladness and joy have been taken away**
  from the fruitful land of Moab;
  I have stopped the wine from the wine presses;
  no one treads them with shouts of joy;
  the shouting is not the shout of joy.

These verses conclude with God's lament over Moab (vv. 31–39), though they begin by remembering Moab's boastful arrogance (vv. 29–30). In fact, Moab's arrogance is presented in an overwhelming manner by a heap of words all stressing the same point (v. 29): "the pride of Moab," "he is very proud," "his loftiness, his pride, his arrogance, and the haughtiness of his heart." We do not know who the speaker of verse 29 is (maybe the prophet?), but the point about Moab's boastfulness is confirmed by God, who asserts, "I myself know his insolence" but then labels Moab's boasts and deeds as false (v. 30).

God's charge that Moab is insolent (audacious, bold) but false prepares the way for the remainder of this oracle. So startling is Moab's demise that even God is moved to join in the weeping over Moab (v. 31; Kir-heres was the capital of Moab). God weeps despite the fact that the Lord is "the destroyer" who has brought Moab to ruin (v. 32; compare vv. 8, 15, 18, where God is identified as "the destroyer"). We have seen the same reaction by God to the destruction of Judah which, though willed by God, nonetheless moved the Lord to weeping (for instance, 4:19–22; 8:18–9:2). Judgment is necessary, but God does not delight in it or ultimately intend it. Even for Moab, the Lord ultimately intended blessing and well-being, land that yielded a bountiful harvest (v. 32) and resulted in "gladness and joy" (v. 33). God was anguished when what was intended could not be (v. 33).

It has been widely noted that these verses are closely related to Isaiah 15:4–6 and 16:11. It is usually assumed that these verses in Jeremiah were based upon the earlier Isaiah material. However, both the books of Isaiah and Jeremiah have had very long and complex histories of development, so one cannot be sure that the editors of the book of Isaiah did not borrow from Jeremiah.

Jeremiah 48:34–39

48:34 **Heshbon and Elealeh cry out; as far as Jahaz they utter their voice, from Zoar to Horonaim and Eglath-shelishiyah. For even the waters of Nimrim have become desolate. 35 And I will bring to an end in Moab, says the LORD, those who offer sacrifice at a high place and make offerings to their gods. 36 Therefore my heart moans for Moab like a flute, and my heart moans like a flute for the people of Kir-heres; for the riches they gained have perished.**

37 For every head is shaved and every beard cut off; on all the hands there are gashes, and on the loins sackcloth. 38 On all the housetops of Moab and in the squares there is nothing but lamentation; for I have broken Moab like a vessel that no one wants, says the LORD. 39 How it is broken! How they wail! How Moab has turned his back in shame! So Moab has become a derision and a horror to all his neighbors.

The destruction of Moab, portrayed vividly in Jeremiah 48, results in lamentation by the Moabites (vv. 34, 37–39) and by God (v. 36). This section of Jeremiah 48, in prose rather than poetry, is usually viewed as a later expansion of the preceding poetic verses. Again, there is connection with the oracles against Moab in the book of Isaiah: Verse 34 is related to Isaiah 15:4–6; verse 36 to Isaiah 16:11; and verses 37–38 to Isaiah 15:2–3.

Throughout these verses we hear reports of the "lamentation" (v. 38) of the Moabites at their destruction. What is described are formal mourning rituals after a military defeat. From all over Moab, there are cries and rituals of mourning (vv. 34, 37–39). The reference to the "flute" of Moab (v. 36), for instance, is likely some part of the Moabites' formal lamentation rituals, and that is also clearly what is behind the shaved heads and beards, gashed hands, and sackcloth (v. 37).

The destruction of Moab is another example of the fulfillment of the word of the Lord. God declared, "I have broken Moab like a pot no one wants" (v. 38). So, proud and haughty Moab (vv. 28–30) is shown to be false and insolent (v. 30). Those who are arrogant (v. 29) are reduced to lamentation and have become a shame, derision, and horror to their neighbors (v. 39).

Yet the lamentations of Moab, surely directed toward their gods, move the God of Israel, who is Moab's destroyer. The Lord's heart also moans over Moab's demise (v. 36; compare 4:19, where God's heart was similarly broken contemplating Judah's demise). The Lord is more than the tribal deity of Israel but is God "over nations and over kingdoms" (1:10), to pluck up and tear down. This anguish over Moab's demise also suggests the well-being of Moab matters to God, and it anticipates the restoration that finally will be promised even to the Moabites (see v. 47, below).

Jeremiah 48:40–47

48:40 **For thus says the LORD:**
    Look, he shall swoop down like an eagle,
    and spread his wings against Moab;
    41 **the towns shall be taken**
    and the strongholds seized.
    The hearts of the warriors of Moab, on that day,
    shall be like the heart of a woman in labor.
    42 **Moab shall be destroyed as a people,**
    because he magnified himself against the LORD.
    43 **Terror, pit, and trap**
    are before you, O inhabitants of Moab!
    says the LORD.

44 Everyone who flees from the terror
    shall fall into the pit,
    and everyone who climbs out of the pit
    shall be caught in the trap.
    For I will bring these things upon Moab
    in the year of their punishment,
    says the LORD.
45 In the shadow of Heshbon
    fugitives stop exhausted;
    for a fire has gone out from Heshbon,
    a flame from the house of Sihon;
    it has destroyed the forehead of Moab,
    the scalp of the people of tumult.
46 Woe to you, O Moab!
    The people of Chemosh have perished,
    for your sons have been taken captive,
    and your daughters into captivity.
47 Yet I will restore the fortunes of Moab
    in the latter days, says the LORD.
    Thus far is the judgment on Moab.

Although a summary of the oracles against Moab, this text looks beyond God's plucking up and tearing down to the building and planting of Moab. In verses 40–44, Moab is portrayed as the prey of an eagle that swoops down in attack (v. 40); while not explicit in the text, this seems a likely reference to the Babylonians' attack on Moab. The destruction of Moab results in terror from which there is no escape (vv. 41, 43–44; the comparison of the Moabite warriors to "a woman in labor" in v. 41 is similar to the reaction of Judah before God's judgment in 4:31 and 30:6). However, as the whole of Jeremiah 48 has claimed, Moab's destruction occurs because Moab has "magnified" itself against God (v. 41).

Verses 45–47 are not found in the Greek version of the Old Testament (the Septuagint), and that suggests they are a later addition to the book by some editor. These verses are related to Numbers 21:21–30, and verses 45–46 are nearly identical to Numbers 21:28–29. Sihon was a Moabite king (Heshbon was his capital city) who attempted to prevent the Israelites from transversing his territory as they journeyed from Egypt to the promised land. The Israelites' defeat of King Sihon is recounted and celebrated in Numbers 21. The repetition of a portion of Numbers 21 in these oracles against the Moabites suggests that God, who has once defeated the Moabites, will do so again. Such a claim has two implications for Judah, which has just been defeated by Babylon.

First, the defeat of Moab asserts that, contrary to the way things may have appeared after the Babylonian exile, the Lord is in control, is powerful as ever, and remains sovereign. Second, God's defeat of Judah's long-standing enemy, Moab, may well hint at Judah's salvation and restoration. When God defeated Moab in the time of Moses, it led the Israelites closer to the Promised Land. Perhaps the Lord's defeat of the Moabites again will signal deliverance and rest for God's exiled and defeated people. God's judgment of the nations points toward salvation for Judah.

Verse 47 moves in a direction that is likely surprising for those Judeans exiled to Babylon. Beyond Moab's woe and captivity (v. 46), God promises to "restore the fortunes of Moab." This concern for Moab is indicated earlier in Jeremiah 48 through God's expressions of grief over Moab's destruction (vv. 31–32, 36). In this verse, the Lord's anguish over Moab's destruction is expressed in a promise of restoration, the same promise announced to Judah and Israel (30:3 and throughout Jeremiah 30–33). While God was concerned for Israel and Judah, we in the church know from the first chapter of the Bible until the last that God's ultimate concern is with the whole of creation. God intends the restoration of Judah, but also of Moab. God, who intends salvation for those in the church gathered in the name of Jesus Christ, also intends "the healing of the nations" (Rev. 22:2).

AGAINST VARIOUS NATIONS
Jeremiah 49:1–39

Jeremiah 49 contains oracles against several nations: Ammon (vv. 1–6); Edom (vv. 7–22); Damascus (vv. 23–27); Kedar and Hazor (vv. 28–33); and Elam (vv. 34–39). Each of these nations was, at one time or another, an enemy of Judah and Israel. Several of the nations mentioned in this chapter also were defeated by Babylon around the time of Judah's destruction in 587 B.C. In some cases, other prophetic books also contain oracles against these nations. Although this chapter announces God's judgment against each of these nations, each nation is presented somewhat differently. In the uniqueness of the discussion of each nation, we can probably hear the different ways Israel and Judah related to each; or we can at least discern the different judgments of those who included this material in the book of Jeremiah (it is not likely that Jeremiah himself was responsible for many of these oracles).

Jeremiah 49:1–6

49:1 Concerning the Ammonites.
    Thus says the LORD:
        Has Israel no sons?
        Has he no heir?
        Why then has Milcom dispossessed Gad,
        and his people settled in its towns?
    ² Therefore, the time is surely coming,
        says the LORD,
        when I will sound the battle alarm
        against Rabbah of the Ammonites;
        it shall become a desolate mound,
        and its villages shall be burned with fire;
        then Israel shall dispossess those who dispossessed him,
        says the LORD.
    ³ Wail, O Heshbon, for Ai is laid waste!
        Cry out, O daughters of Rabbah!
        Put on sackcloth,
        lament, and slash yourselves with whips!
        For Milcom shall go into exile,
        with his priests and his attendants.
    ⁴ Why do you boast in your strength?
        Your strength is ebbing,
        O faithless daughter.
        You trusted in your treasures, saying,
        "Who will attack me?"
    ⁵ I am going to bring terror upon you,
        says the LORD GOD of hosts,
        from all your neighbors,
        and you will be scattered, each headlong,
        with no one to gather the fugitives.
    ⁶ But afterward I will restore the fortunes of the Ammonites, says the
LORD.

Ammon was located east of Judah across the Jordan River. The territory of Ammon was just to the north of Moab (Jer. 48), and, as with Moab,
Judah and Israel had frequent conflicts with the Ammonites (Gen.
19:30–38; Judges 10–11; 2 Samuel 10; 1 Kings 11). During the time of
Jeremiah, Ammon was controlled by Babylon and assisted Babylon in
attacking Judah after King Jehoiakim had rebelled against Babylon
(2 Kings 24:2). Ammon is listed among the nations that gathered in Jerusalem as part of a rebellion against Babylon (Jeremiah 27). For some rea-

son, Ammon seems to have escaped destruction when the Babylonian army was on campaign in the region and defeated Judah in 587 B.C. In fact, we have seen in Jeremiah 41 that Ammon continued to resist Babylon after the fall of Judah and sponsored Ishmael's assassination of Gedaliah because of Gedaliah's willingness to cooperate with the Babylonians (see pages 82–88). Babylon did not defeat Ammon until 582 B.C.

This oracle makes reference to an Ammonite intrusion into the Judean territory of Gad (v. 1), but because border conflicts between Judah and Ammon were frequent, it is not possible to be precise about what event may have given rise to this oracle. Some believe that Jeremiah himself may be responsible for this oracle, but oracles against Ammon are found in other prophetic books (Ezek. 21:20; 28–32; 25:1–7; Amos 1:13–15; Zeph. 2:8–11), so it is difficult to be certain of the origin of this oracle against an old enemy of Judah. Verse 6 is not found in the Greek version of the book of Jeremiah and so is probably a later addition to the text. However, this verse, as we will see, is nonetheless important.

This oracle against Ammon assumes a conflict between the Lord, the God of Israel, and Milcom, the god of the Ammorites. Milcom has apparently won the upper hand because Ammon has invaded Gad in the territory of Judah, the territory of Yahweh (v. 1). The superiority of other gods over the God of Israel was a very real concern to people who had experienced the Babylonian exile of 587 B.C. The Babylonian exile left doubt: Was God really in control? This oracle, though about Ammon, raised the question about God's power that would have been on the minds of those Judeans who had experienced the Babylonians' destruction of Jerusalem and defeat of Judah.

Verses 2–5 offer God's response to Milcom's dispossession of Gad. The Lord will not tolerate the situation. God will make Ammon a desolation, and, as we have seen in some of the other oracles against the nations in Jeremiah, Ammon's defeat means deliverance for Judah (v. 2; compare this reversal of Judah's fortunes with the expression of this same idea in 30:16). Verse 3 presents the consequences of Ammon's defeat as lamentation and exile, though in an interesting manner. The verse imagines the exile of the Ammonite god, Milcom, and not the exile of the actual Ammonite people. Of course, the point is clear enough that the Ammonites are to be exiled since god and people are connected. However, the oracle wants to emphasize that the defeat and exile of the Ammonites will be the victory of the Lord who will be shown superior to the gods of the nations. Such an affirmation was critically important to the people after 587 B.C.

Because it may be confusing, brief mention needs to be made of Heshbon in verse 3 in connection with the Ammonites. In Jeremiah 48:45, Heshbon is associated with the Moabites. Moab and Ammon are neighbors, and it is likely that when this oracle was written, Heshbon, the ancient capital of Moab, had come under Ammonite control.

In the preceding chapter, Moab is punished by God because they are proud and arrogant (48:29). In this oracle, the Ammonites are to be punished because they have boasted in their strength and trusted in their treasures (v. 4). Without naming it as such, Ammon's sin is both arrogance and idolatry, a false sense that they are able to secure themselves (compare 48:30, where God calls Moab's arrogance insolent and "false"). The boast, "Who will attack me?" will be met with attacks that "bring terror" upon Ammon from neighbors and Ammon will be scattered (a more historically grounded description of exile than that found in v. 3).

Given the old conflicts between Judah and Israel and Ammon, and the harshness of God's judgment in verses 1–5, the promised restoration of Ammon announced in verse 6 is somewhat unexpected, except that other oracles against the nations in the book of Jeremiah have also included this promise. The Lord is affirmed to be "over nations and kingdoms" to pluck up and tear down, to build and to plant (1:10), and the primary example of this sovereignty is evident with Judah. God has judged Judah but has promised Judah restoration. The book, however, wants to affirm clearly that God's ways with Judah are the same as with all the nations and kingdoms. God will pluck up and tear down, but God will also built and plant. So Ammon, like Judah, will be restored.

Jeremiah 49:7–22

49:7 **Concerning Edom.**
> **Thus says the LORD of hosts:**
>> **Is there no longer wisdom in Teman?**
>> **Has counsel perished from the prudent?**
>> **Has their wisdom vanished?**
> 8 **Flee, turn back, get down low,**
>> **inhabitants of Dedan!**
>> **For I will bring the calamity of Esau upon him,**
>> **the time when I punish him.**
> 9 **If grape-gatherers came to you,**
>> **would they not leave gleanings?**
>> **If thieves came by night,**
>> **even they would pillage only what they wanted.**
> 10 **But as for me, I have stripped Esau bare,**

I have uncovered his hiding places,
and he is not able to conceal himself.
His offspring are destroyed, his kinsfolk
and his neighbors; and he is no more.
[11] Leave your orphans, I will keep them alive;
and let your widows trust in me.

[12] For thus says the LORD: If those who do not deserve to drink the cup still have to drink it, shall you be the one to go unpunished? You shall not go unpunished; you must drink it. [13] For by myself I have sworn, says the LORD, that Bozrah shall become an object of horror and ridicule, a waste, and an object of cursing; and all her towns shall be perpetual wastes.

[14] I have heard tidings from the LORD,
and a messenger has been sent among the nations:
"Gather yourselves together and come against her,
and rise up for battle!"
[15] For I will make you least among the nations,
despised by humankind.
[16] The terror you inspire
and the pride of your heart have deceived you,
you who live in the clefts of the rock,
who hold the height of the hill.
Although you make your nest as high as the eagle's,
from there I will bring you down,
says the LORD.

[17] Edom shall become an object of horror; everyone who passes by it will be horrified and will hiss because of all its disasters. [18] As when Sodom and Gomorrah and their neighbors were overthrown, says the LORD, no one shall live there, nor shall anyone settle in it. [19] Like a lion coming up from the thickets of the Jordan against a perennial pasture, I will suddenly chase Edom away from it; and I will appoint over it whomever I choose. For who is like me? Who can summon me? Who is the shepherd who can stand before me? [20] Therefore hear the plan that the LORD has made against Edom and the purposes that he has formed against the inhabitants of Teman: Surely the little ones of the flock shall be dragged away; surely their fold shall be appalled at their fate. [21] At the sound of their fall the earth shall tremble; the sound of their cry shall be heard at the Red Sea. [22] Look, he shall mount up and swoop down like an eagle, and spread his wings against Bozrah, and the heart of the warriors of Edom in that day shall be like the heart of a woman in labor.

Edom was also located to the east of Judah, across the Jordan River, south of Moab. In the Old Testament, the animosity between Judah and Edom is attributed to the rivalry between Jacob and his twin brother Esau, who was the ancestor of the Edomites (Gen. 25:25–26). In this oracle,

Edom is referred to as "Esau" (vv. 8, 10). Whatever the origin of the conflict, there is ample evidence that Edom regularly was in conflict with Israel and Judah (Num. 20:14ff.; Judg. 11:17–18; 2 Kings 14:7–10). Nearer the time of Jeremiah, Edom was a vassal of Babylon and participated with Babylon in the invasion that resulted in Judah's destruction in 587 B.C. Sometime after 587 B.C. and Judah's defeat, Edom moved into an area of Judah south of Jerusalem that they occupied for several decades before Edom was significantly weakened by attacks from peoples to the south out of the Arabian peninsula. This oracle is related to the book of Obadiah, and some verses are quite similar to those found in Obadiah (which consists of a single chapter): Verses 14–16 are similar to Obadiah 1–4; verses 9–10 are like Obadiah 5–6.

In many ancient Near Eastern societies, an important group of persons were the wisdom teachers, advisors usually connected with the royal court who were renowned for their discernment. There were such persons in the Jerusalem court, and the book of Proverbs, for instance, reflects such a wisdom tradition within Judah. In the book of Jeremiah, there may be reference to such a group in the comment, "How can you say, 'We are wise, and the law of the Lord is with us' " (8:8; also see 9:23). The oracle against Edom begins by inquiring if there are in the capital city of Edom, Teman, any wise counselors, or if "wisdom [has] vanished" (v. 7). The reason for God's inquiry is developed in verses 8–10. Were there any wisdom left in Edom, then the wise counselors would certainly see that God intends to punish Edom (v. 8). God's punishment is to be quite severe. Unlike grape-pickers who leave gleanings behind, or even thieves who take only what they want, God will strip Edom bare and leave Edom with nothing—no offspring, no kinfolk, no neighbors (v. 10). Verse 11 is difficult. If the "I" is read as the Lord of Israel, then the verse offers some glimmer of hope for Edom that God will protect those who survive the destruction. Another reading is to hear the "I" as the voice of "a kindly survivor promising to help widows and orphans" (Thompson, *The Book of Jeremiah*, p. 721).

Verses 12–16 suggest the reasons that Edom will be punished even while it reinforces the severity of God's judgment. In Jeremiah 25, God is presented as forcing the nations to drink from a cup of God's wrath, and that image is picked up in verse 12. There is a certain mystery about God's ways with the nations, and it is not always clear why any particular nation is judged. Some nations, it seems, have to drink the cup of God's wrath, though they do not deserve to. We have encountered this puzzle in the oracles against the nations, for instance, with the Philistines (especially

47:6). Verses 12–13 make it clear that while some nations may experience wrath for no discernable reason, Edom's punishment is quite deserved, and God will make Edom an "object of horror" and a "waste." Still, verse 12 remains somewhat vague about why God will punish Edom even while asserting that Edom deserves to be punished.

Verses 14–16 are more specific about the reasons for the judgment of Edom. It is because of the "pride" of Edom's heart (v. 16). So Edom, which has inspired terror, will become "least among the nations." Edom, which has held the high position (like an eagle whose nest is high on the rock crevices), will be brought down. The remainder of the oracle reinforces the severity of God's judgment. Ironically, the Edomites, who thought themselves high as the eagle's nest (v. 16), will be destroyed when God sends an eagle to swoop down upon them (v. 22). Who this "eagle" is, is not made explicit, though again Babylon seems likely.

As with the other oracles against the nations, central to this material concerned with Edom is the claim that God is directing history's course, and even Edom, which managed to escape being ravaged by Babylon, will be held accountable. God, who is "over nations and over kingdoms" has a plan and purposes for Edom (v. 20) to which they will have to submit.

Jeremiah 49:23–27

49:23 **Concerning Damascus.**
Hamath and Arpad are confounded,
for they have heard bad news;
they melt in fear, they are troubled like the sea
that cannot be quiet.
²⁴ **Damascus has become feeble, she turned to flee,**
and panic seized her;
anguish and sorrows have taken hold of her,
as of a woman in labor.
²⁵ **How the famous city is forsaken,**
the joyful town!
²⁶ **Therefore her young men shall fall in her squares,**
and all her soldiers shall be destroyed in that day,
says the LORD of hosts.
²⁷ **And I will kindle a fire at the wall of Damascus,**
and it shall devour the strongholds of Ben-hadad.

It is somewhat surprising that Damascus, or Syria of which Damascus is the capital, is mentioned in the oracles against the nations in Jeremiah. Syria was overthrown by Assyria in approximately 732 B.C. and played little role in the history of Israel or Judah after its defeat. In fact, little is known about the territory of Syria after it became an Assyrian province in the late eighth century, and this region seemed to have no role in the events that culminated in Judah's defeat in 587 B.C. One indication of the insignificance of Damascus is that no mention is made of it either in the material about the nations in Jeremiah 25 or in the gathering of Judah's neighbors in Jerusalem to conspire against Babylon (Jeremiah 27).

The oracle against Damascus is quite general and impossible to relate to any events during the time of Jeremiah or following the exile of 587 B.C. Themes of panic, anguish, and destruction are common in the oracles against the nations and evident in this oracle as well. Hamath and Arpad were Syrian cities destroyed by the Assyrians. Ben-hadad was the throne name of several Syrian kings (1 Kings 15:18, 20; 2 Kings 13:24), though there is no indication which particular king is referred to in verse 27. The main point of the oracle is made in its final verse in the explicit claim by the Lord ("I" in v. 27) that Damascus' destruction is God's doing.

Jeremiah 49:28–33

49:28 **Concerning Kedar and the kingdoms of Hazor that King Nebuchadrezzar of Babylon defeated.**

> **Thus says the LORD:**
> **Rise up, advance against Kedar!**
> **Destroy the people of the east!**
29 **Take their tents and their flocks,**
> **their curtains and all their goods;**
> **carry off their camels for yourselves,**
> **and a cry shall go up: "Terror is all around!"**
30 **Flee, wander far away, hide in deep places,**
> **O inhabitants of Hazor!**
> **says the LORD.**
> **For King Nebuchadrezzar of Babylon**
> **has made a plan against you**
> **and formed a purpose against you.**
31 **Rise up, advance against a nation at ease,**
> **that lives secure,**
> **says the LORD,**
> **that has no gates or bars,**
> **that lives alone.**
32 **Their camels shall become booty,**
> **their herds of cattle a spoil.**

I will scatter to every wind
those who have shaven temples,
and I will bring calamity
against them from every side,
 says the LORD.
33 Hazor shall become a lair of jackals,
an everlasting waste;
no one shall live there,
nor shall anyone settle in it.

Kedar was the name for a people who lived in the Arabian desert. They were identified with distant people of the east (v. 28; see Gen. 25:13) and were referred to in Jeremiah 2:10 as among those remote places where one might look to see if ever a people had changed its gods. In Jeremiah 25:24, "the kings of Arabia" are referred to in general, but Kedar is not specifically mentioned. Hazor, not to be confused with the Palestinian city referred to in Joshua 11, is also associated with the Arabian desert, though little is know of it.

Kedar was attacked by Babylon, though just when there were Babylonian campaigns in the Arabian desert region is not clear. As with the other oracles against the nations, this oracle asserts that God directed Babylon "to advance against Kedar" and destroy them (vv. 28–29). So, although Nebuchadrezzar might have a plan and purpose against Kedar (v. 30; compare v. 20), Nebuchadrezzar is no more than God's agent. The cry that goes up from Kedar, "terror all around," has been used several times in the book of Jeremiah to indicate the presence of an enemy sent by God for judgment (most notably in 6:25 by Judah and in 46:5 in reference to Egypt; also see 20:3, 10). The reason for Kedar's destruction is not made clear. They are described as "at ease" and living "secure"; further, "shaven temples" (v. 32) are identified with pagan practices condemned in the Old Testament (9:25–26; see Lev. 19:27). However, compared with the indictment of Moab's pride (48:29) or Egypt's arrogance (46:17), the reasons for God's judgment of Kedar are not clear. Hazor's destruction is announced in verse 33 with no elaboration.

One can only speculate why Kedar and Hazor were included in the oracles against the nations in the book of Jeremiah. These peoples seem to have had little contact with Israel or Judah and were not old enemies over whose destruction those exiled in 587 B.C. might take comfort. It is more likely that Kedar and Hazor were included to indicate the breadth of God's reign. The Lord's reach extended even to distant Kedar and Hazor, so that no kingdom or nation fell outside God's purview.

Jeremiah 49:34–39

49:34 **The word of the LORD that came to the prophet Jeremiah concerning Elam, at the beginning of the reign of King Zedekiah of Judah.**

[35] **Thus says the LORD of hosts: I am going to break the bow of Elam, the mainstay of their might;** [36] **and I will bring upon Elam the four winds from the four quarters of heaven; and I will scatter them to all these winds, and there shall be no nation to which the exiles from Elam shall not come.** [37] **I will terrify Elam before their enemies, and before those who seek their life; I will bring disaster upon them, my fierce anger, says the LORD. I will send the sword after them, until I have consumed them;** [38] **and I will set my throne in Elam, and destroy their king and officials, says the LORD.**

[39] **But in the latter days I will restore the fortunes of Elam, says the LORD.**

Elam was located to the northeast of Israel and Judah. It had once been conquered by Assyria and cooperated with Assyria against Israel (730–20 B.C.; see Isa. 11:11; 21:2; 22:6). The oracle is set during the reign of King Zedekiah, the only one of the oracles against the nations that is directly associated with one of Judah's kings. Some have speculated that those in Judah who hoped for the early demise of Babylon during Zedekiah's reign (see, for instance, Jer. 28–29) may have thought that Elam was capable of overthrowing Babylon. If so, this oracle may represent Jeremiah's effort to dispel any idea that Judah could escape God's intention that they submit to Babylon.

The oracle itself is quite general. The Elamites were known for their skills with the bow (v. 35). Otherwise, the threats against Elam are those common in the book of Jeremiah. God will scatter Elam so that they will be exiled among the nations (v. 36). God will send "disaster" upon them in "fierce anger" and the "sword" until they are "consumed" (v. 37). Just as God summons Babylon to set up thrones at Jerusalem (1:15; compare 43:10 for the same threat against Egypt), so a throne will be established to replace Elam's king (v. 38, "my throne," that is, God's throne; the Lord will determine who reigns over Elam).

Again, as in the other oracles against the nations, God determines what happens to Elam. If this oracle actually did originate during the time of King Zedekiah, the affirmation would have been that the Lord intended the destruction of Elam and the triumph of Babylon; so Judah should not count on Elam to solve the Babylonian problem. After 587 B.C., reflecting on Elam's downfall and Babylon's victory, this oracle asserts to exiles who may have thought otherwise that Babylon's victory over Elam and Judah occurred not because God was powerless but because that is what the Lord intended. God intended to pluck up and pull down Elam, but eventually,

God intended to "restore the fortunes" of Elam along with those of Judah (30:1–3).

AGAINST BABYLON
Jeremiah 50:1–51:64

In the book of Jeremiah, the agent of God's judgment against Judah (Jeremiah 1–45) has been Babylon. Also in the oracles against the nations (Jeremiah 46–49), in each instance Babylon is the instrument by which God judges the nations that surround Judah. In Jeremiah 50–51 it is finally Babylon that is called to account by the Lord. Babylon, the agent of God's judgment, is to be judged.

Babylon's dominance in the ancient Near Eastern world can be traced to its defeat of Egypt at Carchemish in approximately 604 B.C. (see 46:2). Babylonian domination of the region lasted until 538 B.C. when Babylon was defeated by the Persians (also known as the Medes). The book of Jeremiah is largely concerned with this sixty-six year period of Babylonian domination and makes the claim that the Lord intended and allowed Babylon to subjugate Judah and the neighboring nations. Or, to view this matter from a somewhat different perspective, one can say that the plans of the Babylonian empire to expand coincided with God's purposes for Judah and the surrounding nations. For a time, the Lord allowed the Babylonians to do as they intended and, through the prophet Jeremiah, urged Judah to submit to the Babylonians.

With regard to Judah, the book of Jeremiah has made the case again and again that Babylon's invasion was to punish Judah for their long years of apostasy, for turning away from God and violating the covenant. God did not decide to punish Judah arbitrarily but to bring judgment only after they persistently ignored calls through prophets like Jeremiah to repent. With regard to the nations, some of them, like Egypt and Moab, seem to deserve God's judgment because of their arrogance (46:17; 48:26), and Babylon is the agent of this judgment. In other cases, the Philistines, for instance (Jeremiah 47), the book of Jeremiah seems much less clear what prompts God to allow the Babylonians to destroy them. But even if the reasons are not clearly understood, the oracles against the nations insist that Babylonian domination of the ancient Near Eastern region is the Lord's doing.

Jeremiah 50–51 reflects a shift. Historically, these chapters move us close to 539 B.C. and Persia's defeat of Babylon. We see in them indications that whoever wrote this material saw a new world power lurking on the horizon that was a threat to Babylon. Babylon, the foe from the north, is presented in these chapters as itself threatened from the north (50:3, 9, 41; 51:48). Change was occurring in the region, and Babylon was about to be replaced by Persia as the new superpower. It is unlikely that much in these chapters comes from the prophet Jeremiah; the bulk of the material seems to have been written by later editors of the book. Remember that Jeremiah was taken to Egypt shortly after 587 B.C. Near 539 B.C., Jeremiah would have been quite old, and even if he were alive, he would not likely have been in a location where he could know that Persia was emerging as a threat to Babylon far to the northeast of Egypt.

However, the shift in Jeremiah 50–51 is not merely historical. It is also a shift in the theological judgment about Babylon in the book of Jeremiah. Babylon had been the agent of God's judgment against the nations. Jeremiah 50–51 understands that the Lord is about to call Babylon to account. God's intentions coincided with the Babylonians' plans to expand their empire. These final chapters of the book claim that God is not bound to Babylon and is free to direct the course of human events against the Babylonian empire's plans. For a time, Babylon can be used for the Lord's purposes, but then a new people from the north can be raised up who will work God's purposes against Babylon and once more for Judah.

This shift in theological perspective about Babylon reaffirms and strengthens the claims of the book of Jeremiah about the sovereignty of God "over nations and over kingdoms" (1:10). After 587 B.C. it seemed to many in Judah that the Lord was weak and impotent, overpowered by the gods of Babylon and unable to accomplish what God intended. The book of Jeremiah develops the argument that Babylon was the agent of judgment against Judah and that Judah's defeat was exactly what God intended. Still, the real test of the Lord's dominion was Babylon, and Jeremiah 50–51 makes the claim that God directs the course of Babylon's history just as with the other nations. The Lord can use Babylon against Judah and the nations; then God can raise up another people from the north against Babylon. The Lord can work through Babylon toward the captivity of Judah (1:3), but God can then work through Persia toward Babylon's defeat and Judah's restoration.

The two themes, the judgment of Babylon and the restoration of Judah, are thoroughly intertwined in Jeremiah 50–51. God has announced a word of judgment against Judah (Jeremiah 1–39) that is fulfilled in Babylon's victory of 587 B.C. (Jeremiah 39). However, God had also promised restoration for God's people (Jeremiah 30–33), and in Jeremiah 50–51 Judah's restoration is linked with God's judgment of Babylon.

Jeremiah 50:1–10

50:1 The word that the LORD spoke concerning Babylon, concerning the land of the Chaldeans, by the prophet Jeremiah:

2 Declare among the nations and proclaim,
set up a banner and proclaim,
do not conceal it, say:
Babylon is taken,
Bel is put to shame,
Merodach is dismayed.
Her images are put to shame,
her idols are dismayed.

3 For out of the north a nation has come up against her; it shall make her land a desolation, and no one shall live in it; both human beings and animals shall flee away.

4 In those days and in that time, says the LORD, the people of Israel shall come, they and the people of Judah together; they shall come weeping as they seek the LORD their God. 5 They shall ask the way to Zion, with faces turned toward it, and they shall come and join themselves to the LORD by an everlasting covenant that will never be forgotten.

6 My people have been lost sheep; their shepherds have led them astray, turning them away on the mountains; from mountain to hill they have gone, they have forgotten their fold. 7 All who found them have devoured them, and their enemies have said, "We are not guilty, because they have sinned against the LORD, the true pasture, the LORD, the hope of their ancestors."

8 Flee from Babylon, and go out of the land of the Chaldeans, and be like male goats leading the flock. 9 For I am going to stir up and bring against Babylon a company of great nations from the land of the north; and they shall array themselves against her; from there she shall be taken. Their arrows are like the arrows of a skilled warrior who does not return empty-handed.
10 Chaldea shall be plundered; all who plunder her shall be sated, says the LORD.

At the beginning of the book of Jeremiah, the initial verses announce that the word of the Lord came to Jeremiah that led toward "the captivity of Jerusalem" (1:1–3). Babylon is the agent through whom Judah's captivity is to be accomplished. At the end of the book of Jeremiah, these verses announce a shift, and the word of the Lord is concerned with how "Babylon is taken" (v. 2). God called "tribes and kingdoms" from the north against Judah (1:14–15, but pervasively in the book), and these verses announce that "out of the north" a nation will come up against Babylon (v. 3). The Lord has directed that Babylon make Judah "a desolation" (4:27; 6:8; 9:11), and in these chapters it is announced that Babylon is to be made "a desolation" (v. 3). Babylon, the agent of God's judgment of Judah, is now to be judged.

Babylon's judgment is to be publicly and internationally proclaimed (v. 2). Consistently the Bible understands that in events like Persia's defeat of Babylon, God is at work. Again, this is a strange perspective to modern persons who are most likely to interpret world events in terms of causes one can analyze more "objectively": political, military, and economic. Those who wrote Jeremiah 50–51 were as certain that God was involved in Persia's defeat of Babylon in 538 B.C. as they were that God was involved in Babylon's defeat of Judah in 587 B.C.

In the ancient world, the destiny of nations was understood to be linked to the gods of a nation. If Babylon had defeated Judah, a common understanding would have been that the god of Babylon, Merodach (who was also called Bel, v. 2), had defeated Yahweh, the God of Israel and Judah. In fact, many in Judah thought that the Babylonian victory of 587 B.C. signaled the supremacy of the Babylonian deity, so the exile created a faith crisis. That is, Yahweh, the God of Israel and Judah, could no longer be trusted or counted on. The book of Jeremiah claims over and over that the exile does not signal the triumph of the Babylonian gods but, rather, God's use of Babylon to judge Judah. As the book of Jeremiah nears its conclusion and the judgment of Babylon is anticipated, it is asserted that the chief Babylonian god, Merodach or Bel, is about to be shamed and dismayed (v. 2). Yahweh, the God of Israel and Judah, has been in control all along. The Lord was sovereign when Babylon defeated Judah, though it did not seem so to many in Judah. However, when Babylon is finally defeated by another nation from the north, that will be Yahweh's doing, and the Babylonian god will be shamed.

A second major theme of Jeremiah 50–51 is announced in verses 4–7, the restoration of Judah and Israel. The two themes, God's judgment of Babylon and the restoration of Israel and Judah, are linked in verse four. The phrase "In those days and in that time" refers to the time described in verses 2–3 when a nation from the north will make Babylon a desolation. Babylon's demise will mean restoration for God's people. In Jeremiah 50–51 there are many similarities to material found in Jeremiah 30–33, the section of the book that expresses hope for Judah's restoration. The link between the judgment of Babylon and the restoration of Judah and Israel is emphasized by the sequence of material in verses 1–10. First Babylon's defeat is announced (vv. 2–3); then Judah's restoration is portrayed (vv. 4–7); finally Babylon's defeat by nations from the north is announced once more (vv. 8–10).

Verses 4–5 portray the return of Israel and Judah to relationship with "the Lord their God" (v. 4). While there is an indication here of return to the land ("ask the way to Zion," v. 5; compare 31:6), the emphasis is on the restoration of relationship with God. So it is imagined that Israel and Judah will "seek the Lord their God." The prophet Jeremiah had called Judah and Israel to return to God, but they had persistently refused this offer (for instance, 3:12, 14; 4:1). Finally, after the time of their captivity, when God has made Babylon a desolation, these verses imagine that Judah and Israel will at last "seek the Lord their God." Further, the people who broke covenant will "join themselves to the Lord by an everlasting covenant" (v. 5, compare 31:31–34).

In verse 6, God recalls one of the reasons that Judah was taken captive, because "their shepherds had led them astray." As we have seen often in the book, Judah's kings were called shepherds and were held particularly accountable for the exile (see 23:1–4). Even the Babylonians are presented (v. 7) as knowing that the reason for the exile was that Judah had "sinned" against the Lord who was their "true pasture" and "hope of their ancestors." Even in recalling the causes of the exile of which the Babylonians, surprisingly, are aware, these verses affirm that God is the ultimate source of Israel's well-being ("pasture") and hope.

Verses 8–10 build on the hopeful note with which verse 8 concludes and move from the causes of the exile to link again the judgment of Babylon with restoration for God's people. The Lord commands, "Flee from Babylon" and encourages the "lost sheep" (v. 6) to be "like male goats leading the flock" (v. 8). The reason boldness and fleeing are possible for Judah is that God intends to stir up against Babylon "a company of great nations from the land of the north" (v. 9). The Lord is going to judge Babylon, which is to be defeated by Persia, and Judah will then be restored.

Jeremiah 50:11–16

50:11 **Though you rejoice, though you exult,**
    O plunderers of my heritage,
    though you frisk about like a heifer on the grass,
    and neigh like stallions,
    ¹² **your mother shall be utterly shamed,**
    and she who bore you shall be disgraced.
    Lo, she shall be the last of the nations,
    a wilderness, dry land, and a desert.
    ¹³ **Because of the wrath of the LORD she shall not be inhabited,**
    but shall be an utter desolation;
    everyone who passes by Babylon shall be appalled

and hiss because of all her wounds.
¹⁴ Take up your positions around Babylon,
all you that bend the bow;
shoot at her, spare no arrows,
for she has sinned against the LORD.
¹⁵ Raise a shout against her from all sides,
"She has surrendered;
her bulwarks have fallen,
her walls are thrown down."
For this is the vengeance of the LORD:
take vengeance on her,
do to her as she has done.
¹⁶ Cut off from Babylon the sower,
and the wielder of the sickle in time of harvest;
because of the destroying sword
all of them shall return to their own people,
and all of them shall flee to their own land.

The theme of these verses is summarized at the end of verse 15; The Lord will "do to her as she has done." Verse 10 announces that Chaldea, the "plunders of my heritage" (v. 11), will be "plundered"; the Babylonians who rejoiced and exalted (v. 11) will be "utterly shamed" (v. 12; a way to speak of Babylon defeated by Persia); and the rich land of Babylon, compared in verse 11 to a grassy pasture, will become like a barren wilderness that has been overrun by conquerors (v. 12). The text imagines a great reversal that God will effect upon Babylon.

This oracle understands that the judgment of Babylon will occur because Babylon has plundered God's heritage (v. 11). In the book of Jeremiah, both the land of Judah and God's people are referred to as God's "heritage" (2:7; 3:19; 12:7–13; 15; 17:4). In ancient Israel, "heritage" was understood to be the land that was given as a sacred trust by God to a family or tribe and, by extension, to all of the people. God has allowed Babylon to plunder God's heritage, but these verses indicate that the Lord's permission for Babylon to plunder is limited. It is a new time, and the plunders' own heritage will be ruined like Judah: uninhabited and desolate (v. 13), scourged by drought (v. 12), surrounded, besieged, and the walls thrown down (v. 15). Judah has sinned and so has been plundered by Babylon; Babylon has sinned (v. 14) and will also be plundered. The conclusion of this section (v. 16) again links the destruction of Babylon with restoration of captive peoples to their own lands: Judeans, but perhaps also those from other nations who have been plundered by Babylon and exiled.

Jeremiah 50:17–20

50:17 **Israel is a hunted sheep driven away by lions. First the king of Assyria devoured it, and now at the end King Nebuchadrezzar of Babylon has gnawed its bones.** [18] **Therefore, thus says the LORD of hosts, the God of Israel: I am going to punish the king of Babylon and his land, as I punished the king of Assyria.** [19] **I will restore Israel to its pasture, and it shall feed on Carmel and in Bashan, and on the hills of Ephraim and in Gilead its hunger shall be satisfied.** [20] **In those days and at that time, says the LORD, the iniquity of Israel shall be sought, and there shall be none; and the sins of Judah, and none shall be found; for I will pardon the remnant that I have spared.**

In Jeremiah 50:6 God's people are called "lost sheep"; here in verse 17 they are called "hunted sheep." First it was Assyria that hunted them. For over 100 years, from 745 B.C. until after 640 B.C., Assyria had been the dominant power in the ancient Near Eastern world. In 722 B.C., Assyria defeated the northern kingdom, Israel, and made it a vassal state (v. 17, "devoured it"). Judah, the southern kingdom, had to pay tribute to Assyria until the time of King Josiah. Finally Egypt and then Babylon challenged a weakened Assyrian empire and defeated it. Babylon, of course, defeated Judah decisively in 587 B.C. (v. 17, "gnawed its bones"). This text understands that Babylon's defeat of Assyria was God's punishment, and just as Babylon was used to punish Assyria, God will also punish "the king of Babylon" (v. 18). The succession of dominant empires is not merely some geopolitical accident but the way the Lord directs history.

The punishment of Babylon means restoration for Israel and Judah, who will be restored to their "pasture," that is, to their land (v. 19). Babylon's defeat and the restoration of the people to their land signal that the Lord has pardoned the sin and iniquity of the remnant who will experience restoration (v. 20; compare 31:34). Understood the way we are accustomed, Babylon's defeat of Assyria and Babylon's own subsequent demise can be seen as predictable events as over time dominance shifts from one nation to another. In Jeremiah 50, the rise and fall of Babylon are understood to be the Lord's doing connected with the judgment and restoration of Judah. Nations and kingdoms serve God's purposes.

Jeremiah 50:21–27

50:21 **Go up to the land of Merathaim;**
   go up against her,
   and attack the inhabitants of Pekod
   and utterly destroy the last of them,
   says the LORD;

    do all that I have commanded you.
22 The noise of battle is in the land,
    and great destruction!
23 How the hammer of the whole earth
    is cut down and broken!
    How Babylon has become
    a horror among the nations!
24 You set a snare for yourself and you were caught, O Babylon,
    but you did not know it;
    you were discovered and seized,
    because you challenged the LORD.
25 The LORD has opened his armory,
    and brought out the weapons of his wrath,
    for the LORD GOD of hosts has a task to do
    in the land of the Chaldeans.
26 Come against her from every quarter;
    open her granaries;
    pile her up like heaps of grain, and destroy her utterly;
    let nothing be left of her.
27 Kill all her bulls,
    let them go down to the slaughter.
    Alas for them, their day has come,
    the time of their punishment!
28 Listen! Fugitives and refugees from the land of Babylon are coming to declare in Zion the vengeance of the LORD our God, vengeance for his temple.

In Hebrew, "Merathaim" means double rebellion, but the word also sounds like a region in southern Babylon. Similarly, "Pekod" in Hebrew means punishment, but it also sounds like another region of Babylon. By this play on two different words, verse 21 both accuses Babylon of double rebellion and announces God's punishment of Babylon (also see v. 27, where the word punishment is repeated). Babylon fell into the Lord's trap unaware (v. 24). Against the nation that was once the agent of God's judgment, that is, "the hammer of the whole earth" (v. 23), the Lord has "opened his armory and brought out the weapons of his wrath," that is, Persia, who is about to conquer Babylon (v. 25).

Because Babylon "challenged the LORD" (v. 24), it will be destroyed (v. 27). For a time God used Babylon to punish the nations; now the time has come for Babylon to be punished. Verse 28 connects Babylon's punishment with God's vengeance for Babylon's destruction of the Jerusalem temple. Thus "fugitives and refugees" are portrayed returning to Zion from Babylon, able to announce the "vengeance of the LORD," the defeat of Babylon. Of course, elsewhere in the book of Jeremiah, the destruction of the Jerusalem temple is seen as God's judgment on Judah (most notably in Jeremiah 7). It is unlikely that these verses, including the idea that God will punish Babylon for destroying Jerusalem, reflect the ideas of Jeremiah himself; they are most likely those of some editor who wrote well into the exile, perhaps near 538 B.C., when Babylon was defeated by Persia.

Jeremiah 50:29–32

50:29 **Summon archers against Babylon, all who bend the bow. Encamp all around her; let no one escape. Repay her according to her deeds; just as she has done, do to her—for she has arrogantly defied the LORD, the Holy One of Israel.** [30] **Therefore her young men shall fall in her squares, and all her soldiers shall be destroyed on that day, says the LORD.**
> [31] **I am against you, O arrogant one,**
> **says the LORD GOD of hosts;**
> **for your day has come,**
> **the time when I will punish you.**
> [32] **The arrogant one shall stumble and fall,**
> **with no one to raise him up,**
> **and I will kindle a fire in his cities,**
> **and it will devour everything around him.**

The Lord used Babylon to punish Moab and Edom for their pride (48:29; 49:16), but now it is the pride of Babylon (vv. 29, 31, 32; the Hebrew word is translated in these verses as "arrogance") that results in their judgment. Babylon will have done to her "just as she had done" (v. 29). Because Babylon had "defied the LORD, the Holy One of Israel," Babylon would be punished and destroyed (compare v. 24, which charges that Babylon had "challenged" the Lord).

Jeremiah 50:33–34

50:33 **Thus says the LORD of hosts: The people of Israel are oppressed, and so too are the people of Judah; all their captors have held them fast and refuse to let them go.** [34] **Their Redeemer is strong; the LORD of hosts is his name. He will surely plead their cause, that he may give rest to the earth, but unrest to the inhabitants of Babylon.**

Once again the Lord's judgment of Babylon leads to an affirmation of restoration for Israel and Judah. "Rest" for Israel comes when God gives "unrest" to Babylon (v. 34). In these verses, God's people are presented as oppressed by strong and determined captives who refuse to let them go. The comparison between Babylonian captivity and slavery in Egypt is obvious here; Egypt, like Babylon, held the Hebrew slaves fast and refused to let them go (see Exod. 7:14–24; 8:1–7). However, when God punishes Babylon, Israel will know that the Lord is their strong Redeemer (v. 34; see 32:1–16 on redemption). In announcing the end of the Babylonian exile, Isaiah 40–55 often speaks of God as "Redeemer" (43:1; 44:24; 49:7; 54:5). For exiled people who feel that God has deserted them, the claim that the Lord is their Redeemer will have been powerful. On the one hand, the title "redeemer" identifies God as one who is faithful to family, who has not deserted Israel and Judah but is loyal to them. On the other hand, the act of redemption indicates that the exile, a time of forced captivity, is soon to end. In the New Testament, Christ is understood to have redeemed humanity from that which is binding and enslaving (for example, Luke 21:28; Rom. 3:24; 8:23; Eph. 1:7, 14; 4:30; Col. 1:14; Gal. 3:13; 4:5).

Jeremiah 50:35–40

50:35   A sword against the Chaldeans, says the LORD,
      and against the inhabitants of Babylon,
      and against her officials and her sages!
  36   A sword against the diviners,
      so that they may become fools!
      A sword against her warriors,
      so that they may be destroyed!
  37   A sword against her horses and against her chariots,
      and against all the foreign troops in her midst,
      so that they may become women!
      A sword against all her treasures,
      that they may be plundered!
  38   A drought against her waters,
      that they may be dried up!
      For it is a land of images,
      and they go mad over idols.
  39 Therefore wild animals shall live with hyenas in Babylon, and ostriches shall inhabit her; she shall never again be peopled, or inhabited for all generations. 40 As when God overthrew Sodom and Gomorrah and their neighbors, says the LORD, so no one shall live there, nor shall anyone settle in her.

Jeremiah often threatened that Judah would be devoured by the sword (12:12; 14:12–18; 15:2–3; 21:7–9), and the nations were threatened with the same punishment (against Egypt in 46:10, 14; against the Philistines in 47:6; against Moab in 48:2, 10, and so forth). God orders that the sword now be directed against Babylon, and this oracle hammers home its point by a forceful repetition of the phrase "A sword against . . . so that . . ." in verses 35–37. Babylon has been the "sword" that the Lord has used against Judah and the nations, and Babylon will also be punished and destroyed by the sword.

If God's intention to destroy Babylon is not made clear in verses 35–38, verses 39–40 reinforce the idea and finally compare the destruction of Babylon to that of Sodom and Gomorrah (Genesis 17–18). The comparison of Babylon to Sodom and Gomorrah works in two ways: to affirm the completeness of the destruction God intends and to suggest how evil Babylon is. After 587 B.C., Babylon became one of the primary biblical symbols for evil, and later biblical writers invoke the name of Babylon to point to the creation gone wrong (see the book of Daniel, especially Daniel 2–4; and Revelation 18). However, the books of Jeremiah, Daniel, and Revelation all finally affirm that the Lord is "over nations and kingdoms" (1:10), even the mightiest of all, Babylon.

Jeremiah 50:41–46

50:41 **Look, a people is coming from the north;**
    a mighty nation and many kings
    are stirring from the farthest parts of the earth.
  42 **They wield bow and spear,**
    they are cruel and have no mercy.
    The sound of them is like the roaring sea;
    they ride upon horses,
    set in array as a warrior for battle,
    against you, O daughter Babylon!
  43 **The king of Babylon heard news of them,**
    and his hands fell helpless;
    anguish seized him,
    pain like that of a woman in labor.
44 **Like a lion coming up from the thickets of the Jordan against a perennial pasture, I will suddenly chase them away from her; and I will appoint over her whomever I choose. For who is like me? Who can summon me? Who is the shepherd who can stand before me?** 45 **Therefore hear the plan that the LORD has made against Babylon, and the purposes that he has formed against the land of the Chaldeans: Surely the little ones of the flock shall be dragged away; surely their fold shall be appalled at their fate.** 46 **At the sound of the capture of Babylon the earth shall tremble, and her cry shall be heard among the nations.**

Babylon was the dreadful threat from the north Jeremiah announced as coming at the Lord's command to destroy Judah:

> See, a people is coming from the land of the north, . . .
> They grasp the bow and the javelin, they are cruel and have no mercy,
> their sound is like the roaring sea;
> they ride on horses, equipped like a warrior for battle,
> against you, O daughter Zion!
>
> (6:22–23; compare 50:42)

This oracle, however, anticipates a new day when God will send a threat from the north against Babylon. Babylon caused Judah and the nations to be seized with anguish as irresistible as a woman's labor (13:21; 30:6; 48:41; 49:22); soon it is to be the king of Babylon who will writhe in irresistible anguish (v. 43). Babylon rose because God intended that, but it will also fall because of the "the plan" and "the purposes" of the Lord, which not even Babylon can resist (vv. 44–45).

Jeremiah 51:1–4

51:1   **Thus says the LORD:**
       I am going to stir up a destructive wind
       against Babylon
       and against the inhabitants of Leb-qamai;
   2   **and I will send winnowers to Babylon,**
       and they shall winnow her.
       They shall empty her land
       when they come against her from every side
       on the day of trouble.
   3   **Let not the archer bend his bow,**
       and let him not array himself in his coat of mail.
       Do not spare her young men;
       utterly destroy her entire army.
   4   **They shall fall down slain in the land of the Chaldeans,**
       and wounded in her streets.

The strange name in verse one, "Lab-qamai," literally means "the heart of those who rise up against me," an apt description for the Babylonians, at least as they are viewed after 587 B.C. in Jeremiah 50–51. Many scholars have also seen in this name a combination of Hebrew letters that when reversed spell Chaldeans (that is, Babylonians; see Jer. 25:26 where we encounter something similar). The point is clear: The Lord intends the destruction of Babylon, which, though once the agent of judgment, is viewed as being in rebellion against God (compare 50:24, 29–32).

This oracle uses several images to speak of Babylon's destruction. First Babylon's destruction is attributed to wind (vv. 1–2). At verse 3, the image shifts and becomes archers. Thus an advancing enemy is imagined as wind, but then the assault of the army is described more directly as archers who bend their bows (vv. 3–4). God's judgment against Judah is also imagined as a winnowing, hot wind (4:11; also see 13:24; 18:17 in which judgment against Judah is portrayed in images of wind). Again, these verses indicate that even as Babylon has been a winnowing wind against Judah, Babylon will soon be winnowed by an enemy that will "utterly destroy her entire army" (v. 3). Though these verses do not make the connection directly, the Lord, who used Babylon to destroy Judah, will use Persia to destroy Babylon.

Jeremiah 51:5–10

51:5 **Israel and Judah have not been forsaken**
    by their God, the LORD of hosts,
    though their land is full of guilt
    before the Holy One of Israel.
6 **Flee from the midst of Babylon,**
    save your lives, each of you!
    Do not perish because of her guilt,
    for this is the time of the LORD's vengeance;
    he is repaying her what is due.
7 **Babylon was a golden cup in the LORD's hand,**
    making all the earth drunken;
    the nations drank of her wine,
    and so the nations went mad.
8 **Suddenly Babylon has fallen and is shattered;**
    wail for her!
    Bring balm for her wound;
    perhaps she may be healed.
9 **We tried to heal Babylon,**
    but she could not be healed.
    Forsake her, and let each of us go
    to our own country;
    for her judgment has reached up to heaven
    and has been lifted up even to the skies.
10 **The LORD has brought forth our vindication;**
    come, let us declare in Zion
    the work of the LORD our God.

The Lord's judgment of Babylon means restoration for Judah. God's people are urged to "flee from the midst of Babylon" (v. 6). After 587 B.C., it may have seemed that Judah and Israel had been forsaken by God. However, when Babylon is defeated, then it will be clear that the Lord can repay Babylon what it is due for destroying Zion (v. 6) and bring "vindication" to God's people (v. 10). Verse 7 refers to Jeremiah 25 and the cup of God's wrath. In these verses, Jeremiah 25 is interpreted to mean that Babylon is the cup of God's wrath by which the earth was made drunk and the nations mad. However, soon Babylon will be judged (vv. 8–9), and from Zion God's people will declare Babylon's judgment to be "the work of the LORD our God" (v. 10). Before the exile of 587 B.C., Jeremiah announces that the work of the Lord is judgment upon Judah and the nations by Babylon. After the exile of 587 B.C., the editors of the book of Jeremiah can see that Persia is the agent of judgment of Babylon. God is not bound to Babylon but is sovereign "over nations and over kingdoms" (1:10), including Babylon.

Jeremiah 51:11–19

51:11   **Sharpen the arrows!**
           Fill the quivers!
   The LORD has stirred up the spirit of the kings of the Medes, because his purpose concerning Babylon is to destroy it, for that is the vengeance of the LORD, vengeance for his temple.
           [12] **Raise a standard against the walls of Babylon;**
               make the watch strong;
               post sentinels;
               prepare the ambushes;
               for the LORD has both planned and done
               what he spoke concerning the inhabitants of Babylon.
           [13] **You who live by mighty waters,**
               rich in treasures,
               your end has come,
               the thread of your life is cut.
           [14] **The LORD of hosts has sworn by himself:**
               Surely I will fill you with troops like a swarm of locusts,
               and they shall raise a shout of victory over you.
           [15] **It is he who made the earth by his power,**
               who established the world by his wisdom,
               and by his understanding stretched out the heavens.
           [16] **When he utters his voice there is a tumult of waters in the heavens,**
               and he makes the mist rise from the ends of the earth.
               He makes lightnings for the rain,

and he brings out the wind from his storehouses.

17 Everyone is stupid and without knowledge;
   goldsmiths are all put to shame by their idols;
   for their images are false,
   and there is no breath in them.

18 They are worthless, a work of delusion;
   at the time of their punishment they shall perish.

19 Not like these is the LORD, the portion of Jacob,
   for he is the one who formed all things,
   and Israel is the tribe of his inheritance;
   the LORD of hosts is his name.

The poetic images used to portray Babylon's defeat in Jeremiah 50–51 point to the conquest of the Babylonians by Persia (or the Medes) in 538 B.C. It is likely that those who edited these chapters of the book of Jeremiah, if not aware of the Persian victory over Babylon, could at least see it coming. The Lord's "purpose" concerning the Babylonians was to stir up "the kings of the Medes" to destroy them (v. 11; compare 50:45). The Persian victory is then imagined in poetic images in verses 12–14.

Verses 15–19 are a repetition of Jeremiah 10:12–16 and place God's purposes against Babylon in a larger context. The Lord God of Israel is the One "who made the earth by his power" (v. 15). If God can stretch out the heavens (v. 14), then God can surely stir up the Medes to defeat the Babylonians (v. 11). Judah may have imagined that the gods of Babylon had defeated "the LORD, the portion of Jacob" (v. 19). Against such an idea, these verses scoff at the idols as "false" (v. 17) and "worthless" (v. 18). God's "power" (v. 15) will be evident when Persia is victorious over Babylon as "the LORD of hosts [had] sworn by himself"! (v. 14). The word of the Lord will be fulfilled.

Jeremiah 51:20–24

51:20 You are my war club, my weapon of battle:
     with you I smash nations;
     with you I destroy kingdoms;

21 with you I smash the horse and its rider;
   with you I smash the chariot and the charioteer;

22 with you I smash man and woman;
   with you I smash the old man and the boy;
   with you I smash the young man and the girl;

23 with you I smash shepherds and their flocks;
   with you I smash farmers and their teams;

with you I smash governors and deputies.
²⁴ I will repay Babylon and all the inhabitants of Chaldea before your
very eyes for all the wrong that they have done in Zion, says the LORD.

This poem is made intense by the constant repetition of the assertion "I smash," and it is much like the poem in 50:35–38, which gains its intensity by the repetition of "sword." The Lord is the speaker of these verses and addresses a "you" (v. 20) who is not directly identified but who is usually identified as Cyrus, the Persian king who defeated Babylon. In Isaiah 40–55, also concerned with the restoration of Israel after the exile, Cyrus is directly named (44:28; 45:1; also see Ezra 1:1–8; 5:13–17). However, while Cyrus is to be God's "club, my weapon of battle," the real agent of restoration is the Lord, the "I" who uses the weapon to "smash." At a time before Jeremiah, the prophet Isaiah called Assyria the "rod of my [God's] anger" (Isa. 1:5). Jeremiah knew that Babylon was God's agent to punish Judah. The editors who included this poem in the book of Jeremiah understood that once again the Lord's purposes were to be accomplished by a human, historical agent.

Verse 24, which is not part of the poem but stands beside it, makes clear that the Lord who called Babylon from the north against Judah will in time call a weapon, that is, Persia, against Babylon. As we have seen at the beginning of Jeremiah 51, God's motive for smashing Babylon, at least as these verses come to us in the final form of the book of Jeremiah, is to "repay Babylon . . . for all the wrong they have done" (v. 24).

A text such as this, with its portrayal of a brutally vengeful God, must be interpreted with great caution in our own setting because it seems to invite us to seek revenge. While it may be possible to hear the sentiment of this text in an historical setting where one group has been harshly oppressed by another, the text is clear that it is God, working through the processes of history in which nations rise and fall, who "repays Babylon" and not the people of Judah and Israel themselves. The text attempts to understand how the Lord works (or was about to work) through geopolitical events, the emergence of Persia and the collapse of Babylon. The text is not proposing a personal ethic or even reflecting on the ethics of war. This text does understand that nations—all nations—finally stand accountable before God. Most helpfully, the text may raise for us Christian citizens of the United States questions about what we have done with our tremendous military and economic power (like Babylon), for which God may "repay" us "for all the wrong" we have done.

Jeremiah 51:25–33

51:25 I am against you, O destroying mountain,
    says the LORD,
    that destroys the whole earth;
    I will stretch out my hand against you,
    and roll you down from the crags,
    and make you a burned-out mountain.
26 No stone shall be taken from you for a corner
    and no stone for a foundation,
    but you shall be a perpetual waste,
    says the LORD.
27 Raise a standard in the land,
    blow the trumpet among the nations;
    prepare the nations for war against her,
    summon against her the kingdoms,
    Ararat, Minni, and Ashkenaz;
    appoint a marshal against her,
    bring up horses like bristling locusts.
28 Prepare the nations for war against her,
    the kings of the Medes, with their governors and deputies,
    and every land under their dominion.
29 The land trembles and writhes,
    for the LORD's purposes against Babylon stand,
    to make the land of Babylon a desolation,
    without inhabitant.
30 The warriors of Babylon have given up fighting,
    they remain in their strongholds;
    their strength has failed,
    they have become women;
    her buildings are set on fire,
    her bars are broken.
31 One runner runs to meet another,
    and one messenger to meet another,
    to tell the king of Babylon
    that his city is taken from end to end:
32 the fords have been seized,
    the marshes have been burned with fire,
    and the soldiers are in panic.
33 For thus says the LORD of hosts, the God of Israel:
    Daughter Babylon is like a threshing floor
    at the time when it is trodden;
    yet a little while
    and the time of her harvest will come.

The destroyer of nations, mighty Babylon, is about to be destroyed. The Lord summoned Babylon from the north to judge Judah and the nations. In these verses, God is imagined to have sounded the battle cry that calls together nations against Babylon (v. 27). Babylon's time as God's agent has passed, and "the king of the Medes" (Persia) is designated to overthrow Babylon (v. 29). Babylon has struck terror into the warriors of many nations (46:12, 21; 48:14–15, 41; 49:24), but soon it will be Babylon's warriors who are terrified (v. 30). The Lord, who for a season used Babylon to judge the nations, is about to judge Babylon.

The phrase in verse 33 that indicates that Babylon's destruction will occur in "yet a little while" suggests that this text was written by someone who, close to 538 B.C., was aware that Persia was a significant threat to Babylonian power even before Persia had actually defeated Babylon. However, what interested the person who wrote these verses was not the political or military intrigue of shifting world power but the certainty that God was directing the course of history against Babylon and toward Persia. For those who had experienced the tragedy of 587 B.C. and who might have doubted that the Lord was sovereign, this announcement that God was doing a new thing with Persia and against Babylon would have been "good news," the gospel of God's reign.

Jeremiah 52:34–44

51:34 **"King Nebuchadrezzar of Babylon has devoured me,**
    he has crushed me;
    he has made me an empty vessel,
    he has swallowed me like a monster;
    he has filled his belly with my delicacies,
    he has spewed me out.
  35 **May my torn flesh be avenged on Babylon,"**
    the inhabitants of Zion shall say.
    "May my blood be avenged on the inhabitants of Chaldea,"
    Jerusalem shall say.
  36 **Therefore thus says the LORD:**
    I am going to defend your cause
    and take vengeance for you.
    I will dry up her sea
    and make her fountain dry;
  37 **and Babylon shall become a heap of ruins,**
    a den of jackals,
    an object of horror and of hissing,
    without inhabitant.

38 Like lions they shall roar together;
   they shall growl like lions' whelps.
39 When they are inflamed, I will set out their drink
   and make them drunk, until they become merry
   and then sleep a perpetual sleep
   and never wake, says the LORD.
40 I will bring them down like lambs to the slaughter,
   like rams and goats.
41 How Sheshach is taken,
   the pride of the whole earth seized!
   How Babylon has become
   an object of horror among the nations!
42 The sea has risen over Babylon;
   she has been covered by its tumultuous waves.
43 Her cities have become an object of horror,
   a land of drought and a desert,
   a land in which no one lives,
   and through which no mortal passes.
44 I will punish Bel in Babylon,
   and make him disgorge what he has swallowed.
   The nations shall no longer stream to him;
   the wall of Babylon has fallen.

These verses link the Lord's intention to defeat Babylon with God's power as creator to bring order out of chaos. Verses 34–35 state charges or accusations against Babylon; beginning with the "therefore" in verse 36, judgment is announced upon Babylon. The portrayal of God's judgment of Babylon concludes in verses 41–44 that celebrate Babylon's defeat.

One image used in the accusation against Babylon is that they have been to Judah "like a monster" that has "filled his belly with . . . delicacies" (v. 34). The understanding of creation common in Babylon included stories about the great sea monster who caused chaos and had to be subdued for there to be order and a creation (see Psalms 87:4; 89:10, and Isa. 51:9, which mention this monster, Rahab). In these verses, Babylon is accused of being the great chaos monster which "devoured," "crushed," and "swallowed" Judah. In another image, Babylon is accused of shedding the blood of Judah, which God needs to avenge (v. 35).

Because Babylon has acted like the chaos monster, God will respond, and Babylon itself will be thrown into chaos (vv. 36–37). What God has allowed Babylon to do to the other nations, God will allow to be done to Babylon. For instance, the judgment against Babylon described in verse 37 has been used previously to describe what Babylon will do to Judah (see

2:15). To the nations it has destroyed, Babylon may have seemed to be a mighty monster, but at the end of these verses, when subdued by God, the monster will become no more ferocious than baby lions ("lion whelps," v. 38) or like lambs and goats ready for the slaughter (v. 40). Verse 39 also suggests that Babylon at last will be forced to drink from the cup of God's wrath (see 25:26).

The concluding verses of this section begin as if they are a lament over the terrible fall of Babylon (v. 41, "How Sheshach is fallen . . . "). However, in the concluding verse (v. 44), the tone of a lament is absent, and God celebrates the fall of Babylon. "Sheshach" is a cipher for Babylon also used in Jeremiah 25:26 to announce God's judgment upon Babylon. There is an interesting contrast between the way God's judgment is imagined in verses 36 and 42. In verse 36, God announces, "I will dry up her sea, and make her fountain dry," a threat that God will make Babylon an arid desert without water (remember the threats of drought against Judah, see Jeremiah 14; also Gen. 2:5 imagines that before God's creating, the world was an unwatered desert). In verse 42, God's judgment is that the "sea" will cover Babylon. This latter image is of watery, primal chaos engulfing Babylon and is most like images of chaos found in Genesis 1:2, or in the story of the flood in Genesis 6–8. God's judgment of Babylon will bring order to God's creation and signal the defeat of the Babylonian god, Bel.

To Judah and those who experienced the exile of 587 B.C., Babylon may have seemed like the incarnation of chaos, a monster that has swallowed up Judah and the nations. It may have even seemed to those who experienced the exile that God's creation was in collapse or that the Babylonian gods had triumphed over the Lord of Israel. These verses announce the good news that the Lord will subdue the monster Babylon (which will become like a lion cub or a sheep to be slaughtered), triumph over the gods of Babylon, and restore order in creation. The Lord is not sovereign merely "over kingdoms and over nations" (1:10) but over the entire creation (see 10:1–16).

Jeremiah 51:45–53

> 51:45 **Come out of her, my people!**
> **Save your lives, each of you,**
> **from the fierce anger of the LORD!**
> 46 **Do not be faint-hearted or fearful**
> **at the rumors heard in the land—**
> **one year one rumor comes,**
> **the next year another,**

rumors of violence in the land
and of ruler against ruler.
47 Assuredly, the days are coming
when I will punish the images of Babylon;
her whole land shall be put to shame,
and all her slain shall fall in her midst.
48 Then the heavens and the earth,
and all that is in them,
shall shout for joy over Babylon;
says the LORD.
49 Babylon must fall for the slain of Israel,
as the slain of all the earth have fallen because of Babylon.
50 You survivors of the sword,
go, do not linger!
Remember the LORD in a distant land,
and let Jerusalem come into your mind:
51 We are put to shame, for we have heard insults;
dishonor has covered our face,
for aliens have come
into the holy places of the LORD's house.
52 Therefore the time is surely coming, says the LORD,
when I will punish her idols,
and through all her land
the wounded shall groan.
53 Though Babylon should mount up to heaven,
and though she should fortify her strong height,
from me destroyers would come upon her,
says the LORD.

The themes of these verses repeat much of what we have found already in Jeremiah 50–51. Because Babylon has "fallen" (v. 44), the Lord calls, "Come out of her, my people" (v. 45). The reversal of Babylon's fortunes for ill will also result in the reversal of fortunes for Israel and mean their restoration.

Babylon, the enemy from the north that was the agent of judgment, will itself be destroyed by "destroyers" sent by God from the north (v. 48), and Babylon will be unable to resist what the Lord intends (v. 53). These verses stress particularly that the judgment of Babylon is in response to what Babylon did to Judah. Thus the Lord announces that "Babylon must fall for the slain of Israel" (v. 49). Or again, the punishment of Babylon is linked with the desecration of the "holy places of the LORD's house" (vv. 51–52).

The restoration of Israel and Judah, made possible by Babylon's defeat, is specifically connected with their return to the land and to Jerusalem (v. 50). There are echoes of Jeremiah 30–33 in the idea that restoration means return to the land. The way Israel and Judah are addressed as "survivors of the sword" (v. 50) is very similar to the way they are addressed in Jeremiah 31:2–6 where they are promised that they will return to Judah and Jerusalem.

The book of Jeremiah affirms that the Lord allowed Babylon to pluck up and tear down Judah. However, when the judgment of Judah is accomplished, the book imagines that God will also pluck up and tear down Babylon, and the judgment of Babylon will make possible Judah's restoration, God's long-awaited building and planting.

Jeremiah 51:54–58

51:54 **Listen!—a cry from Babylon!**
       A great crashing from the land of the Chaldeans!
   55 **For the LORD is laying Babylon waste,**
       and stilling her loud clamor.
       Their waves roar like mighty waters,
       the sound of their clamor resounds;
   56 **for a destroyer has come against her,**
       against Babylon;
       her warriors are taken,
       their bows are broken;
       for the LORD is a God of recompense,
       he will repay in full.
   57 **I will make her officials and her sages drunk,**
       also her governors, her deputies, and her warriors;
       they shall sleep a perpetual sleep and never wake,
       says the King, whose name is the LORD of hosts.
   58 **Thus says the LORD of hosts:**
       The broad wall of Babylon
       shall be leveled to the ground,
       and her high gates
       shall be burned with fire.
       The peoples exhaust themselves for nothing,
       and the nations weary themselves only for fire.

The oracles against Babylon began with the Lord's announcement, "Declare . . . Babylon is taken" (50:2). The oracles against Babylon conclude with the admonition, "Listen!—a cry from Babylon! . . . For the LORD is laying Babylon waste" (vv. 54–55). Because Judah has broken its relationship with God, the Lord announces through Jeremiah the destruction of Judah by Babylon. That word of the LORD has been fulfilled in 587 B.C. In time, God has also declared that Babylon will be taken, and these final verses of the oracles against Babylon want it clear that what God has declared will also be accomplished.

More directly and more emphatically than throughout Jeremiah 50–51, these verses stress that Babylon's demise is the Lord's doing. Of course, God uses historical agents, "a destroyer," which we know to be the Persians (v. 56). However, these verses want it clear that Babylon's fall is not a historical accident. Three times in these five verses, "the Lord" is credited with Babylon's defeat:

1. "the LORD is laying Babylon to waste" (v. 55);
2. "her warriors are taken, their bows are broken; for the Lord is a God of recompense" (v. 56);
3. "they shall sleep a perpetual sleep and never wake, says the King, whose name is the Lord of hosts" (v. 57).

Most of the book of Jeremiah is concerned with why and how God has directed Judah's history toward the "captivity" (1:3). However, there has been a broader concern in the book about the Lord who is sovereign "over nations and kingdoms" (1:10), even mighty Babylon. Judah can not resist judgment, plucking up and tearing down; but then, neither can Babylon, and all the empire's striving against the Lord's intentions will be "for nothing" (v. 58; compare v. 53).

In both the Old and the New Testaments, Babylon, God's agent of judgment against Judah, becomes a symbol for earthly power that may challenge even the Lord of hosts. The claim that God can direct the course of Babylon's history comes to be an affirmation that the Lord is sovereign, a litmus test of the Lord's reign. So, in the prophetic books of the Old Testament, oracles against Babylon are eventually attributed to prophets who lived before Babylon became a power in the ancient Near Eastern world as a way to say that God ruled over all the nations (for instance, Isaiah 13; Micah 4:10). In the book of Revelation, centuries after Babylon ceased to be an important world power, an affirmation that God caused the downfall of Babylon is used to reassure Christians who are being persecuted by Rome (Revelation 18). The writer of Revelation remembers that the Lord judged mighty Babylon "in one hour" (Rev. 18:10, 17, 19), and the clear implication is that God will do the same to Rome.

The oracles against Babylon in the book of Jeremiah call for us in the church to trust that the Lord reigns even where that claim is not so evident. The Lord's reign was not evident to those who had experienced the exile of 587 B.C. Indeed, it seemed as if Babylon reigned. Not so! retorts the book of Jeremiah. In our world, too, it is not always so clear that the Lord reigns when we see how guns and violence infest our society, observe the use of military force instead of diplomacy to solve international conflicts, and notice that in our staggering opulence we are easily blind to grinding and dehumanizing poverty. Death seems to rule in our world. Not so, retorts the book of Jeremiah, for even mighty Babylon will fall. In this spirit, we in the church gather week by week, and no matter how the Babylon of our time may have had its way during the preceding days, we find the courage to say, "The earth is the Lord's and all that is in it, the world and those who live in it" (Psalm 24:1).

Jeremiah 51:59–64

51:59 **The word that the prophet Jeremiah commanded Seraiah son of Neriah son of Mahseiah, when he went with King Zedekiah of Judah to Babylon, in the fourth year of his reign. Seraiah was the quartermaster.** [60] **Jeremiah wrote in a scroll all the disasters that would come on Babylon, all these words that are written concerning Babylon.** [61] **And Jeremiah said to Seraiah: "When you come to Babylon, see that you read all these words,** [62] **and say, 'O LORD, you yourself threatened to destroy this place so that neither human beings nor animals shall live in it, and it shall be desolate forever.'** [63] **When you finish reading this scroll, tie a stone to it, and throw it into the middle of the Euphrates,** [64] **and say, 'Thus shall Babylon sink, to rise no more, because of the disasters that I am bringing on her.'"**

Thus far are the words of Jeremiah.

This conclusion to the oracles against the nations reports that the oracles were dictated to Seraiah, the brother of Baruch. The indication in verse 59 is that in the fourth year of King Zedekiah's reign (about 593 B.C.), Zedekiah was summoned to Babylon. Such an occurrence is certainly plausible, likely as an occasion when the Babylonians might have required Zedekiah, whom they had appointed as king in 598 B.C., to reaffirm his allegiance to Babylon in the midst of plots among Judah's neighbors to rebel against Babylon (see Jeremiah 27). Seraiah, it is claimed, accompanied Zedekiah, and Jeremiah prevailed upon him to carry a scroll to Babylon.

Of course, we have no way of knowing what actually transpired. This story, placed at the conclusion of the oracles against the nations, leaves readers with the impression that Seraiah's role with the oracles against the nations was extensive and parallel to Baruch's role with the oracles against

Judah (Jeremiah 36). Since it is likely that many of the oracles against the nations originated not with Jeremiah but with later editors of the book of Jeremiah, it does not seem likely that we should read these verses as an entirely accurate account of Seraiah's role in the development of book of Jeremiah. We need to search for the point of this material not so much in the historical accuracy of its report but in what is meant to be conveyed as Seraiah is presented as a character in the book of Jeremiah alongside his brother, Baruch.

It seems that each of the brothers functions in the book as the scribe for one of the ways that God is affirmed to be "over nations and over kingdoms to pluck up and pull down . . . to build and to plant" (1:10). Baruch is the scribe for the part of the book that announces the disaster that God brings upon Judah and views Babylon as God's agent to pluck up and pull down Judah (1:14). Baruch represents the pro-Babylonian stance that dominates the book of Jeremiah. Seraiah is the scribe of that part of the book that finally announces the "disasters that would come on Babylon" (v. 60) and that make possible Judah's restoration, God's eventual building and planting. Seraiah represents the voice against Babylon, which the book withholds until very late. Thus, Baruch and Seraiah represent the two perspectives about Babylon found in the book of Jeremiah. Baruch represents the dominant view, which sees Babylon serving the Lord to "pluck up and tear down" Judah. Seraiah represents the less dominant perspective, which is not given much play until near the book's conclusion. Finally, God will bring "disasters" upon Babylon, which will be plucked up and pulled down so that Israel and Judah can be restored, built, and planted. Together, the brothers present the whole claim of the book of Jeremiah that the Lord reigns over the nations—over Judah to be sure, but also over mighty Babylon.

As with Baruch, Seraiah is to write down the words of Jeremiah. The implication is that the written words will endure and serve as a witness to the fulfillment of the word of the Lord when Babylon finally does fall. Interestingly, once in Babylon, Seraiah is to read the words and it is the Lord who is to be reminded of them by Seraiah's reading (v. 61). Perhaps the rainbow at the conclusion of the flood story is similar, a reminder to God not to destroy again the world (see Gen. 9:14–15: "When I bring clouds over the earth and the bow is seen in the clouds, I will remember my covenant . . . and the water shall never again become a flood to destroy all flesh."). Finally, Seraiah is to throw the scroll tied to a stone into the Euphrates so it will sink. This is to be another symbolic action, indicating that Babylon is to sink and rise no more (v. 64).

From the beginning, the book of Jeremiah has understood that God's word directs history. God directs disasters against Judah through Babylon to bring judgment upon God's people. Yet, finally, God directs disasters against Babylon to allow Judah's restoration. We need both Baruch and Seraiah to have the words of Jeremiah. With Babylon's end certain, the book of Jeremiah comes full circle and witnesses to the Lord, who is "over nations and kingdoms to pluck up and pull down . . . to build and to plant."

"King Evil-merodach . . . Showed Favor to King Jehoiachin"
Jeremiah 52

This final chapter in the book of Jeremiah is nearly identical to 2 Kings 24:18–25:30. It is widely held that this material was a late addition to the book. To call this chapter a summary is apt, since little new ground is covered. We are told of that which we already know, albeit in greater detail—the siege of Jerusalem, the Babylonian breach of the city's walls, the plunder and destruction of the Temple and king's residence, and the brutal treatment of Zedekiah by the Babylonians. We do learn of the numbers of persons exiled in 597, 587, and 582 B.C. (vv. 28–30). The final verses of the chapter (vv. 31–34) also move beyond what we already know from the book of Jeremiah, that in 561 B.C. King Evil-merodach of Babylon "showed favor to King Jehoiachin of Judah," who had been exiled twenty-four years earlier. The exiled King Jehoiachin, we learn, was released from prison, "dined regularly at the king's table," and received a daily allowance until his death. The report is tantalizing and modestly stated. These verses may be intended as more than just a summary, to offer one last hint as the book of Jeremiah concludes that the Lord continues to direct history not only for plucking up and tearing down but also for building and planting.

Jeremiah 52:1–3a

> 52:1 **Zedekiah was twenty-one years old when he began to reign; he reigned eleven years in Jerusalem. His mother's name was Hamutal daughter of Jeremiah of Libnah. ² He did what was evil in the sight of the LORD, just as Jehoiakim had done. ³ Indeed, Jerusalem and Judah so angered the LORD that he expelled them from his presence.**

The language of verse 1 reflects the standard manner in which the kings of Israel and Judah are introduced in 1 and 2 Kings. Verses 2–3 offer a theological judgment about King Zedekiah and his reign, a judgment that is entirely consistent with the book of Jeremiah. About King Zedekiah, the judgment is that he did "evil" and so "angered the Lord" who "expelled" the king and people from "his presence," that is, from the land. This three-step sequence—did evil, angered the Lord, and expelled—offers a nice summary of the book of Jeremiah, for which we have been prepared from the book's initial verses indicating an overriding concern with "the captivity of Jerusalem" (1:3). Throughout the book, "the captivity of Jerusalem" has been explained as God's response to having been forsaken by Judah (1:16). These verses, then, offer a judgment that links Judah's evil, God's anger, and the exile in ways that are entirely consistent with the book to this point.

Jeremiah 52:3b–11

52:3b **Zedekiah rebelled against the king of Babylon. [4] And in the ninth year of his reign, in the tenth month, on the tenth day of the month, King Nebuchadrezzar of Babylon came with all his army against Jerusalem, and they laid siege to it; they built siegeworks against it all around. [5] So the city was besieged until the eleventh year of King Zedekiah. [6] On the ninth day of the fourth month the famine became so severe in the city that there was no food for the people of the land. [7] Then a breach was made in the city wall and all the soldiers fled and went out from the city by night by the way of the gate between the two walls, by the king's garden, though the Chaldeans were all around the city. They went in the direction of the Arabah. [8] But the army of the Chaldeans pursued the king, and overtook Zedekiah in the plains of Jericho; and all his army was scattered, deserting him. [9] Then they captured the king, and brought him up to the king of Babylon at Riblah in the land of Hamath, and he passed sentence on him. [10] The king of Babylon killed the sons of Zedekiah before his eyes, and also killed all the officers of Judah at Riblah. [11] He put out the eyes of Zedekiah, and bound him in fetters, and the king of Babylon took him to Babylon, and put him in prison until the day of his death.**

The logic of these verses is different from the preceding verses. God is not mentioned once. The charge against Zedekiah is not, as in the prior verses, that he did evil that angered the Lord but that "Zedekiah rebelled against the King of Babylon" (v. 3a). It is not the Lord who responds to Zedekiah's rebellion but King Nebuchadrezzar and the Babylonian army. There is no mention that Judah forsook the Lord, but it is noted that Zedekiah's army deserted him just before he was tortured and exiled (vv. 8–11).

These verses are not directly theological but focus on political, diplomatic, and military developments that led to Judah's defeat by Babylon.

Those for whom the book of Jeremiah was originally intended, persons living in the midst of the exile, would have been quite familiar with the events reported in these verses. It is also likely that those who survived the exile of 587 B.C. had drawn their own theological conclusions about the meaning of these events. The kings of Judah, even Zedekiah who came to power as a puppet of Babylon, were considered God's agents for the well-being of Judah. It was understood that God had established kings on the throne of David "forever" (2 Samuel 7). By the time Babylon sacked Jerusalem and tortured and exiled Zedekiah, King Jehoiakim of Judah has already been exiled in Babylon for a decade. It would have been difficult for those in Judah, who had seen two of their kings deposed, not to conclude that the Lord had either reneged on promises made to David or had been overpowered by the gods of Babylon.

However, this chapter points in another direction. Though verses 4–11 make an explicit reference to verses 1–3, we who have been reading the book of Jeremiah can hardly help making a connection. The Lord's anger (v. 3) finds expression in the specificity of historical events, through King Nebuchadrezzar and the Babylonian army. Zedekiah is "expelled" (v. 11) through the agency of the Babylonians but through the intention of the Lord. Furthermore, as we know, the "evil" Zedekiah did was in part his failure to submit to the Babylonians and instead to seek rescue by the Egyptians (see 37:3–10). These verses, which make no direct mention of God, seem to function as a quiz for readers who have come to the end of the book of Jeremiah: Why do you imagine now that Zedekiah was "expelled"?

Jeremiah 52:12–27

52:12 **In the fifth month, on the tenth day of the month—which was the nineteenth year of King Nebuchadrezzar, king of Babylon—Nebuzaradan the captain of the bodyguard who served the king of Babylon, entered Jerusalem.** [13] **He burned the house of the LORD, the king's house, and all the houses of Jerusalem; every great house he burned down.** [14] **All the army of the Chaldeans, who were with the captain of the guard, broke down all the walls around Jerusalem.** [15] **Nebuzaradan the captain of the guard carried into exile some of the poorest of the people and the rest of the people who were left in the city and the deserters who had defected to the king of Babylon, together with the rest of the artisans.** [16] **But Nebuzaradan the captain of the guard left some of the poorest people of the land to be vinedressers and tillers of the soil.**

[17] **The pillars of bronze that were in the house of the LORD, and the stands and the bronze sea that were in the house of the LORD, the Chaldeans broke**

in pieces, and carried all the bronze to Babylon. [18] They took away the pots, the shovels, the snuffers, the basins, the ladles, and all the vessels of bronze used in the temple service. [19] The captain of the guard took away the small bowls also, the firepans, the basins, the pots, the lampstands, the ladles, and the bowls for libation, both those of gold and those of silver. [20] As for the two pillars, the one sea, the twelve bronze bulls that were under the sea, and the stands, which King Solomon had made for the house of the LORD, the bronze of all these vessels was beyond weighing. [21] As for the pillars, the height of the one pillar was eighteen cubits, its circumference was twelve cubits; it was hollow and its thickness was four fingers. [22] Upon it was a capital of bronze; the height of the one capital was five cubits; latticework and pomegranates, all of bronze, encircled the top of the capital. And the second pillar had the same, with pomegranates. [23] There were ninety-six pomegranates on the sides; all the pomegranates encircling the latticework numbered one hundred.

[24] The captain of the guard took the chief priest Seraiah, the second priest Zephaniah, and the three guardians of the threshold; [25] and from the city he took an officer who had been in command of the soldiers, and seven men of the king's council who were found in the city; the secretary of the commander of the army who mustered the people of the land; and sixty men of the people of the land who were found inside the city. [26] Then Nebuzaradan the captain of the guard took them, and brought them to the king of Babylon at Riblah. [27] And the king of Babylon struck them down, and put them to death at Riblah in the land of Hamath. So Judah went into exile out of its land.

The initial focus of Jeremiah 52 is on King Zedekiah, but these verses expand that focus in three ways, incorporating an account of the destruction of Jerusalem (vv. 12–16), an account of the pillage of the Temple (vv. 17–23), and an account of what the Babylonians did to some of the leading citizens of Jerusalem (vv. 24–27). For those in ancient Judah, the city of Jerusalem, the Temple, and the key religious and political leaders (remember that the monarch, King Zedekiah, was already considered in earlier verses) were all understood to have been established by the Lord and secure forever as signs of God's commitment to Judah.

Jerusalem was the great city of David and understood in Judah to be the city God had chosen for a dwelling. It was unimaginable that Jerusalem could be invaded by outsiders, sacked, and burned. Yet, in careful detail so that the reality would be unmistakable, that is what is described in verses 12–16. The Temple was considered the Lord's house, and the Holy of Holies the very throne of God. The Temple was that place where God's presence with the people was most evident, where the Lord's reign over the whole of creation was given vivid symbolic expression (hence, the pillars, the sea, the lampstands, and so forth). The destruction of the Temple by foreigners was unthinkable. Finally, even beyond the king, the religious and political leaders of Judah were considered agents and representatives ordained for their functions by God. Their deportation, like that of the king himself, would have been interpreted as a grave sign.

The events recounted in detail within Jeremiah 52—King Zedekiah being "expelled," Jerusalem being burned, the Temple being looted, key officials being deported—all would have been popularly interpreted as an indication that God had either broken promises with Judah or that God was overpowered by the gods of the Babylonians. However, this chapter invites readers to an alternative reading of "the captivity of Jerusalem" (1:3) that summarizes the book as a whole. Without ever making the connection explicit, Jeremiah 52 invites readers to link the logic of verses 1–3 to the descriptions of verses 4–27. Zedekiah and the others were "expelled," Jerusalem was burned, the Temple looted because God's people had done evil and angered the Lord. In the particular events that befell Judah at the hand of Babylon, God was not defeated but was directing the course of history toward the captivity of Jerusalem.

Jeremiah 52:28–30

52:28 **This is the number of the people whom Nebuchadrezzar took into exile: in the seventh year, three thousand twenty-three Judeans; 29 in the eighteenth year of Nebuchadrezzar he took into exile from Jerusalem eight hundred thirty-two persons; 30 in the twenty-third year of Nebuchadrezzar, Nebuzaradan the captain of the guard took into exile of the Judeans seven hundred forty-five persons; all the persons were four thousand six hundred.**

The book of Jeremiah began with the notice that it was concerned with "the captivity of Jerusalem" (1:3). Just a few verses before the book's conclusion, we are provided a detailed account of the numbers of those exiled:

—3,023 in 597 B.C.
—842 in 587 B.C.
—745 in 582 B.C.

Even including the exile of 582 B.C., usually thought to be Babylon's response to Gedaliah's murder (see Jeremiah 41), the total number exiled was quite modest, only 4,600. Some factors suggest that the impact of the exile may have been greater than numbers suggest. Obviously, for those exiled and their families, the impact of the deportation would have been profound. The key positions in Judean society occupied by many of those exiled would also have heightened its impact. There are also indications even within the book of Jeremiah that many beyond those deported by the Babylonians left Judah, like the group that fled to Egypt taking Jeremiah with them.

Yet, even when account is taken of these factors, the quantitative scope of the exile was rather small compared with its enormous impact on the way Judah and Israel thought of themselves and of God. The book of Jeremiah has engaged us in a sustained reflection about God, who is "over nations and over kingdoms to pluck up and tear down, . . . to build and to plant" (1:10). It may have seemed to those who experienced the catastrophic events of deportations between 597 and 582 B.C. that they were God-forsaken. The book of Jeremiah reads these events in another way, as God using nations and kingdoms to direct the course of Judah toward plucking up and tearing down. Through the words of the prophet Jeremiah, the Lord spoke a word that led to "the captivity of Jerusalem" (1:1–3). This word of the Lord was fulfilled. The statistical summary of those exiled is a pointed way to underscore that God accomplished what God intended. Judah did evil, angered God, and was expelled (vv. 1–3). The captivity of Jerusalem occurred concretely and specifically in the midst of history, in years that could be remembered, involving persons who could be counted, through Babylon, whom God had sent.

The book might well conclude here, in 582 B.C., remembering God's plucking up and tearing down. However, the summary of those exiled is not quite the final word.

Jeremiah 52:31–34

52:31 **In the thirty-seventh year of the exile of King Jehoiachin of Judah, in the twelfth month, on the twenty-fifth day of the month, King Evil-merodach of Babylon, in the year he began to reign, showed favor to King Jehoiachin of Judah and brought him out of prison;** [32] **he spoke kindly to him, and gave him a seat above the seats of the other kings who were with him in Babylon.** [33] **So Jehoiachin put aside his prison clothes, and every day of his life he dined regularly at the king's table.** [34] **For his allowance, a regular daily allowance was given him by the king of Babylon, as long as he lived, up to the day of his death.**

The last date referred to in the preceding verses is 582 B.C., the date of the final Babylonian exile (v. 30). These final verses of the book jump ahead over twenty years, to the thirty-seventh year of the exile of Jehoiachin, sometime near 561 B.C. There was a new king in Babylon, and we are told of this new king's favorable actions toward King Jehoiachin of Judah, who was in his fourth decade of exile. King Evil-merodach of Babylon released Jehoiachin from prison, "spoke kindly to him and gave him a seat above . . . the seats of the other kings who were with him in Babylon" (v. 32). This report is in contrast with the dominant perspective of the book of Jeremiah, which understands Babylon to be "evil from the north" sent by God to pluck up and tear down Judah.

The "favor" of Evil-merodach is a surprising turn of events. At the same time, what is reported in these verses is modest, not the end of King Jehoiachin's exile (in fact, it is clear from these verses Jehoiachin died in Babylon—v. 34) but his rehabilitation as a prisoner by the king of Babylon. No reasons are given for the unexpected kindness of Evil-merodach. There is only a modest hint that the "favor" shown Jehoiachin might suggest some change from the dominant perspective of the book of Jeremiah, which has insisted that Babylon is God's agent of plucking up and tearing down. However, with this report of Babylon's "favor" the book of Jeremiah abruptly ends, leaving us to wonder what it means. Might this report suggest that God's word of building and planting, like God's word of plucking up and tearing down, will also be fulfilled?

The book of Jeremiah concludes without providing a definitive answer about the precise ways the "favor" of the king of Babylon played out for Jehoiachin and Judah toward the fulfillment of God's promise about building and planting. Yet the hint is clear that the Lord who was "over nations and kingdoms" was about that which once again was unimaginable, "favor" for Judah from Babylon. Exiles whose reality was remote from God's promise of building and planting were finally asked to trust this incredible word of the Lord with only a hint that it might be true. That is how the word of the Lord is among God's people, who gather week by week in the midst of the brokenness of our world and our lives and, with only a hint that it might be true, dare to say, "The Lord is risen, the Lord is risen indeed."

Works Cited

Anderson, Bernhard W. "The Lord Has Created Something New." *Catholic Biblical Quarterly* 40 (1978): 463–78.

Brueggemann, Walter. *To Build, To Plant: A Commentary on Jeremiah 26–52*. International Theological Commentary. Grand Rapids: Wm. B. Eerdmans Publishing Co., 1991.

Buechner, Frederick. *Listening to Your Life: Daily Meditations with Frederick Buechner*. Compiled by George Connor. San Francisco: Harper-Collins, 1992.

Carroll, Robert. *Jeremiah*. Old Testament Library. Philadelphia: Westminster Press, 1986.

Clements, Ronald E., *Jeremiah*. Interpretation: A Bible Commentary for Teaching and Preaching. Edited by James Luther Mays. Atlanta: John Knox Press, 1988.

Habel, Norman C. *Jeremiah, Lamentations*. Concordia Commentary. St. Louis: Concordia Publishing House, 1968.

Luther, Martin. *The Large Catechism*, translated by J. N. Lenker. Minneapolis: Augsburg Publishing House, 1935.

Newbigin, Lesslie. *Foolishness to Greeks: The Gospel and Western Culture*. Grand Rapids: Wm. B. Eerdmans Publishing Co., 1986.

Pritchard, J. B., ed. *Ancient Near Eastern Texts Relating to the Old Testament (ANET)*. Princeton, N.J.: Princeton University Press, 1950.

Sakenfeld, Katharine Doob. *Faithfulness in Action: Loyalty in Biblical Perspective*. Overtures to Biblical Theology. Minneapolis: Fortress Press, 1985.

Thompson, John A. *The Book of Jeremiah*. New International Commentary on the Old Testament. Grand Rapids: Wm. B. Eerdmans Publishing Co., 1980.

The hymn "If You But Trust in God to Guide You" is by Georg Neumark, 1641, and is found in *The New Century Hymnal*, 410. Cleveland: Pilgrim Press, 1995.

Lamentations

Introduction to Lamentations

The five poems that comprise the book of Lamentations seek to grasp the meaning of the tragedy that befell Israel in 587 B.C. when Babylon destroyed Jerusalem. A biblical account of this event is found in 2 Kings 25:1–12, and its close parallel is in Jeremiah 52 (also Jeremiah 39). The concern of the book with Jerusalem's destruction is evident from its very first verse:

> How lonely sits the city that was once full of people!
> How like a widow she has become,
>   she that was great among the nations!
> She that was a princess among the provinces has become a vassal.

The connection of Lamentations with the exile of 587 B.C. is further attested by the use of the book as part of the Jewish liturgy for the 9th of Ab (July–August), which commemorates Jerusalem's fall.

The five poems of Lamentations, one in each chapter, reflect upon the events of 587 B.C. in slightly different ways and deal with a variety of issues: sin and God's wrath, human suffering and divine retribution, despair and the possibility of hope. In many ways, the book of Lamentations is like the book of Job in that both ponder issues of suffering. However, Lamentations is concerned with communal suffering rather than Job's more individual concern. While the five poems of Lamentations are related to Jerusalem's destruction, the issues addressed by these poems transcend the particular event that occasioned them. The book addresses human experiences of suffering and tragedy that are not readily reconciled with a good and caring God. In the Christian tradition, readings from Lamentations have been included as part of Tenebrae, the worship service used in some church traditions on Good Friday. As we read the book of Lamentations, we will be invited to reflect about those occasions when we and the communities of which we are a part cry out to God, but God seems silent.

THE NAME OF THE BOOK AND ITS PLACEMENT IN THE BIBLE

In the Hebrew Bible, the name of the book we call "Lamentations" is *'ekah*, meaning "how," and is taken from the first word of the book: *"How* lonely sits the city . . ." (1:1). Some early Jewish manuscripts, however, called the book another name, *qinot*, meaning "lamentations." The Greek translation of the Hebrew text of the Old Testament, called the Septuagint, followed those manuscripts that designated the book "lamentations," a practice followed also in later Latin versions of the Bible. Since English language versions of the Bible have used the names of books from Greek and Latin versions, we know the book as Lamentations.

Again, because English language versions of the Bible follow the order of the books in Greek and Latin versions of the Bible, the book of Lamentations follows the book of Jeremiah in our Bibles. The reason for this order is that for a long time Jeremiah was thought to be the author of the book. However, as the discussion that follows will indicate, this is not likely. In the Hebrew language texts of the Old Testament, the book of Lamentations does not follow the book of Jeremiah. Instead, it is found in a section of the Hebrew Bible called "the Writings" (which includes not only Lamentations but also books such as Psalms, Proverbs, Job, and Ecclesiastes; in English-language Bibles these poetic books are clustered together after the so-called historical books and before the prophetic books). In the Hebrew Bible, the book of Lamentations is part of a collection of five books called the *Megilloth* ("scrolls"), which are read at important Jewish festivals. Lamentations, as mentioned, is read as part of the commemoration of the destruction of the Temple in Jerusalem in 587 B.C. This festival is called the 9th of Ab. The four other books that were part of the *Megilloth* and the festivals to which they are connected are Song of Songs (Passover); Ruth (Festival of Weeks); Ecclesiastes (Tabernacles); and Esther (Purim).

THE DATE OF COMPOSITION AND AUTHOR

Even though there is no description of the deportation from Judah to Babylon in Lamentations (see Jer. 52:28–30 for a direct description), there are numerous references to circumstances that are difficult to associate with any event except the Babylonian destruction of Jerusalem in 587 B.C. (for instance, see Lam. 1:1, 3, 6, 10; 2:1–2, 5–7, 8–9). It is also widely held that the poignancy of the poems in Lamentations reflects a fresh experience of the tragic events of 587 B.C. However, there is no sense that these poems are aware of Babylon's defeat by Persia (also known as the Medes) and the subsequent efforts to restore Judah that began in 538 B.C. One can detect such awareness of Persia's threat to Babylon, for instance, in Isaiah 40–55, the so-called Second Isaiah, where the end of Judah's exile and Cyrus' defeat of Babylon are anticipated (see Isa. 40:2; 43:1–7, and especially 44:24–45:8). This lack of awareness that Persia presented a threat to Babylon, or any mention of efforts to restore Judah after 538 B.C., suggests that much of Lamentations was composed closer to 587 B.C. than to 538 B.C.

Even though this dating of Lamentations is widely accepted, at least some caution about this conclusion is necessary. For example, Iain Provan has argued that while Lamentations seems to reflect upon the events of 587 B.C., this is not decisive evidence as to the date of the poems' composition. He writes:

> It is clear . . . that the "freshness" and "vividness" of a poem may have more to tell us about the creativity and imagination of the author than about when he lived. (Provan, p. 12)

In other words, Provan allows that the subject matter and tone of the book of Lamentations could be the result of skilled writers and are not necessarily a sure indication that the book was written as an immediate reflection by persons who had experienced the exile of 587 B.C.

With regard to the author of the book of Lamentations, nothing in the book itself suggests who wrote it. However, Lamentations has long been attributed to the prophet Jeremiah. Jeremiah is first identified as the author of Lamentations in the Greek translation of the Hebrew Bible, where the book has a heading that reads: "And it came to pass after Israel had gone into captivity, and Jerusalem was laid waste, that Jeremiah sat weeping and composed this lament over Jerusalem and said . . ." In the Greek version of the Old Testament, the book of Lamentations is also placed in order behind the book of Jeremiah. In the later writings of the Jewish rabbis, who were undoubtedly influenced by the Greek version of the Old Testament, Jeremiah is again identified as the author of Lamentations. For instance, in writings called the Peshitta, dated from the first to second centuries and attributed to rabbis from Syria, the heading for the book of Lamentations reads, "The book of Lamentations of Jeremiah the prophet."

How might it have happened that Jeremiah was identified as the author of the book of Lamentations? There are two likely reasons. First, in 2 Chronicles 35:25 it is reported that "Jeremiah . . . uttered a lament for Josiah, and all the singing men and singing women have spoken of Josiah in their laments to this day." This passage from Chronicles has been interpreted to suggest that Jeremiah was the author of Lamentations. Second, there is material in the book of Jeremiah that closely resembles the mournful tone of the poetry of Lamentations. For instance, in the book of Jeremiah the prophet cries:

> Cut off your hair and throw it away;
>   raise a lamentation on the bare heights,
> for the LORD has rejected and forsaken
>   the generation that provoked his wrath.
>   (7:29)

Or again:

> Is there no balm in Gilead?
>   Is there no physician there?
> Why then has the health of my poor people not been restored?
> O that my head were a spring of water, and my eyes a fountain of tears,
>   so that I might weep day and night for the slain of my poor people!
>   (8:22–9:1)

During his lifetime, the prophet Jeremiah is reported to have wept and mourned over the imminent destruction of Judah and Jerusalem. So the book of Lamentations, which does the same, could readily be identified with the prophet.

Still there is considerable evidence to suggest that Jeremiah was not the author of Lamentations. There is nothing in the book of Lamentations itself that indicates directly who its author might have been. Furthermore, in the Hebrew version of the Old Testament, the books of Lamentations and Jeremiah are not placed together: Jeremiah is in the second section of the Hebrew Bible, which is called "the Prophets"; Lamentations is in the third section called "the Writings." Had the books both been written by Jeremiah, it is likely that they would have been found together in the Hebrew Bible. Also, despite the reference in 2 Chronicles to Jeremiah's lament over Josiah, no lament over Josiah can be identified in the book of Lamentations. Finally, comparing some of the ideas in Lamentations with those found in the book of Jeremiah makes it unlikely that both had the same author. For example, the book of Lamentations views an unidentified king of Judah as "the breath of our life, . . . the one of whom we said, 'Under his shadow we shall live among the nations' " (4:20). This positive view of Judah's monarchy contrasts sharply with the dominant view in the book of Jeremiah, which blames the monarchy for Judah's destruction (see particularly Jer. 21:11–22:8; but also various other texts such as 2:8; 8:1–3; Jeremiah 36). Similarly, Lamentations' perspective that the Jerusalem temple was protected by God (1:10) is hardly compatible with the harsh condemnation in the book of Jeremiah of those in Judah who falsely trusted in the Temple of the Lord to keep them secure (7:1–16). While we cannot be certain, it is unlikely that the prophet Jeremiah was the author of the book of Lamentations.

However, if Jeremiah was not the author of Lamentations, then who was? This is a very difficult question to answer. Some have suggested that there was a single author for Lamentations and others that there were multiple authors of the book. However, the most likely proposal is that it is simply not possible to determine who wrote the book.

LITERARY FEATURES

There are several literary features to the poems in the book of Lamentations that are worth noting before we begin to read the book.

1. *Alphabetical Poems.* Though it is not evident as one reads the book of Lamentations in English translation, the four poems in Lamentations 1–4 (each chapter is a separate poem) are based on the Hebrew alphabet (poems organized according to the alphabet are called acrostic). The poem in Lamentations 3 is even more strictly ordered; in this chapter, the first word of each of the three lines of every stanza, and not just the first word of the first line, begins with the same letter of the alphabet. Thus, in these four chapters of Lamentations (but not Lamentations 5), each stanza of the poem has an initial word whose first letter follows the letters of the Hebrew alphabet in order. There are twenty-two letters in the Hebrew alphabet, so the poems of Lamentations 1–4 are each twenty-two stanzas long. However, in the four poems of Lamentations whose stanzas are arranged alphabetically, the number of lines per stanza varies.

In the Old Testament, other examples of poems arranged alphabetically can be found in Nahum 1:2–8; Proverbs 31:10–31; and frequently in the Psalms, including Psalms 9–10, 25, 34, 37, 111, 112, 119, 145. There has been much speculation about the purpose of the alphabetical arrangement of biblical poetry. It has been suggested that such poems were developed as an aid to memorization; others have proposed that something magical was implied; a few have argued that such poems were an attempt to express completeness, as we might say it, everything from A to Z. Regarding this latter point, for instance, it has been written:

> The function of the acrostic was to encourage completeness in the expression of grief, the confession of sin and the instilling of hope. (Gottwald, p. 28)

None of these explanations, however, has been widely accepted. Perhaps, as another scholar has suggested, "A simple aesthetic explanation works best: shaping the poems in this fashion must have had a pleasing effect on early audiences" (Westermann, p. 99).

2. *Many Voices in the Poems*. As we read the book of Lamentations, it will sometimes be confusing because there will be more than one "speaker" in a poem. For example, in Lamentations 1, the first eleven verses seem to be offered by someone we might call a narrator, one in a position to provide a descriptive account of what happened: "How lonely sits the city . . . she weeps bitterly in the night . . . Judah has gone into exile . . . ," and so forth. However, starting at verse 12, there is a shift, and it is the city of Jerusalem (Zion) that speaks as if a person: "Is it nothing to you, all you who pass by? . . . My transgressions were bound into a yoke . . . The Lord has rejected all my warriors . . . " At places, the speaker seems to be the people of Judah, as in Lamentations 4:17–19. In Lamentations 3, the speaker is an individual whose address is in the first person, "I."

It will be important as we read through the book of Lamentations to give attention to who is speaking and to be particularly alert for changes in speakers within a single chapter or poem.

3. *The Kind of Poetry*. There has been considerable discussion about how best to understand the intent or purposes of the poems of Lamentations. What kind of poems are found in the book? Some have seen a close connection between some of the poems of Lamentations and dirges. A dirge is a song of mourning heard at the time of a death and at funerals. Dirges contain the following elements:

> An opening cry of ah! alas!, or the equivalent; a mournful cry as such . . . ; a summons to mourn . . . ; a proclamation that a death has occurred . . . ; a comparing of the former with the present state of affairs . . . including a eulogizing of the deceased; a description of the mourner's pain or of the general state of misery; reference to the effect all this is having on the

bystanders; questions expressing bewilderment at what has happened. (Westermann, p. 7)

Those who have seen a connection between the poems of Lamentations and dirges have suggested that the purpose of the poems in the book of Lamentations is to mourn the "death" of Jerusalem, figuratively understood to have occurred at the time of the Babylonian exile. Certainly there is material in Lamentations that suggests the poems might be dirges. For instance, within Lamentations 1, that which suggest a dirge include the following:

—It is noted of Zion, "How like a widow she has become" (v. 1);
—Zion's grief is observed as "she weeps bitterly" (v. 2), "the roads to Zion mourn" (v. 4), and Zion declares, ". . . I weep, my eyes flow with tears" (v. 16).

Certainly portions of Lamentations resemble a dirge, material that expresses grief and mourning at the time of a death.

However, a more common conclusion is that while containing elements of dirges, the dominant form of poetry in Lamentations is best understood as a communal lament. Communal laments are also found the book of Psalms, for instance in Psalms 74, 79, 137. Portions of Lamentations 1, 2, 4, and 5 are widely held to be communal laments. Some see much of Lamentations 3 as an individual lament (Re'emi, p. 80) and others see this poem as an expression of confidence whose purpose was instruction (see Westermann, p. 191–93). Observing that a communal lament was developed for a "solemn assembly convened in response to a public emergency," Claus Westermann concludes:

The occasion for such a solemn assembly was always some calamity that had befallen—or was about to befall—the land or the city. Given the kind of situation which constituted its life-setting, the communal lament sought to implore God for help. (*Lamentations*, p. 96)

As we read the book of Lamentations, we will repeatedly find pleas to God for help:

"See, O Lord, how distressed I [Zion] am" (1:20)

"Cry aloud to the Lord" (2:18)

"Arise, cry in the night . . ." (2:19)

"Look, O Lord, and consider" (2:20)

"Pay them back for their deeds, O Lord, according to the work of their
     hands" (3:64)

"Remember, O Lord, what has befallen us; look, and see our disgrace"
     (5:1)

"Why have you forgotten us completely?
     Why have you forsaken us these many days?
Restore us to yourself, O Lord, that we may be restored;
     renew our days as of old" (5:20–21)

The poems of Lamentations repeatedly portray a community imploring
God for help, and significant portions of the book are best understood as
communal laments.

In Lamentations, God is implored for help for a variety of reasons. To
be sure, as in a dirge, God's help is sought because the destruction of Jerusalem that is spoken in Lamentations is as if a "death" had occurred. But
God is also implored because of the triumph of an enemy (for example, 1:5,
10; 2:2, 4–5, 16; 3:52–54); God's anger and harsh, unbearable judgment
(1:15; 2:1–8, 17, 22; 3:1–20; 4:11, 16; 5:21–22); the absence of anyone to
help or comfort the people (1:7, 16–17, 21); the sin and iniquity of Zion
that have brought about its ruin (1:8–9, 14, 20, 22; 2:14; 3:42; 4:13–15, 22).
The poems of Lamentations express the multi-faceted brokenness and
despair of a community in a time of crisis and implore God for help.

4. *The Language of Lamentations.* While it seems likely that the occasion
for the communal laments of Lamentations was the destruction of Jerusalem by Babylon in 587 B.C., the language of Lamentations is quite general and difficult to relate exactly to the situation that may have occasioned
the poems in the first place. Even if it was the fall of Jerusalem to Babylon
in 587 B.C. that inspired the book of Lamentations, the language of the
book invites hearing and praying its poems in a variety of circumstances of
distress and disaster.

Thinking about the language of Lamentations in another way, one
notes that the book was intended to be used in worship, and, as mentioned,
it is so used in both Jewish and Christian traditions. The book of Lamentations shares with the language of worship an openness that allows different persons to hear what is being said as related to their own
circumstances. For example, a prayer of confession may invite all of those
present to say, "O God, forgive us, for we have sinned against you and our

neighbors." Through these words each one present may recall quite particular ways that he or she has sinned. The language of the confessional prayer is open and can be heard in different ways. The language of Lamentations is similar. In Lamentations we read, for instance:

> He [God] has made my teeth grind on gravel,
>   and made me cower in ashes;
> my soul is bereft of peace;
>   I have forgotten what happiness is;
> so I say, "Gone is my glory, and all that I had hoped for from the LORD."
>
> (Lam. 3:16)

It is certainly possible to imagine that those who experienced Babylon's invasion of Jerusalem, the burning of the city, and the destruction of the Temple might have said these words. However, these words from Lamentations might express the sentiments of many communities who have experienced a disaster—a flood, destruction caused by a storm, the ravages of war, the death of a beloved leader—and help these communities say honestly how it feels that God has dealt with them.

THEOLOGY OF THE BOOK OF LAMENTATIONS

What does the book of Lamentations say about God? There have been numerous efforts to discern what the theological theme or claims of the book of Lamentations might be. Here are some examples from more recent scholarship:

1. One perspective on the book is that it deals with a particular problem created by the catastrophe of the Babylonian exile in 587 B.C. (Gottwald). The problem was this. A popular theology in Judah at the time of the exile asserted that God rewarded people for doing good and punished them for disobedience. Just prior to the Babylonian invasion of Judah, there had been a significant effort within Judah, led by King Josiah, to reform the ills of the nation. Such reform, it was perceived, should have resulted in good for Judah, but instead Judah experienced a very harsh punishment. The book of Lamentations was an attempt to deal with the question of why those who sincerely attempted to obey God (through their efforts at reform) should suffer so. This question is answered by the book's "steadfast insistence on God's righteousness and goodness [that] declares itself in the conviction that as there has been a past glory and a present pain there will be a future marked by God's favor (3:31–36; 4:22; 5:21)" (Gottwald, p. 62).

2. Another slant on the theology of the books identifies Lamentations 3 as the key to understanding what the book wants to say about God (Hillers and Re'emi). Lamentations 3 was written to present the point of view of an unnamed sufferer who "wins through to confidence that God's mercy is not at an end" (Hillers, p. xvi). The book of Lamentations intends to affirm hope beyond immediate suffering, hope that is grounded in God's mercy. The book calls a suffering people to a penitent waiting for the Lord's deliverance.

3. Others who have studied the book of Lamentations are less confident that hope is the dominant theme (Provan). Lamentations 3 itself ends not on a note of hope (see 3:31–33) but with an expression of hope mixed with despair (see 3:43–54), and finally, with a plea for God to act (3:64–66). Further, the book as a whole does not end with Lamentations 3 but in Lamentations 5 with a prayer and plea for God to remember what had befallen Israel. The book of Lamentations is much more complicated than a straightforward affirmation of hope in God's mercy. It invites us to ponder the meaning of suffering for faith without providing a clear answer.

If we are honest, suffering does not always yield to a quick resolution and a clear sense of hope. Even if persons find a way to continue with their lives, some experiences of suffering last a lifetime and can never be forgotten: the death of a spouse or child, the impact of a serious illness or injury, the memories of some traumatic event. The book of Lamentations can be seen to deal with the way hope and despair, suffering and faith, are thoroughly intertwined without easy resolution.

4. Finally, it has been suggested that the book of Lamentations was perhaps not intended to provide answers to questions raised by suffering but to give voice and expression to it even if the suffering could not be explained until later, if at all (Westermann).

As we read the book of Lamentations, we should not expect the book to provide answers about suffering. Instead, the book of Lamentations gives us words with which to address God about suffering. Such expression of suffering is not common in our culture or in our churches. Our culture is optimistic and values certainty and confidence. To speak of suffering is a sign of weakness and pessimism, out of character in "can-do" America. Our churches are eager to hear of God's triumph and our Lord's resurrection. In many churches, attendance on Easter morning is greater than attendance at all Lenten and Holy Week services combined. Joy is fine, but we have little patience for suffering. So suffering is unmentioned, unacknowledged, and kept apart from our relationship with God or one another.

The book of Lamentations invites us to speak honestly before God of the pain that afflicts us as we live in communities. Lamentations is a book to be prayed because in those communities where we live there is suffering of which God needs to know even if it is not immediately evident that God is paying attention or cares. Perhaps, as we pray through Lamentations, we may discover anew God's reign even when God seems absent.

"How Lonely Sits the City"
Lamentations 1

Lamentations 1 is a poem concerning the desolation of Jerusalem. The most obvious circumstance to which this poem points is the destruction of Jerusalem by the Babylonians in 587 B.C. The poem is in two parts:

1. Verses 1–11 offer a description of the city by an observer, a narrator who recounts what happened to Jerusalem. Often in this section of the poem, the city is presented as a woman in distress or peril. The reversal of the city's fortunes from prosperity to distress is emphasized. The descriptive tone of these verses is interrupted at only two places. At the end of verses 9 and 11, we hear Jerusalem, portrayed as a woman, cry out for God to notice what has happened to her: "the enemy has triumphed" (v. 9); "see how worthless I have become" (v. 11).

2. The cries of verses 9 and 11 prepare us for the second part of Lamentations 1. In verses 12–22, the city, speaking as a person, expresses to God the pain and sense of rejection caused by the tragedy described in the earlier verses of the poem. The reasons for what has occurred are probed and attributed to the Lord's fierce anger (vv. 12–13) and "my transgressions" (v. 14), the Lord's rejection (v. 15) and Jerusalem's rebellion against God (v. 18). The prayer concludes with a petition (vv. 18–22) asking God to act on Jerusalem's behalf against the enemies who have destroyed the city. One senses in this passionate prayer not a systematic analysis of the tragedy that had befallen Jerusalem but, as with most honest prayer in a time of crisis, a raw outpouring of pain and confusion.

While it is easy to imagine that Lamentations 1 is a poem reflecting upon the tragic destruction of Jerusalem at the hands of the Babylonians, the language of the poem is not tightly tied to the events of 587 B.C. Babylon, for instance, is never named as Jerusalem's enemy or the place of deportation for exiles; the burning of the Jerusalem Temple is not mentioned; and the nature of Jerusalem's sin and rebellion is not specified. So the language of this poem is open for our praying, too, and invites our use of its words and images in our own moments of pain and confusion as we seek ways to express to God that for which our own words fail us.

Lamentations 1:1–11

1:1 **How lonely sits the city**
   that once was full of people!
How like a widow she has become,
   she that was great among the nations!
She that was a princess among the provinces
   has become a vassal.
2 **She weeps bitterly in the night,**
   with tears on her cheeks;
among all her lovers
   she has no one to comfort her;
all her friends have dealt treacherously with her,
   they have become her enemies.
3 **Judah has gone into exile with suffering**
   and hard servitude;
she lives now among the nations,
   and finds no resting place;
her pursuers have all overtaken her
   in the midst of her distress.
4 **The roads to Zion mourn,**
   for no one comes to the festivals;
all her gates are desolate,
   her priests groan;
her young girls grieve,
   and her lot is bitter.
5 **Her foes have become the masters,**
   her enemies prosper,
because the LORD has made her suffer
   for the multitude of her transgressions;
her children have gone away,
   captives before the foe.
6 **From daughter Zion has departed**
   all her majesty.
Her princes have become like stags
   that find no pasture;
they fled without strength
   before the pursuer.
7 **Jerusalem remembers,**
   in the days of her affliction and wandering,
all the precious things

that were hers in days of old.
When her people fell into the hand of the foe,
    and there was no one to help her,
the foe looked on mocking
    over her downfall.
⁸ Jerusalem sinned grievously,
    so she has become a mockery;
all who honored her despise her,
    for they have seen her nakedness;
she herself groans,
    and turns her face away.
⁹ Her uncleanness was in her skirts;
    she took no thought of her future;
her downfall was appalling,
    with none to comfort her.
"O LORD, look at my affliction,
    for the enemy has triumphed!"
¹⁰ Enemies have stretched out their hands
    over all her precious things;
she has even seen the nations
    invade her sanctuary,
those whom you forbade
    to enter your congregation.
¹¹ All her people groan
    as they search for bread;
they trade their treasures for food
    to revive their strength.
Look, O LORD, and see
    how worthless I have become.

A description of what has happened to Jerusalem is here recounted by an observer of the tragedy, a narrator. Throughout these verses, the dramatic change in Jerusalem's circumstances is stressed, and the reversal of Jerusalem's fortunes is presented again and again: The city, once full of people, is "lonely" (v. 1); the roads to the city and its gates, once crowded with throngs coming to celebrate festivals at the Temple, are desolate and deserted and mourned (v. 4); foes became masters who mocked the city's downfall (vv. 5, 7); Zion's majesty had departed (v. 6), and the good old days were but a fond memory (v. 7). Clearly what is being described in these verses is a great tragedy, yet the description is surprisingly vague. It is difficult to say exactly who did what and when it happened. Perhaps the clearest indication of just what occurred is found in verse 3, where we are told that "Judah has gone into exile." This verse suggests that we are hearing a report of the destruction of Jerusalem by Babylon in 587 B.C. and the awful reversals in the city's welfare brought about by this defeat.

The scene of reversal, of stunning loss, that these verses lay out is not unfamiliar to us. We know of the reality of which these verses speak. Television has brought into our living rooms poignant pictures of victims of tragedies revisiting what had once been sacred space for them. We have seen those who have survived a tornado or hurricane sifting through the scattered debris with anguish on their faces at the site that was once home for them. We have witnessed persons whose churches have been burned recounting with tears streaming down their cheeks how the smoldering rubble behind them was the place where marriages were celebrated, where infants were received into the church through baptism, and where their precious dead were remembered. We have seen war refugees fleeing burning cities in long lines with what few possessions they could salvage strapped on their backs. In these scenes we have ourselves seen the great reversal of fortune described in these initial verses of Lamentations. The joy and glory of the former days are quickly lost and become fond memories of what will never be again.

The initial verse of Lamentations 1 introduces us to one of the particular ways that this chapter will present what happened to Jerusalem. The city is portrayed as a woman who has experienced loss or been dishonored and humiliated. In these images, and they are numerous, it is important to understand that in the ancient Near Eastern world in which Israel lived, cultures were highly patriarchal, and women were vulnerable in many ways. Women's roles and status in the world of ancient Israel were a harsh and regrettable reality. This chapter uses images of women's vulnerability in the ancient world to portray the devastating impact on Jerusalem of Babylon's victory over Judah in 587 B.C.

Jerusalem is portrayed in three ways in verse 11. One obvious way is the reference to the city as a "widow" in contrast to one who was "great among the nations." In the world of ancient Israel, as is evidenced often in the Old Testament, widows were quite vulnerable. The ancient Near Eastern world was unquestionably patriarchal; so a woman's social status and financial security were dependent upon her husband. Israel's prophets often insisted that a measure of social justice was how well the widows and orphans—persons who had lost their social status, legal standing, and means of economic survival—were cared for. In Lamentations 1:1, Jerusalem's downfall is portrayed by describing the city as a "widow." Jerusalem once had significant status and security and so was "great among the nations." By referring to the city as a "widow," the loss of that status and security by defeat at the hands of Babylon is indicated. A second way that Jerusalem is presented as a woman who has lost her status occurs at the end of verse 1, where Jerusalem is described as a princess who has become a vassal. This image stresses the political nature of what happened to Jerusalem. The city was once the capital of an independent state but has become a vassal of another country, Babylon (compare 1 Kings 20:14–15). The third way that Jerusalem is portrayed as a woman who has lost her status and security is less obvious. The beginning of verse 1 contrasts the city "once . . . full of people" with one that has become "lonely." At least some have suggested that this image is of a mother "robbed of her children," much like the image of Rachel weeping for her lost children in Jeremiah 31:15–21. We will find throughout the first half of Lamentations 1 that Jerusalem's defeat is often portrayed as a woman who has experienced loss, dishonor, or humiliation.

The image of Jerusalem as a widow continues in verses 2–3. At the beginning of verse 2, Jerusalem is portrayed as crying in the night with "no one to comfort her." In our contemporary experience, widows can often feel isolated and alone, and widows in the patriarchal world of the ancient Near East were even more abandoned and isolated than widows in our time. Yet whatever the personal grief we might identify in this verse, it is important to remember that the "widow" is a poetic image being applied to Jerusalem. The phrase "no one to comfort," when applied to the corporate experience of Judah and Jerusalem in the exile, points beyond a sense of personal isolation in grief. What is implied is that there was no political, military, or economic ally who might intervene to save Judah from Babylon. Frequently in the Old Testament, "lovers" is a term that is used to refer to political allies (Jer. 4:30; 22:20–22; Ezek. 16:36–37; Hos. 8:9–10). Further, those who had once been Judah's "friends," another way of speaking of political and military allies, had betrayed her and become enemies. Before the threat of a super power like Babylon, it is very likely that surrounding nations that had supported Judah chose to align themselves with Babylon against Judah. A significant consequence of Babylon's invasion was that Judah was left without allies, or in the poetic language of these verses, she became a widow with no one to comfort her. That Judah had "no one to comfort her" becomes an important theme of Lamentations 1 (vv. 2, 9, 16, 17, 21).

The poetic imagery used to describe Judah's defeat in verse 2 is given a more explicit interpretation in verse 3. The beginning of verse 3 is difficult to associate with any event other than the Babylonian exile of 587 B.C.

Thus this verse is one of the clearest in the entire book of Lamentations in linking it to Babylon's defeat of Judah. However, even in this verse there is no explicit reference to Babylon. This restraint in not naming Babylon prevents a narrow identification of this poem with the disaster of 587 B.C. In this way the poem can help other communities who have experienced a disaster that has left them bereft of allies and any hope of help to express their anguish.

The sense of grief and loss continues (v. 4), and for the first time in this poem there is a reflection about God's role in Jerusalem's suffering (v. 5). It is not the city itself that mourns but the "roads to Zion." (In the Old Testament, Jerusalem is sometimes called Zion because this was the name of the hill in the city upon which the Temple stood, Mount Zion.) The roads to Jerusalem were once traveled by pilgrims coming to festivals at the Jerusalem Temple (on Zion). However, after 587 B.C. that all changed. The Temple was burned, the city walls were severely damaged, festival celebrations ceased, and the "roads to Zion" were abandoned.

The description of Judah's enemies in verse 5 draws upon covenant curses from Deuteronomy 28. Basically, Deuteronomy 28 affirms that if the people obeyed, they would be blessed by God and prosper (Deut. 28:1–14). However, if God's people did not obey, they would be cursed and suffer (Deut. 28:15–68). The connection of verse 5 to Deuteronomy 28 is evident when we translate the Hebrew of verse 5 literally, "her foes have become the heads." The NRSV quite appropriately translates "the heads" as "masters," but this translation does not pick up the relationship of verse 5 to Deuteronomy 28:44, which, in describing the consequences of disobeying God, declares "they [aliens, v. 43] shall be the head and you will be the tail." From the perspective of Deuteronomy 28, that Judah's enemies had become their masters could only mean that Judah had disobeyed God and was suffering as a consequence. For the first time in Lamentations 1, there is a shift from a description of Judah's suffering to an interpretation of it. Judah's suffering is God's punishment for its transgressions.

The triumph of Judah's enemies (v. 5a), the exile of Judah's citizens (v. 5c), and the flight of Judah's leaders (v. 6) are attributed to God's punishment of Judah's transgressions. Even though there is no indication about how Judah might have disobeyed, the first explanation for Judah's suffering offered in the book of Lamentations is as a punishment for transgressions. Bad things happen to bad people! Judah rebelled against God and was punished. But a caution is needed. This is only the first of several reflections about suffering in Lamentations, and before we reach the book's conclusion, we will be invited to ponder several other views of this matter. Further, it is doubtful many would find it convincing if the viewpoint of verse 5 were the only explanation of suffering offered. Sometimes bad things happen to bad people, but sometimes bad people get by with their evil, and it is the innocent who suffer. Over the entire book, Lamentations will show awareness of the complexity of the problem of suffering.

The theme that runs through verses 7–11 is the triumph of Jerusalem's enemies, who now mock the fallen city. The mocking or derision of enemies is a notion that is common in lament psalms (see Psalms 13:4; 41:5; 55:3; 71:10). The situation in which foes mock Jerusalem's downfall is contrasted to memories of "precious things" that were Jerusalem's in the "days of old (v. 7). As in the earlier verses of this poem, there is a before and after comparison. Regretfully, that to which "precious things" refers is difficult to discern. Recognizing the vagueness of the phrase, one commentator has suggested that it

> may simply be everything in general which the city had in the past . . . and has now lost, or something in particular such as temple treasure to which 1:10 may also allude ["precious things"]. We might also translate this word 'precious ones', however, again interpreting the line as referring to the people who had once inhabited the city . . . . Such an interpretation fits the context well. (Provan, p. 43)

If this interpretation is correct in connecting "precious things" to the loss of inhabitants, then this verse may well be related to the first line of verse 1 as well as to verse 5, verses that speak of the loss of children. The downfall of Jerusalem and the mocking of her enemies were all the worse because, once again, it is recognized that there was "no one to help her" (vv. 2, 10).

The mockery of those who have conquered the city is picked up in verse 8 where it is seen as the result of Jerusalem's sin. This view of suffering is much like that of verse 5; sin leads to punishment, here the mocking of an enemy which results in Jerusalem's humiliation. Jerusalem's humiliation is first described relationally. Those who once honored the city now despise her. This is worse than the mocking of an enemy; even former friends have turned on the city. While expressed in a way that suggests personal relationships, the relationships referred to are surely political: Judah's former allies had turned away as the nation fell to Babylon. Jerusalem's humiliation is also described with the phrase "they have seen her nakedness." Being stripped naked, which was sometimes an image for punishing an enemy, was a cause of great disgrace.

The beginning of verse 9 is difficult to understand. The image of "uncleanness in her skirts" is drawn from the laws of ritual purity from Leviticus 15:16–24 and concerns menstrual blood. But how might this apply to the situation of Jerusalem after 587 B.C.? That is difficult to determine. In the books of Jeremiah and Ezekiel, a similar phrase is used to speak of Judah's idolatry (Jer. 2:23; Ezek. 23:7, 13). For both Jeremiah and Ezekiel, the people had committed harlotry by worshiping other gods (compare Hosea 1) and so were made unclean. Perhaps this phrase concerning Jerusalem's uncleanness means to suggest the nature of Judah's grievous sin in verse 8, namely, idolatry. Thus the description of Jerusalem that emerges is of a city, a people, who had sinned, perhaps through idolatry. Jerusalem's sin resulted in defeat by an enemy that mocked and humiliated the city. Much of verses 10 and 11 continues in this same vein.

However, at two places in this first half of Lamentations 1, the descriptive nature of the poem is broken, and we hear the city cry or pray to God. These cries or prayers are found at the end of verses 9 and 11. In both instances, the plea that is directed toward God is simple, a request that God "look." One plea begs God to take notice that the enemy has triumphed (v. 9). The other wants God to see "how worthless I have become" (v. 11). No action or intervention is requested in these prayers. Rather, they are cries for God to notice, to be aware of the awful situation of the once great Jerusalem. What is ironic, of course, is that Lamentations 1 understands that Jerusalem's suffering is God's punishment for sin. Yet it is to the Lord that Jerusalem cries out. To whom else might the people turn in their suffering? These two brief cries to God anticipate the second half of Lamentations 1, a long complaint by Jerusalem directed to God.

Lamentations 1:12–22

1:12 **Is it nothing to you, all you who pass by?**
     Look and see
if there is any sorrow like my sorrow,
     which was brought upon me,
which the LORD inflicted
     on the day of his fierce anger.
   13 **From on high he sent fire;**
        it went deep into my bones;
     he spread a net for my feet;
        he turned me back;
     he has left me stunned,
        faint all day long.
   14 **My transgressions were bound into a yoke;**

by his hand they were fastened together;
they weigh on my neck,
    sapping my strength;
the LORD handed me over
    to those whom I cannot withstand.
15 The LORD has rejected
    all my warriors in the midst of me;
he proclaimed a time against me
    to crush my young men;
the LORD has trodden as in a wine press
    the virgin daughter Judah.
16 For these things I weep;
    my eyes flow with tears;
for a comforter is far from me,
    one to revive my courage;
my children are desolate,
    for the enemy has prevailed.
17 Zion stretches out her hands,
    but there is no one to comfort her;
the LORD has commanded against Jacob
    that his neighbors should become his foes;
Jerusalem has become
    a filthy thing among them.
18 The LORD is in the right,
    for I have rebelled against his word;
but hear, all you peoples,
    and behold my suffering;
my young women and young men
    have gone into captivity.
19 I called to my lovers
    but they deceived me;
my priests and elders
    perished in the city
while seeking food
    to revive their strength.
20 See, O LORD, how distressed I am;
    my stomach churns,
my heart is wrung within me,
    because I have been very rebellious.
In the street the sword bereaves;
    in the house it is like death.
21 They heard how I was groaning,
    with no one to comfort me.

All my enemies heard of my trouble;
   they are glad that you have done it.
Bring on the day you have announced,
   and let them be as I am.
²² Let all their evil doing come before you;
   and deal with them
as you have dealt with me
   because of all my transgressions;
for my groans are many
   and my heart is faint.

In the second half of Lamentations 1, the city of Jerusalem, Zion, is portrayed as a person. These verses contain two speeches uttered by Jerusalem/Zion. In the first speech (vv. 12–16), Jerusalem describes what has happened to her. It is not exactly clear to whom this speech is directed. The second speech (vv. 18–22) is a prayer directed to God. It reminds us of the brief cries to God uttered by Jerusalem at the end of verses 9 and 11. While verses 1–11 are dominated by a narrator's description or report, similar material is found in the second half of the chapter only in verse 17. Thus the approach of the two halves of Lamentations 1 is nearly opposite: Verses 1–11 are almost totally a narrator's description, with only two brief prayers uttered by Jerusalem; verses 12–22 are almost totally speeches of Jerusalem, with only one verse of narrator's description. However, themes from the first half of the poem continue in the second half: the sin of Judah, God's wrath and punishment, the triumph and jeering of Judah's enemies, the desertion of Judah's lovers (allies), and the refrain that Jerusalem has no one to comfort her.

Jerusalem cries out plaintively to "all you who pass by" (v. 12). This verse assumes that other nations are observing the destroyed city of Jerusalem. Both the observer nations and Jerusalem are presented as if they were persons. The onlookers are addressed by the city. Jerusalem's complaint is that the city's sorrow is taken lightly or disregarded by those who see what has happened: "Is it nothing to you?" cries Jerusalem. However, the main concern of this verse is not the disregard of the onlookers but what the Lord has done to bring sorrow upon the city. What the Lord "has brought upon me" is described at length as Jerusalem speaks to the uncaring onlookers.

The severity of what the Lord has done becomes clear when one lifts out from verses 12–15 all the descriptions of God's actions against Jerusalem. According to the city's complaint, the Lord inflicted sorrow on the day of his wrath (v. 12);

bound Judah's transgressions together as a weight on her neck (v. 13);

handed the city over to those it could not withstand (v. 13);

rejected all of the city's warriors (v. 14);

crushed the city's young men (v. 14);

trod upon Judah as in a wine press (v. 14).

Together, these actions signal God's rejection of Jerusalem and account for the city's destruction.

The Lord's primary action against Jerusalem was to inflict anger on "the day of his wrath" (v. 12). This refers to the day of the Lord, a tradition to which Israel's prophets appealed regularly. Amos 5:18 is particularly helpful in understanding the day of the Lord. Apparently, a popular idea about the day of the Lord was that on it, God would set the world right and punish all the enemies of Israel and Judah. Amos warned that those in Israel who longed for the day of the Lord would be shocked when it was the people themselves whom the Lord would judge, and not their enemies. Thus, Amos used the tradition of the day of the Lord and turned it against the people of Israel, who had seen the day as one of hope (compare Isa. 10:3; Ezek. 7:7–12). The cry in verse 12 identifies the disaster Jerusalem experienced with the judgment of the day of the Lord, and verse 13 speaks of the consequences of God's judgment. The language of the verse is stereotypical and is found frequently in lament psalms: some malady of the bones, the source of strength (compare Psalms 6:2; 22:14; 51:8; 102:3; Jer. 20:9), and a net, suggesting capture by enemies (compare Psalms 10:9; 31:4; 57:6). God's judgment, complains Jerusalem, has robbed the city of its strength and allowed it to become prey for its enemies.

The consequences of the judgment announced in verses 12–13 are played out in verses 15–16 through images of political and military defeat. They specify what God's fierce anger entails. These verses also pick up ideas from the first half of the poem, so that Jerusalem's condition, described by a narrator in verses 1–11, is confirmed by Jerusalem's own speech. For instance, Jerusalem's admission of weeping in verse 16 confirms the report of the narrator in verse 2. Jerusalem's description of the defeat of her warriors, the loss of her children, and the victory of an enemy in verses 15–16 also confirm details of the narrator's description that are pervasive in verses 1–11. The complaint that Judah and Jerusalem had no one to comfort them (v. 16) is also prominent in the first half of the chapter (vv. 2, 7, 9). Thus on the one hand verses 15–16 describe in concrete and specific ways how God's fierce anger was enacted. On the other hand, these verses, spoken by Jerusalem herself, confirm the descriptions offered by the narrator in the first verses of this chapter and give emphasis to the awful condition of the city.

Standing between Jerusalem's recognition of judgment (vv. 12–13) and descriptions of the political and military consequences of that judgment (vv. 15–16), verse 14 links God's judgment and Judah's sin. The sorrow and judgment that Jerusalem experienced were not arbitrarily imposed but were God's response to Judah's transgressions. No indication is given as to what those transgressions may have been. However, the Lord's judgment is imagined as binding together Judah's sins as a weight upon her neck so that enemies could not be resisted. This verse stands as a confession and suggests that Jerusalem recognized two reasons for the disaster that had befallen her. Sorrow had been brought upon Jerusalem because of the Lord's fierce anger but also because of her own transgressions. Thus the basic theological claim in verses 1–11 is confirmed by Jerusalem herself. Judah's transgression leads to God's judgment.

The impact of verse 17 within Lamentations 1 is to pile up descriptions that emphasize what has happened to the city and why. First a narrator describes the situation for us (vv. 1–11); then the narrator's description is confirmed in Jerusalem's own words (vv. 12–16); finally, the narrator reconfirms that which we have been told already from both his own perspective and that of Jerusalem herself (v. 17). This piling up of descriptions makes Jerusalem's circumstances vivid, heavy, and hopeless. What might Jerusalem do? What might any community do that comes to see unmistakably that its situation is desperate—not only in a social, political, and military sense—and that, theologically, disaster is the result of its own transgression which has resulted in God's judgment?

Jerusalem's response to the dire circumstances in which the community found itself is a prayer to God (vv. 18–21), a prayer that provides words for other communities that, in the midst of disasters, may seek to address God. This prayer has complex concerns which do not relate to each other easily. In the initial petition (v. 18), Jerusalem affirms that "The Lord is in the right" for punishing the city for its rebellion; nonetheless, it cries out that the suffering caused by the exile be noticed. The premise of the prayer is that suffering, even if deserved, needs to be addressed by someone. But to whom might Jerusalem turn? Political allies ("lovers," v. 19; compare v. 2) have already proven fickle and cannot be counted upon; the religious and political leadership (priests and elders, v. 19) has perished seeking food (perhaps a reference to v. 11 which indicates a famine). The prayer suggests that there are no human helpers in view.

Thus it is to the Lord, whose righteous judgment has caused Jerusalem to suffer, that the community must turn for comfort, and the lamenting voice of chapter 1 prays for God to intervene on Jerusalem's behalf (vv. 20–22). Jerusalem experienced God's judgment but had no one but the Lord to whom it could turn for grace. The city's situation is described by Jerusalem once more, but this time the Lord is addressed directly. Familiar themes from earlier in the chapter reoccur: the city's distress, its rebellion, the violence and death that have beset Jerusalem, and groaning with no one to bring comfort. However, much of this appeal concerns Jerusalem's enemies. The prayer reminds God, "they are glad you have done it" (v. 21). More than a cry for help, the tone of the prayer is almost a challenge to the Lord's sense of what is right. God was right in judgment (v. 18), but is it right that Judah's enemies gloat over Jerusalem's demise while the evil perpetrated by these enemies goes unpunished? The prayer asks God, who has punished Jerusalem for her transgressions (vv. 8, 14) with "the day of his fierce anger" (v. 12), to punish the evil of Jerusalem's enemies with a similar day (v. 21). In this petition, there is some challenge to the theological viewpoint that has dominated the chapter, the view that the disaster that befell Jerusalem was God's punishment. The disaster may have been God's righteous judgment, but a question is at least raised about how "right" God's way with the enemies was. Did not they, too, deserve judgment?

Yet at its conclusion, Jerusalem's petitions return to the theme with which they began. The petitions began with the cry for God to notice "how distressed I am" (v. 21); they conclude with an appeal for God to intervene because of the community's "groans" (v. 22). Even as God was attentive to the transgressions and rebellion of Jerusalem through judgment, the concluding prayer of Lamentations 1 makes the case that God should also be attentive to the distress and groans of the city to bring comfort. The theological premise of this chapter, first offered by the narrator in the first half of the chapter (vv. 5–8), is that God rightly punishes those who transgress and rebel. Jerusalem deserved to be punished. However, as the chapter concludes, the voice of Jerusalem protests this theological premise in two ways: (a) the prayer of Jerusalem raises the issue that those enemies that gloat over the city's demise should also be punished for their evil; (b) further, Jerusalem's prayer suggests that God, who was attentive to the transgressions of Jerusalem in judgment, should be equally attentive to the suffering of Jerusalem to bring comfort.

Lamentations 1 connects to the biblical concern for the relationship to God of persons who suffer. This is a theme that occurs repeatedly in scripture. The shaping event for ancient Israel was the exodus. The exodus showed God's compassion for those suffering and oppressed. When God witnessed how the Israelites "groaned under their slavery, and cried out" (Exod. 2:23), God "took notice of them" (Exod. 2:25) and resolved to set them free. In the exodus, the suffering of slaves claimed God's attention and led to God's intervention. It is upon this tradition that at least in part Lamentations 1 depends. Those who suffer matter to God and should expect God to act to comfort them.

The Day of Your Anger
Lamentations 2

As in Lamentations 1, there are two voices in Lamentations 2, a narrator and the city itself. The narrator dominates this chapter and is the speaker for the first nineteen verses. These verses themselves can be subdivided:

a. In verses 1–10, the narrator describes what has happened to Jerusalem. However, the concern here differs from that provided in Lamentations 1. Lamentations 1 has as its primary concern *what* happened to Jerusalem: she became like a widow when an enemy had exiled Judah. Secondarily, Lamentations 1 was concerned with why Zion had suffered disaster. Lamentations 2, by contrast, has as its primary concern *why* disaster befell Jerusalem, and answers this question by repeated affirmations about what the Lord had done. God's actions against Jerusalem are the cause of the city's destruction and of its people's suffering.

b. In verses 11–19, the narrator speaks very personally, sometimes in the first person (I or me) about what the city's destruction means. The narrator views Jerusalem as a beloved city and is personally anguished by its destruction. The narrator concludes by urging that the city appeal to God.

Lamentations 2 concludes (vv. 20–22) as the city itself, heeding the advice of the narrator, prays to God. The request of this prayer is quite simple and stated in the petition's first line: "Look, O LORD, and consider!" (v. 20). The remainder of the prayer presents a graphic and shocking description of the results of God's judgment.

Lamentations 2:1–10

2:1 **How the LORD in his anger**
    has humiliated daughter Zion!
He has thrown down from heaven to earth
    the splendor of Israel;
he has not remembered his footstool
    in the day of his anger.

2 The LORD has destroyed without mercy
     all the dwellings of Jacob;
   in his wrath he has broken down
     the strongholds of daughter Judah;
   he has brought down to the ground in dishonor
     the kingdom and its rulers.
3 He has cut down in fierce anger
     all the might of Israel;
   he has withdrawn his right hand from them
     in the face of the enemy;
   he has burned like a flaming fire in Jacob,
     consuming all around.
4 He has bent his bow like an enemy,
     with his right hand set like a foe;
   he has killed all in whom we took pride
     in the tent of daughter Zion;
   he has poured out his fury like fire.
5 The LORD has become like an enemy;
     he has destroyed Israel;
   He has destroyed all its palaces,
     laid in ruins its strongholds,
     and multiplied in daughter Judah
     mourning and lamentation.
6 He has broken down his booth like a garden,
     he has destroyed his tabernacle;
   the LORD has abolished in Zion
     festival and sabbath,
   and in his fierce indignation has spurned
     king and priest.
7 The LORD has scorned his altar,
     disowned his sanctuary;
   he has delivered into the hand of the enemy
     the walls of her palaces;
   a clamor was raised in the house of the LORD
     as on a day of festival.
8 The LORD determined to lay in ruins
     the wall of daughter Zion;
   he stretched the line;
     he did not withhold his hand from destroying;
   he caused rampart and wall to lament;
     they languish together.
9 Her gates have sunk into the ground;
     he has ruined and broken her bars;

> her king and princes are among the nations;
>   guidance is no more,
> and her prophets obtain
>   no vision from the LORD.
> 10 The elders of daughter Zion
>   sit on the ground in silence;
> they have thrown dust on their heads
>   and put on sackcloth;
> the young girls of Jerusalem
>   have bowed their heads to the ground.

Reading these verses, one cannot possibly be confused about *why* Jerusalem was destroyed. Twenty-eight times in these ten verses, the Lord is the subject of a verb that indicates actions taken against Jerusalem and its inhabitants. The verbs convey the terrible destruction that from the narrator's perspective the Lord has imposed upon Jerusalem. A brief sampling from the first three verses makes the point. The narrator asserts that the Lord acted to humiliate, throw down, not remember (v. 1), destroy, break down, bring down (v. 2), cut down, withdraw from, and burn Jerusalem (v. 3). By the time readers make their way through ten verses of similar affirmations, the cumulative weight is overwhelming. Lamentations 1 was concerned with enemies that had invaded Jerusalem and gloated over her. In Lamentations 2, the long recital of God's actions against the city make clear that Jerusalem's most dreaded enemy was the Lord. In fact, verses 4 and 5 explicitly liken the Lord to an enemy with bow bent, determined to destroy Jerusalem. The image of the Lord with bow bent contrasts to Gen. 9:13–17, where the sign of God's covenant with Noah is a rainbow, that is, an undrawn bow, to remind God not to destroy again the creation. Creation was spared, but Jerusalem, as the narrator of this chapter recognizes, was certainly not. These verses stress the Lord's destruction of Jerusalem by presenting a cascade of verbs describing God's actions against the city.

The destructive actions of the Lord against Jerusalem are intensified by repeated references to God's anger. The first line of this poem asserts, "How the Lord in his anger has humiliated daughter Zion" (v. 1), and there follow several similar references: "the day of his [the LORD's] anger" (v. 1); "his wrath" (v. 2); "in his fierce anger" (v. 3); "he has poured out his fury" (v. 4); "in his fierce indignation" (v. 6). What emerges is an image of the Lord, enraged at Jerusalem, wreaking destruction. Such a view of God likely offends Christian piety, which stresses God's love and compassion more. The difficulty may be that we have overemphasized God's caring and have not taken seriously enough God's capacity for anger and judgment. Recently during a Sunday in Lent at the church where I belong, a church school children's drama reminded worshipers of Jesus' rage at the money changers in the Temple. There was some surprise in the congregation at the anger displayed by the boy playing Jesus. It is not how we are used to thinking about God. Surely those who had witnessed the destruction of Jerusalem in 587 B.C. would have been keenly aware that God could be angry.

The narrator of this poem stresses that in anger God destroyed Jerusalem. Whereas some references to that which is destroyed are clear enough, a few are worth brief comment:

- God "has not remembered his footstool" (v. 1). In Psalm 99:5 and 132:7, "footstool" refers to the ark of the covenant or perhaps to Mount Zion, where the Temple was located. The footstool is God's throne, the place from which God exercised sovereignty. Obviously, in this poem God's footstool refers to Zion or Jerusalem. It was surprising that God did not remember his throne.
- The Lord has thrown down the "splendor of Israel" (v. 1). A similar phrase occurs in Isaiah 13:19 to refer to the capital of Babylon. Again, in this poem the "splendor of Israel" refers to Jerusalem, the place that symbolized God's special relationship with Judah.
- The Lord "has withdrawn his right hand from them" (v. 3). Verses 3–5 present the Lord as a divine warrior, an image drawn from the religious world of the ancient Near East to speak of gods who defended their people. Elsewhere in the Old Testament, the Lord as a divine warrior uses his right hand to save or protect Israel (for instance, Exod. 15:6, 12; Psalms 16:8; 17:7; 44:3; 60:5). The withdrawal of God's right hand and the declaration that the Lord would no longer be a warrior willing to protect Judah but would instead be "an enemy" (v. 5) signal God's unwillingness to save or protect Jerusalem any longer.
- The reference to God's booth (v. 6) is probably connected to the temporary dwellings of the Israelites when they left Egypt (see Lev. 23:42–43). Judah believed that the temple was established forever and secured by God. The idea that God would view the temple as a mere "booth" and break it down as one might uproot a garden would have been a shocking image. In a similar vein, priests and kings (v. 6) were deemed indispensable by those in Judah. That these would be "spurned" by God would have been unimaginable.

This poem's initial section is quite overstated and makes its point by exaggeration. In anger the Lord totally destroyed Judah.

There is really no other way for this section of the poem to conclude but with a picture of everyone in Jerusalem, from its elders to the city's young girls, bowed to the ground in grief (v. 10), the traditional posture of mourning after some calamity.

Lamentations 2:11–19

2:11 My eyes are spent with weeping;
            my stomach churns;
        my bile is poured out on the ground
            because of the destruction of my people,
        because infants and babes faint
            in the streets of the city.
12 They cry to their mothers,
            "Where is bread and wine?"
        as they faint like the wounded
            in the streets of the city,
        as their life is poured out
            on their mothers' bosom.
13 What can I say for you, to what compare you,
            O daughter Jerusalem?
        To what can I liken you, that I may comfort you,
            O virgin daughter Zion?
        For vast as the sea is your ruin;
            who can heal you?
14 Your prophets have seen for you
            false and deceptive visions;
        they have not exposed your iniquity
            to restore your fortunes,
        but have seen oracles for you
            that are false and misleading.
15 All who pass along the way
            clap their hands at you;
        they hiss and wag their heads
            at daughter Jerusalem;
        "Is this the city that was called
            the perfection of beauty,
            the joy of all the earth?"
16 All your enemies
            open their mouths against you;
        they hiss, they gnash their teeth,
            they cry: "We have devoured her!

Ah, this is the day we longed for;
  at last we have seen it!"
¹⁷ The LORD has done what he purposed,
  he has carried out his threat;
as he ordained long ago,
  he has demolished without pity;
he has made the enemy rejoice over you,
  and exalted the might of your foes.
¹⁸ Cry aloud to the Lord!
  O wall of daughter Zion!
Let tears stream down like a torrent
  day and night!
Give yourself no rest,
  your eyes no respite!
¹⁹ Arise, cry out in the night,
  at the beginning of the watches!
Pour out your heart like water
  before the presence of the Lord!
Lift your hands to him
  for the lives of your children,
who faint for hunger
  at the head of every street.

In this section, the poet offers personal reflections about the disaster that befell Jerusalem. These personal reflections of the poet complement Lamentations 1, in which we hear the city, presented as human, crying out in her anguish because of the disaster that occurred.

The poet speaks quite personally (note the use of "my" and "I") about the ruin of Jerusalem and how it has affected him (vv. 11–13). He is physically sickened by what he has witnessed. Particularly disturbing is the sight of children who cry out for food that their mothers cannot provide and who eventually die in their mother's arms (v. 12; see also 1:11). It is difficult to know if the Babylonian invasion of Jerusalem in 587 B.C. caused a food shortage as severe as is suggested here, though that is certainly possible. The poet regards the ruin of Jerusalem to be of incomparable magnitude, and so it is beyond his ability to give any comfort. Those of us who now read this text may find the claim that Jerusalem's destruction was a world-class disaster somewhat farfetched given what we know of history. However, for the poet who surely regarded Jerusalem with its temple as the very center of the universe, the city's fall signaled an unprecedented collapse of order. The poet compares Jerusalem's destruction to the vastness of the sea, a comparison in the ancient Near Eastern world that would have suggested chaos. The final question of verse 13, "who can heal you?" points toward the conclusion of the poem. The only one who could "heal" chaos is the Lord.

The poet addresses Jerusalem (so the pronouns shift from "me" and "I" to "you" and "your") and specifically the causes of Jerusalem's ruin (vv. 14–16). This is attributed to the "false and deceptive visions" of Judah's prophets. These prophets failed to expose Judah's "iniquity" and so failed to speak a word that might have "restored" the city. The implication is clear that Judah's prophets had the capacity to direct Jerusalem's course to either ruin or restoration, and the false visions they offered had meant ruin. A similar charge against Judah's prophets is a prominent theme in the book of Jeremiah. In a passage much like the accusation here in Lamentations, it is said of Judah's prophets:

> Thus says the LORD of hosts: Do not listen to the words of the prophets who prophesy to you; they are deluding you. They speak visions of their own minds, not from the mouth of the LORD. They keep saying to those who despise the word of the LORD, "It shall be well with you"; and to all who stubbornly follow their own stubborn hearts, they say, "No calamity shall come upon you." (Jer. 23:16–17; compare 14:13–14 and the story of Hananiah in Jeremiah 28)

Thus the poet in Lamentations, in laying blame for Jerusalem's destruction upon Judah's prophets, offers a common interpretation of the events of 587 B.C.

Verses 15–16 return to a familiar concern of Lamentations, "enemies" that deride the fallen Jerusalem. Each verse mentions a taunting action of the enemies: hissing, clapping their hands, wagging their heads in verse 15; hissing, shouting, and gnashing their teeth in verse 16. Further, each verse reports the ridiculing words of the enemies: in verse 15, berating the extent of the city's fall from its status of "perfection of beauty, the joy of all the earth"; in verse 16, gloating over their long-hoped-for victory over Jerusalem. This section of Lamentations 2 is framed by two differing reactions to the city's ruin. The physical revulsion of the poet at the fall of Jerusalem (v. 11) contrasts sharply with the rejoicing of Jerusalem's enemies (vv. 15–16).

The Lord's role in Jerusalem's fall becomes the focus in verse 17 as the poet declares, "The LORD has done what he purposed . . . ." Enemies may have breached the city's walls, and the false visions of prophets may have been a primary cause for Jerusalem's downfall. But finally, the poet understands that Jerusalem fell because the Lord "purposed . . . carried out his threat . . . ordained . . . demolished . . . and made the enemy rejoice" (v. 17). The claim of this verse is decisive and surely must have been shocking to those who survived 587 B.C. Other Old Testament literature from the time of the Babylonian exile gives us some idea of how the fall of Jerusalem was popularly regarded. For instance, in Isaiah 40, widely assumed to have been written to assure those who had been exiled to Babylon, the prophet asks:

> Why do you say, O Jacob,
>   and speak, O Israel,
> "My way is hidden from the LORD,
>   and my right is disregarded by my God"?
>   (Isa. 40:27)

This question suggests that those exiled thought that Jerusalem was destroyed because God was not paying attention or intentionally had chosen to disregard Judah. What a shock, then, to hear that what had happened to Jerusalem was what God had purposed and ordained. If the ruin of Jerusalem, vast as the sea, was God's doing, it was clear that only the Lord, who purposed and ordained Jerusalem's ruin, could also purpose and ordain its health. The Lord was Judah's only hope. So the poet concludes by urging the city to throw itself upon God's mercy. In the last line of the poet's reflection, he returns to the image that seems to have haunted him, the image of children faint with hunger on every street corner (see v. 12). The logic that seems to be at work is that if the poet found the sight of starving and dying children repulsive, then surely the Lord, too, would be moved by such a sight.

The poet's personal reflections about the disaster of 587 B.C. are honest. The poet is honest about his own pain and revulsion and names specifically that which troubles him the most, the plight of hungry children. The poet is honest about the failure of Judah's prophets, unafraid to lay blame where it belongs or to face the humiliating taunts of the enemies. The poet risks an honest theological assessment of the situation and is willing to say to those who did not want to hear it, God purposed this.

Too often our way of handling difficult circumstances in church and society is to sugarcoat the realities, to gloss over awful events with polite language and euphemisms that refuse to say directly what has happened. The tendency to be less than forthright in dealing with terrible events carries into our prayer life, too. We tend to address God politely and with proper decorum. The poet in Lamentations 2 "lets it all hang out," and that suggests that the only way to move through tragedy is to do so with honesty—honesty with each other and with God.

Lamentations 2:20–22

2:20 **Look, O LORD, and consider!**
To whom have you done this?
Should women eat their offspring,
the children they have borne?

> Should priest and prophet be killed
>   in the sanctuary of the Lord?
> 21 The young and the old are lying
>   on the ground in the streets;
> my young women and my young men
>   have fallen by the sword;
> in the day of your anger you have killed them,
>   slaughtering without mercy.
> 22 You invited my enemies from all around
>   as if for a day of festival;
> and on the day of the anger of the LORD
>   no one escaped or survived;
> those whom I bore and reared
>   my enemy has destroyed.

These concluding verses of Lamentations 2 are the prayer of Jerusalem offered at the urging of the poet. The prayer is honest and confronts God with images whose intent seems to be to shame God into action. The question with which this prayer begins sets the tone: "Look, O LORD, and consider! To whom have you done this?" (v. 20) In other words, Jerusalem challenges the Lord to look at who is suffering as a result of what God purposed and ordained (see v. 17). In a sometimes graphic and shocking manner, the remainder of the prayer presents what should concern God. It is difficult to imagine that the events of 587 B.C. actually drove women to eat their children as verse 20 suggests, though this was imagined as a curse for those who violated God's covenant (see Deut. 28:53–57; Lev. 26:29). If what happened to the residents of Jerusalem was covenant curse, then this prayer raises the question about how far God was willing to go in punishing Judah. As the prayer proceeds, the death of the inhabitants of the city is directly attributed to the Lord's anger ("you have killed them") and to enemies whom the Lord had invited "from all around." The prayer presents a scene of pervasive death for which God is blamed. Without saying so directly, the prayer raises the question about what kind of God purposes and ordains such horror. The prayer ends, but the question lingers unanswered.

It is not possible to read Lamentations apart from the horror of the Holocaust or apart from the horror of all the holocausts that have scarred the history of recent decades. Even if we would deny that God would purpose and ordain the atrocities we have witnessed, in honesty we have to raise with God the question of the horror of the death camps, the horror of starving children, and the horror of senseless acts of terrorism spawned by cruel acts of injustice. How can God allow it? That is what honest prayer must ask even as the question often lingers unanswered.

"I Am One Who Has Seen Affliction"
Lamentations 3

Lamentations 3 is often identified as the heart of the book of Lamentations, the chapter with the greatest theological depth and insight. The reason for this judgment is the hope in the Lord expressed through the middle verses of this chapter. Lamentations 3 begins in the tone of the prior chapters. It expresses the afflictions of the one who prays these verses. However, these complaints finally yield, and confidence is expressed that "the steadfast love of the Lord never ceases" (v. 22). Then the one who prays in this chapter expresses hope in God in other ways: confidence that "the Lord will not reject forever," faith that all that happens God sees and ordains (vv. 36–37), recognition that the appropriate response to punishment is not complaint but repentance (vv. 38–40). In Lamentations 3, we find expressions of confidence in the Lord that are largely missing from the preceding chapters. When Lamentations 3 is read as the theological heart of the book, the book "fits" the way the church usually imagines God and makes the book as a whole easier to comprehend.

Caution is needed, however, in hearing the expressions of hope in Lamentations 3 as the core message of the book. Even before Lamentations 3 itself concludes, the hopeful tone of the chapter's middle verses disappears. Furthermore, the book of Lamentations concludes not with a resounding affirmation of God's steadfast love and mercy (3:22) but with a question about God's faithfulness: ". . . have you utterly rejected us? Are you exceedingly angry with us?" (5:22). When we move beyond Lamentations 3 to the two concluding chapters of the book, little of the confident tone of Lamentations 3 is found again. The hope we find in Lamentations 3 is best understood as but one response to affliction by those who have shaped the book. Judged from the perspective of the whole, it is difficult to argue that the confidence of Lamentations 3 is the book's dominant response to affliction. Complaints far outweigh the few verses of hope in Lamentations 3.

Complaint dominates the book and is found at the beginning and the end of Lamentations 3. In response to affliction, however, there are glimmers of hope such as we hear in this chapter. The responses to affliction found in the book of Lamentations are much like our own responses to grief and loss. Many days there are tears and loneliness and much hurt. Some days we may be more hopeful and see God's goodness and mercy experienced through those who have been attentive to us through our difficulty. Then on another day hurt and hopelessness return. The pain of affliction does not cease all at once, if at all. Confidence in God's faithfulness comes only slowly after loss. The book of Lamentations invites us to face affliction honestly and to acknowledge hurt as well as glimpses of hope such as we find in Lamentations 3.

In the chapter itself there is an alternation between sections that express deep doubt and despair and sections that are more confident and hopeful, that express the normative faith of ancient Israel confident of God's sovereignty and faithfulness. In verses 1–18, the petitioner complains to God about his affliction, though in these initial verses there is no clear indication of the nature of the affliction suffered. In verses 19–21, there is a shift in tone from complaint to hope, a shift that is particularly evident in verses 22–41. Instead of the despair of the early part of the chapter, these verses express trust in God and a hopeful confidence. This section of Lamentations 3, assured of God's steadfast love and mercy and about God's sovereignty, expresses the normative faith of ancient Israel. These hopeful verses conclude with a call for the community to cease complaint and to repent instead. Verses 42–51, although they flow from the call for repentance which have preceded them, mark another transition. The mood again shifts, and the petitioner questions the ways of the Lord. There is no indication of forgiveness or that the Lord has seen and comes with salvation. The confidence of verses 21–41 dissolves into tears. The conclusion of the chapter is complicated by problems with translating the Hebrew text but is probably a series of pleas that the Lord deal with the enemies of the community. Reflecting on the concluding verses of Lamentations 3, Provan observes, "We are entitled to see . . . a retreat from the confident position adopted in the middle of the poem. Faith and reason have for the moment been overwhelmed by experience" (83–84).

Lamentations 3:1–20

> 3:1 **I am one who has seen affliction**
>   **under the rod of God's wrath;**
>   2 **he has driven and brought me**
>   **into darkness without any light;**

³ against me alone he turns his hand,
    again and again, all day long.
⁴ He has made my flesh and my skin waste away,
    and broken my bones;
⁵ he has besieged and enveloped me
    with bitterness and tribulation;
⁶ he has made me sit in darkness
    like the dead of long ago.
⁷ He has walled me about so that I cannot escape;
    he has put heavy chains on me;
⁸ though I call and cry for help,
    he shuts out my prayer;
⁹ he has blocked my ways with hewn stones,
    he has made my paths crooked.
¹⁰ He is a bear lying in wait for me,
    a lion in hiding;
¹¹ he led me off my way and tore me to pieces;
    he has made me desolate;
¹² he bent his bow and set me
    as a mark for his arrow.
¹³ He shot into my vitals
    the arrows of his quiver;
¹⁴ I have become the laughingstock of all my people,
    the object of their taunt-songs all day long.
¹⁵ He has filled me with bitterness,
    he has sated me with wormwood.
¹⁶ He has made my teeth grind on gravel,
    and made me cower in ashes;
¹⁷ my soul is bereft of peace;
    I have forgotten what happiness is;
¹⁸ so I say, "Gone is my glory,
    and all that I had hoped for from the LORD."
¹⁹ The thought of my affliction and my homelessness
    is wormwood and gall!
²⁰ My soul continually thinks of it
    and is bowed down within me.

The first section of Lamentations 3 is a long personal complaint or lament. The speaker is identified as "one who has seen affliction" because of "God's wrath" (v. 1). The one who prays in these verses is an individual who in the context of the book of Lamentations can be identified most readily as the narrator of the preceding chapters. In Lamentations 1–2, this narrator speaks descriptively of that which happened to Jerusalem. Here the narrator speaks personally about what has happened to him or her because of God's wrath. Thus, Lamentations 3 begins where the prior chapter ends. At the conclusion of Lamentations 2, "daughter Jerusalem" complains that on "the day of the anger of the Lord" all the children of Jerusalem were killed (2:22). Through verse 18, the narrator contemplates the personal consequences of God's wrath using a variety of images. There is a pattern to the narrator's complaint in these verses in which the Lord ("He") is accused of doing something to the narrator that has had negative consequences.

The image of the Lord as a shepherd dominates verses 2–6. As one commentator notes, however, in this section of the poem the complaint is that the Lord is the reverse of the shepherd of Psalm 23: "the Lord is a shepherd who misleads, a ruler who oppresses and imprisons" (Hillers, 65). In this text, where light and darkness are traditional symbols for good and evil, the petitioner complains that the Lord has driven him out into darkness (in Isa. 20:4, the verb "driven" is used to describe exile). The pastoral sense is developed further in verse 4. Flocks are driven to pasture so they can be well fed; in this poem the complaint is that the Lord has driven the petitioner to a place where there is no food, so starvation results. In fact, this complaint ends with the accusation that God's wrath has brought death, the darkness of the nether world of Sheol (v. 6; compare Psalm 88:6).

After verse 6, the poem jumps from one picture to another to express complaint against the Lord. Verses 7–9 portray imprisonment by which the petitioner is cut off not just from the human community but also from God, who does not respond to cries for help. There are parallels to Jeremiah's experience as a prisoner in a dry well (Jeremiah 37–38). In verse 9, the Lord is portrayed as blocking the petitioner's way and forcing him off the road where there are wild animals with which to contend. Then the poem shifts images again, and the Lord's hostility is compared to an aggressive, hostile animal lying in wait and ready to rip apart its prey (vv. 10–11; especially in the prophetic books, God's judgment is sometimes described as the attack of a wild animal, as in Amos 5:19 and Hos. 13:7–8). There follows a complaint that the Lord has hunted the petitioner down (vv. 12–13); and, with yet one more shift, the petitioner complains of becoming a laughing-stock, the object of taunt and derision (compare Jer. 20:7). Finally, if the shepherd of Psalm 23 sees that the flock is well fed (see Psalm 23:2), the one who offers this prayer complains that the Lord has offered only bitterness and wormwood.

This long section of complaint against the Lord's lack of care moves to a conclusion with the declaration, "my soul is bereft of peace" (v. 17). For the one who offers this prayer, the Lord has not been the good shepherd who restores the soul (Psalm 23:2) but a troubler of the soul who has "made me desolate" (v. 11) and bitter (vv. 5, 15). The NRSV translates verse 18 as "Gone is my glory," though the Hebrew is difficult and in recent commentaries it has been suggested that the phrase may be better translated to mean that my strength is gone. Whatever the exact translation, there is no mistaking that verse 18 is a cry of utter despair. The one who has provided a long catalog of afflictions brought about by God's wrath (v. 1) is broken and can no longer depend upon the Lord, a most unreliable shepherd.

Interestingly, we are given no indication about what specific situation or circumstances have caused the affliction. While the petitioner may be describing the personal impact of the experience of the exile of 587 B.C., there is little in these verses to lead us to this connection. The petitioner has experienced an unspecified affliction and, in response, complains to the Lord. These reflections, however, are not concluded with complaint.

Lamentations 3:21–24

3:21 **But this I call to mind,**
  and therefore I have hope:
 22 **The steadfast love of the LORD never ceases,**
  his mercies never come to an end;
 23 **they are new every morning;**
  great is your faithfulness.
 24 **"The LORD is my portion," says my soul,**
  "therefore I will hope in him."

When the poem reaches the point of despair, we discover that the petitioner has another thought that is the seed of hope (v. 21). The poem seems to present a person alone in thought. As the person reflects, there is an initial sense of overwhelming despair, of darkness and not light (vv. 1–6). But then another thought comes, and the person's mind races off in a new direction. This chapter presents a stream of thoughts not necessarily coherent, the kind of thoughts that one has lying awake at 3:00 A.M.

At the point of despair, the petitioner remembers God's steadfast love and mercies (v. 22). It would be difficult to imagine a sharper contrast than this affirmation alongside verses 1–20. Initially, Lamentations 3 concerns the ways the Lord was an undependable shepherd who led those who followed into trouble and toward death. The poet's new thought concerns God's "steadfast love," a term used in the Old Testament to affirm the Lord's faithfulness and loyalty. "Steadfast love" is rarely used in the Old Testament to describe humans, whose unfaithfulness and lack of loyalty to

God are a dominant biblical theme. In the Old Testament, God's "stead-fast love" and "mercy" are perhaps most clearly illustrated in Exodus 32–34. Israel, having been delivered from Pharaoh's oppression, becomes anxious when Moses is delayed on the mountain. A golden calf is fashioned. Despite the Lord's deliverance, Israel is quickly ready to desert God for an idol. God rages and threatens to wipe out the rebellious people, preserving only Moses. Finally, with Moses' intervention, the Lord relents and pledges to continue with Israel. In the context of these events, it is affirmed:

> The LORD, the LORD,
> a God merciful and gracious,
> slow to anger,
> and abounding in steadfast love and faithfulness,
> keeping steadfast love for the thousandth generation,
> forgiving iniquity and transgression and sin.
>
> (Exod. 34:6–7a)

Israel remembered that the Lord related in "steadfast love" and "mercy," sustaining relationship despite the people's rebellion. This memory of the Lord's character is totally the opposite of the petitioner's experience of God recounted so vividly in verses 1–18. Whereas the petitioner's initial experience of God's wrath led to hopelessness, recalling God's steadfast love and mercy leads the petitioner to hope (vv. 21, 24).

The affirmation of verse 24, "The Lord is my portion," refers to the dividing of the Promised Land when each family received a "portion" (Joshua 13ff.) from God that was a gift to sustain them. However, the priests did not receive a portion, for God declared, "I am your portion" (Num. 18:20). That is, the priests would be sustained by the Lord, tangibly through the offerings God commanded that they were to receive. The memory of the petitioner that the Lord "is my portion" affirms a dependence upon and confidence in God. The Lord will provide for him (see Psalms 73:26; 119:57; 142:5 for similar affirmations about the Lord as portion).

To this point, then, Lamentations 3 moves in two distinct ways. Reflecting upon affliction because of the Lord's wrath, the petitioner is overwhelmed by despair and hopelessness (vv. 1–18). Having experienced the Lord as an undependable shepherd who led him toward death (v. 6), the petitioner has another thought. It is a recollection of the central and enduring memory of Israel about God's ways and character, the ways of the Lord known through the exodus, the wilderness sojourn, and the entrance into the Promised Land. This memory was the orthodox view and dominant perspective about the Lord in Israel. This normative faith of the community undergirds the petitioner's reflections in the verses that follow.

Lamentations 3:25–41

3:25 **The LORD is good to those who wait for him,**
      to the soul that seeks him.

26 **It is good that one should wait quietly**
      for the salvation of the LORD.

27 **It is good for one to bear**
      the yoke in youth,

28 **to sit alone in silence**
      when the Lord has imposed it,

29 **to put one's mouth to the dust**
      (there may yet be hope),

30 **to give one's cheek to the smiter,**
      and be filled with insults.

31 **For the Lord will not**
      reject forever.

32 **Although he causes grief, he will have compassion**
      according to the abundance of his steadfast love;

33 **for he does not willingly afflict**
      or grieve anyone.

34 **When all the prisoners of the land**
      are crushed under foot,

35 **when human rights are perverted**
      in the presence of the Most High,

36 **when one's case is subverted**
      —does the Lord not see it?

37 **Who can command and have it done,**
      if the Lord has not ordained it?

38 **Is it not from the mouth of the Most High**
      that good and bad come?

39 **Why should any who draw breath complain**
      about the punishment of their sins?

40 **Let us test and examine our ways,**
      and return to the LORD.

41 **Let us lift up our hearts as well as our hands**
      to God in heaven.

Verses 21–24, introduced by the phrase "But I call this to mind," seem to be a private reflection, the insight from a moment of introspection. The tone of the poem beginning at verse 25 suggests that a community of believers is being addressed, that the prayer is public and has its purpose to admonish.

Reflecting upon the implications of the Lord's steadfast love (vv. 25–33), the petitioner first affirms that "The LORD is good to those who wait for him" and then urges those addressed "to wait quietly for the salvation of the LORD" (v. 26). This affirmation and admonition is repeated in various ways throughout these verses. For instance, there is an admonition to "bear the yoke in youth" (v. 27). From verses 29–30, this yoke seems to be some kind of punishment from God that results in isolation and insult (compare v. 14 regarding the petitioner's own experience). The assurance given is that this "yoke," whatever punishment is meant, can be endured because "the Lord will not reject forever" (v. 31). Also, grief is to be endured (v. 32), and two reasons are given: (a) steadfast love will bring God to act in mercy (v. 32); and (b) God does not willingly afflict anyone (v. 33). Since this poem began with the petitioner's claim to have experienced affliction under God's wrath (v. 1), the contrast with this section of the chapter is stark. Thus there is a tension in the poem. In the petitioner's experience, the affliction suffered leads to despair and grave doubt about the goodness of the Lord. However, for one who shares the normative faith of the community, that affliction can be endured in the confidence that God does not willingly afflict and hopeful that God will finally act in mercy born of steadfast love.

This tension between lived experience and normative faith is evident to anyone who is honest. We who have been nurtured in the life of the church know the "right" answers, know that God is sovereign and good, know that God will end tears and that death will be no more (Rev. 21:4). However, there are those moments in life when the normative faith of the community is hardly credible. A petty dictator practices genocide, and thousands of innocent victims lose their lives; their lifeless bodies greet us on the evening news. A promising young teen is killed by a drunk driver, and her family searches in vain to discern God's mercy. There is a report of a baby bitten by rats in its crib, and waiting patiently for the Lord's salvation does not seem a very good idea. This chapter of Lamentations invites us into the deep tensions between the church's normative confessions about God's goodness and the ways we experience our world; between our confidence in God's sovereignty and our knowledge of injustice where God seems silent. One of my teaching colleagues talks of life being "messy." This poem sees life as "messy" and reflects that messiness in its untidy darting from confidence to doubt about the goodness of the Lord.

It is possible to read verses 34–36 in quite opposite ways. One way is reflected in the NRSV translation. There the concluding question in verse 36 suggests an affirmative answer: "Does the Lord not see it?" Yes, of course! The question is rhetorical. As translated in the NRSV, these verses affirm that when injustices occur, the Lord is attentive. Again, the contrast between this normative expression of Israel's faith and the experience of the petitioner in the initial verses of Lamentations 3 is quite marked. In the petitioner's experience, it seemed that the Lord had ignored all the cries for help and prayers (v. 8). In contrast, the normative expression of Israel's faith affirms that the Lord sees and responds to injustice.

A different but possible translation of the Hebrew of the final phrase of verse 36 sees it as a declarative sentence: "The Lord does not see!" If one follows this translation, then these verses are an objection that is being raised to the confident expressions of this section of the chapter. Provan has suggested that when read as an objection or protest, the speaker in verses 34–36 needs to be understood as one from the wider community who has heard the confidence of the petitioner but who does not find that hopeful perspective convincing. Such an objection is not surprising. After all, the petitioner has viewed the Lord with much less confidence than expressed in this section of the poem.

Yet another normative conviction about God comes to the fore in verses 37–41. These verses affirm that the Lord is sovereign, and all that happens, good and bad, God ordains (vv. 37–38). Of course, an affirmation of God's sovereignty would respond to verses 34–36 if these are read as an objection, as some have proposed (above). Beyond the immediate context of the chapter, the book of Lamentations is a response, probably to the exile of 587 B.C., when God's sovereignty was in doubt. So, the assurances of these verses, rooted deeply in Israel's normative understanding of God, match well the concerns and context of Lamentations.

The affirmation of God's sovereignty in verses 37–38 is used in the verses that follow to urge the community to repent and seek God's forgiveness. The logic of verses 39–41 is this: God ordains all that happens, both good and bad. If there is bad, it must signal God's judgment, the punishment of sin. Therefore, complaint is useless, and what is needed is self-examination and repentance. Israel needs to "return to the Lord" (v. 40). This way of imaging God then ties to the affirmations of verses 21–31. "The steadfast love of the Lord never ceases, his mercies never come to an end." Surely those who return to the Lord could expect forgiveness. When the community had repented, they then needed to wait for the Lord's salvation (vv. 25–26), rescue from the desperate situation that God had imposed as a punishment. After all, "the Lord will not reject forever" (v. 31).

We find in the middle of Lamentations 3 a clear statement of the normative faith of ancient Israel. Verses 21–41 say about God what everyone assumed to be so. God is in charge of all that happens, is loving and forgiving, and, although angry for a season, will forgive those who acknowledge their sin. In the church, we also have a normative way of thinking about God, assumptions that we imagine everyone shares. For some congregations, the normative way of thinking about God may be expressed through one of the historic creeds of the church, such as the Nicene or the Apostles' Creed, or a denominational statement of belief. Other congregations may find their normative beliefs about God expressed in words and phrases often used by a beloved pastor. Sometimes our normative ideas about God come from simple teachings we learned as children from our parents or in church school: "God is Love" or "God never gives us burdens too heavy to carry." These normative ideas about God are deeply rooted in us and likely to come to mind quickly as we confront a difficult situation about which we are attempting to make sense.

That is the experience of the petitioner in Lamentations 3. Dealing with a very difficult, almost overwhelming situation, the poet's experience has raised all kinds of questions about God and has led him to despair that there may be any hope in the Lord (vv. 1–20). However, just at the moment when despair comes to the surface, the poet remembers the normative faith of the community that he had heard from childhood. This lamenting one "knows" about God's steadfast love and mercy, about God who ordains good and bad, about God who forgives and expects repentance (vv. 21–41).

Lamentations 3:42–51

3:42   We have transgressed and rebelled,
      and you have not forgiven.
43   You have wrapped yourself with anger and pursued us,
      killing without pity;
44   you have wrapped yourself with a cloud
      so that no prayer can pass through.
45   You have made us filth and rubbish
      among the peoples.
46   All our enemies
      have opened their mouths against us;
47   panic and pitfall have come upon us,
      devastation and destruction.
48   My eyes flow with rivers of tears
      because of the destruction of my people.
49   My eyes will flow without ceasing,
      without respite,
50   until the LORD from heaven
      looks down and sees.

⁵¹ **My eyes cause me grief**
at the fate of all the young women in my city.

Another shift occurs, and what follows seems to develop from the admonition for the community to repent (vv. 40–41). The tone differs significantly from that of the preceding section. In fact, the mood of this section is much like that found in the first twenty verses of the chapter in which the petitioner made harsh accusations against the Lord. The shift from confidence to complaint is evident immediately (v. 42). The petitioner, who had urged the community to "return to the Lord" (v. 40), addresses the Lord with the accusation "you have not forgiven." The normative faith of Israel was hopeful in God's steadfast love and mercy that "the Lord will not reject forever" (v. 31). The petitioner's words, however, suggest that in experience it seemed different, and there was no evidence of the Lord's forgiveness.

That experience suggests that in anger the Lord brought death "without pity" (v. 43; compare v. 6). Once again, then, we encounter a significant tension between the assumed faith of Israel and lived experience where God's mercy is far from clear. The accusation of verse 44, that God is isolated from hearing prayers, echoes a nearly identical charge from the beginning of the chapter (v. 6), and calls into question the point of raising one's hands to heaven (the posture of prayer) as was earlier urged (v. 41). The Lord has made the community "filth and rubbish" (v. 45), and enemies taunt at the "devastation and destruction" they observe (vv. 46–47). With this accusation, Lamentations 3, for the first time, picks up the theme of Israel's defeat at the hands of an enemy, so prominent in Lamentations 1–2. This concern will continue through the conclusion of the chapter. These accusations, rooted in the experience of defeat by an enemy, echo the beginning of Lamentations 3 (vv. 1–18) and stand in tension with the confidence that the Lord "does not willingly afflict or grieve anyone" (v. 33).

Finally, the petitioner is reduced to tears and weeps over the destruction of the community (v. 48) and over the "fate" of the city's young women (perhaps victims of the enemy's brutality). The waiting for the Lord (vv. 25–26) is a painful waiting, a waiting in grief. Given the circumstances of the community, its normative faith, confident of the Lord's sovereignty and hopeful because of God's steadfast love and mercy, is not convincing. The petitioner of Lamentations 3 honestly faces and gives expression to the faith crisis in which the community lives. This is the value of Lamentations for the church, that it faces and gives expression to that which we too often gloss over, that there are times when the faith we confess and our experience are in considerable tension. Lamentations is a book for those willing to risk honesty and who are able to admit that sometimes our experiences call into question our deepest held beliefs about God. Yet, even in such a moment, the petitioner of Lamentations 3 turns to God in prayer, a prayer that might not even matter to God (vv. 8, 44). The one who prays in Lamentations 3, despite all the doubts about the Lord, is, in the language of the street, in God's face. The prayer of this chapter suggests a depth of relationship between the petitioner and God that is rare and risky in its honesty and forthrightness.

Lamentations 3:52–66

3:52   Those who were my enemies without cause
      have hunted me like a bird;

53   they flung me alive into a pit
      and hurled stones on me;

54   water closed over my head;
      I said, "I am lost."

55   I called on your name, O LORD,
      from the depths of the pit;

56   you heard my plea, "Do not close your ear
      to my cry for help, but give me relief!"

57   You came near when I called on you;
      you said, "Do not fear!"

58   You have taken up my cause, O Lord,
      you have redeemed my life.

59   You have seen the wrong done to me, O LORD;
      judge my cause.

60   You have seen all their malice,
      all their plots against me.

61   You have heard their taunts, O LORD,
      all their plots against me.

62   The whispers and murmurs of my assailants
      are against me all day long.

63   Whether they sit or rise—see,
      I am the object of their taunt-songs.

64   Pay them back for their deeds, O LORD,
      according to the work of their hands!

65   Give them anguish of heart;
      your curse be on them!

66   Pursue them in anger and destroy them
      from under the LORD's heavens.

This concluding section of Lamentations 3 concerns the enemies first mentioned in verse 46. How these final verses of Lamentations 3 are understood depends upon a difficult problem about how the Hebrew should be translated beginning in verse 56. The NRSV translates verses 56–61 with past tense verbs, indicating that the Lord had already responded to the petitioner. Translated in this way, these concluding verses sound an optimistic note and suggest that in the end, God was responsive after all and came to rescue the petitioner. Thus, the doubts of the petitioner would be put to rest and the normative faith of Israel (vv. 21–41) confirmed. This interpretation certainly makes sense and brings resolution to the difficult questions raised by the honesty of the petitioner in reflecting upon the affliction suffered. Perhaps we are part of the church because, in our own experience more often than not, we have found God to be faithful and our doubts dissipated by God's merciful intervention in our lives.

The proper translation of the Hebrew beginning at verse 56, however, may not be as declarative sentences (for instance, in verse 56, "you heard my plea") but as imperatives, so that the verses may be read as a plea for God to act rather than a description of how God acted. Thus it is suggested that these verses be translated like this:

> 56 Hear my plea . . .
> 57 Come near when I call on you,
>   tell me not to be afraid!
> 58 Take up my cause . . .
>   redeem my life.
> 59 See the wrong done to me, O LORD,
>   judge my cause.
> 60 See all their malice . . .
> 61 Hear their taunts . . .

Translated in this way, Lamentations 3 concludes without clear resolution. In the first two-thirds of Lamentations 3, the petitioner has held in tension the normative faith of Israel—confident of God's steadfast love—and doubts and despair that grew out of the experience of suffering. Then, at the end of his prayer, he addresses God with his hopes and needs for God to act against the enemies. The petitioner asks that once more the Lord demonstrate steadfast love and sovereign power. However, when read as petitions rather than descriptions, Lamentations 3 concludes without clear resolution, and questions raised through the chapter remain open. So, with the petitioner we must wait and hope for the salvation of God (vv. 25–26), with no quick resolution of how the crisis will be resolved. This reading of the conclusion of Lamentations 3 also may resonate with our experience, with occasions when a crisis lingered long and we hovered the whole while between despair rooted in painful experience and the faith we learned in the laps of our parents.

"The Lord Gave Full Vent to His Wrath"
Lamentations 4

Like the previous poems of the book, the first word of each stanza in Lamentations 4 begins with a Hebrew letter arranged in alphabetical order (a total of 22 stanzas). In many other ways, however, this chapter is different from those already considered. This poem is shorter. Whereas in Lamentations 1–3 each stanza of the poems had three lines (a total of 66 lines), in Lamentations 4 the stanzas of the poem are only two lines long (a total of 44 lines). The preceding poems are mostly prayers through which God is addressed. Lamentations is not a prayer, at least in the sense that God is not addressed. In fact, the Lord is only mentioned explicitly in two verses, and in these verses God is spoken of descriptively (in the third person): in verse 11, "The Lord gave full vent to his wrath . . ." and in verse 16, "The splendor of the Lord destroyed them . . ." The previous chapters are often characterized as complaints or laments, that is, as prayers of an individual or community that recount trouble and plead with God to intervene. Lamentations 4 is most often characterized as a dirge, that is, a song or poem that is used to express grief at the time of death.

In Lamentations 1–2, Jerusalem is personified, spoken of, or even speaks as if a person. This technique is not evident in Lamentations 4. The persons described in this poem are the city's inhabitants. Much of Lamentations 4 concerns the suffering of Jerusalem's residents as a result of an invasion. The poem presents scenes "in the streets" of the sacked city (vv. 5, 8, 14, but also 1). Even though the Babylonians are not mentioned directly, more than any poem in Lamentations, this chapter is most evidently concerned with the destruction of Jerusalem by Babylon in 587 B.C. Frequently, Lamentations 4 emphasizes the tragedy that has befallen the residents of Jerusalem by comparing how life was for them before and after the city's destruction. While there is a good deal of simple description of the consequences caused by the invasion of Jerusalem, Lamentations 4 is also interested in the causes of Jerusalem's fall. In particular, Lamentations

4 attributes the city's destruction to the Lord's anger (vv. 11, 16), the sin of Judah's priests and prophets (vv. 13–15), and the failure of allies to come to Judah's rescue (v. 17).

This chapter concludes on a surprising note. After vividly recounting the destruction of the city and its terrible aftermath, the final two verses of Lamentations 4 sound a hopeful note about Zion's future and announce punishment for Edom, one of Judah's traditional enemies. The concluding verses of Lamentations 4 may be the most hopeful about Jerusalem's restoration in the entire book.

Lamentations 4 :1–10

4:1 **How the gold has grown dim,**
    how the pure gold is changed!
The sacred stones lie scattered
    at the head of every street.

2 **The precious children of Zion,**
    worth their weight in fine gold—
how they are reckoned as earthen pots,
    the work of a potter's hands!

3 **Even the jackals offer the breast**
    and nurse their young,
but my people has become cruel,
    like the ostriches in the wilderness.

4 **The tongue of the infant sticks**
    to the roof of its mouth for thirst;
the children beg for food,
    but no one gives them anything.

5 **Those who feasted on delicacies**
    perish in the streets;
those who were brought up in purple
    cling to ash heaps.

6 **For the chastisement of my people has been greater**
    than the punishment of Sodom,
which was overthrown in a moment,
    though no hand was laid on it.

7 **Her princes were purer than snow,**
    whiter than milk;
their bodies were more ruddy than coral,
    their hair like sapphire.

8 **Now their visage is blacker than soot;**
    they are not recognized in the streets.
Their skin has shriveled on their bones;

it has become as dry as wood.
9 Happier were those pierced by the sword
    than those pierced by hunger,
whose life drains away, deprived
    of the produce of the field.
10 The hands of compassionate women
    have boiled their own children;
they became their food
    in the destruction of my people.

These verses are descriptive of the sacked city of Jerusalem. The initial verse of the poem refers to the physical state of the city, or more precisely the Jerusalem temple that was destroyed by the Babylonians in 587 B.C. (compare 2:5–9; also see 2 Kings 25:8–17 as well as Jer. 52:12–23). The destroyed Temple is strewn about, its rubble scattered about in the streets of the city. Even its gold ornamentation lies around, now tarnished (gold, of course, would not rust or erode but would lose its luster when exposed to the weather). Since the "sacred stones" seem to be scattered over some distance, it has been suggested that these were not the stones of the exterior walls of the Temple, but precious jewels from the Temple treasury.

At verse 2, the focus shifts to the people of the city, who become the primary concern of the poem through verse 10. A contrast of the state of the residents of Jerusalem before and after the fall of the city is the primary means used to stress their deplorable circumstances. Verse 2 provides a general statement about the reversal of the citizenries' fortunes, which is then elaborated on in verses 3–7. Picking up the reference to gold from verse 1, the residents of Jerusalem are characterized as initially "worth their weight in gold," but following the fall of the city, like "earthen pots," common, everyday vessels of no particular value. In Lamentations 4, the "earthen pots" image is clearly intended to convey a regrettable loss of status. Interestingly, the apostle Paul uses the image of "clay jars" in a very positive manner. He asserts that the church has the ministry of Jesus Christ "in clay jars so it may be made clear that . . . power belongs to God and not ourselves" (2 Cor. 4:7). Clearly there is a difference between surrendering oneself to be a servant of Christ (so, an inconspicuous "clay jar") and being forcibly enslaved by an oppressive foreign power.

The portraits of the residents of Jerusalem developed in verses 3–10 continue to make extensive use of before and after contrasts and offer a bleak assessment of life in the fallen city. The impact of this section of the poem is enhanced by the way it heaps one picture of life in the city on top of another:

1. Mothers were not able to nurse their infants who begged for food (vv. 3–4; compare 2:11–12). The scene presented is tragic. (It is not clear why jackals and ostriches are held in such low regard in these verses).

2. Those described in verse 5 seem to be of an upper social and economic class. In the ancient Near East, the color purple (sometimes translated scarlet) was associated with royalty. The NRSV translation of this verse has these once affluent citizens perishing and clinging to ash heaps. Another translation may convey better the sense of the Hebrew and the dramatic reversals experienced by those in Jerusalem who once lived well (Hillers, 75):

> Those who once fed on delicacies are destitute in the streets;
>> Those brought up in scarlet clothing pick through the garbage.

The verse portrays the affluent reduced to the status of beggars, like street people searching the trash for food, as all in Jerusalem are forced to scrounge for something to eat.

3. The residents of Jerusalem are compared to those of Sodom (Gen. 18:17–19:28), and the residents of Sodom are seen to have had it better (v. 6). The point seems to be that Sodom was destroyed in a moment while the residents of Jerusalem lingered to suffer under the hand of their enemies. The concluding phrase of verse 6 is puzzling, and there is no consensus about its meaning.

4. It is also indicated that the residents of Jerusalem who were once well fed were nearly starving following the fall of the city to Babylon (vv. 7–8). The translation in the NRSV indicates that those referred to in these verses are nobility, perhaps the crown princes of Judah (compare v. 5). There is a marked deterioration in these persons' physical appearance. The consequences of Jerusalem's demise were severe.

5. Those whose death came by starvation are compared with those whose death came by sword (v. 9). Clearly, "happier" here implies more fortunate, certainly not joy or blessing as in the beatitudes. In announcing God's judgment upon Judah, the prophet Jeremiah threatened that death would come by "sword, famine, and pestilence" (Jer. 14:12, and pervasively in the book thereafter). This poem, reflecting upon the city after the Babylonian victory, judges that those who died quickly by the sword were better off than those whose death came slowly by famine.

6. The most distressing portrayal of the city's plight appears in verse 10. Women consume their infants for food. The effect of describing the women as compassionate is to enhance the desperation of the situation,

that even "compassionate women" would be driven to such an extreme. It is difficult to imagine that what is described actually occurred, though there is no way of knowing. In the book of Deuteronomy, among the covenant curses is the warning that "in desperate straits," Israel and Judah would be driven to "eat the fruit of your womb, the flesh of your own sons and daughters" (Deut. 28:53–57). This verse at least wants to say that in defeat the residents of Jerusalem experienced the most terrible of covenant curses.

Lamentations 4 :11–20

4:11 The LORD gave full vent to his wrath;
　　　　he poured out his hot anger,
　　　and kindled a fire in Zion
　　　　　that consumed its foundations.
12 The kings of the earth did not believe,
　　　　nor did any of the inhabitants of the world,
　　　that foe or enemy could enter
　　　　　the gates of Jerusalem.
13 It was for the sins of her prophets
　　　　and the iniquities of her priests,
　　　who shed the blood of the righteous
　　　　　in the midst of her.
14 Blindly they wandered through the streets,
　　　　so defiled with blood
　　　that no one was able
　　　　　to touch their garments.
15 "Away! Unclean!" people shouted at them;
　　　　"Away! Away! Do not touch!"
　　　So they became fugitives and wanderers;
　　　　it was said among the nations,
　　　"They shall stay here no longer."
16 The LORD himself has scattered them,
　　　　he will regard them no more;
　　　no honor was shown to the priests,
　　　　　no favor to the elders.
17 Our eyes failed, ever watching
　　　　vainly for help;
　　　we were watching eagerly
　　　　　for a nation that could not save.
18 They dogged our steps
　　　　so that we could not walk in our streets;
　　　our end drew near; our days were numbered;
　　　　　for our end had come.

¹⁹ **Our pursuers were swifter**
  than the eagles in the heavens;
 they chased us on the mountains,
  they lay in wait for us in the wilderness.
²⁰ **The LORD's anointed, the breath of our life,**
  was taken in their pits—
 the one of whom we said, "Under his shadow
  we shall live among the nations."

This second section of Lamentations 4 has a different emphasis than the first ten verses. There is much less description of the changed (and worsened) circumstances of the city. Instead, the concern is with why Jerusalem was destroyed and its citizens' fortunes so dramatically reversed. At least four reasons are given as to why Jerusalem was destroyed:

1. The first reason given is that "the Lord gave vent to his wrath." The theme of the Lord's wrath or anger has been part of other poems in Lamentations (2:3; 3:1) and must have been widely understood as a major cause of the Babylonian exile. The book of Jeremiah, shaped at a time close to the exile, frequently related God's judgment to God's anger or wrath (see Jer. 4:8, 26; 7:20; 12:13; 15:14, and so forth). One way to account for the catastrophic and unthinkable fall of Jerusalem was to attribute it to God's wrath. In Judah, there was a deeply rooted assumption that Zion was inviolable. The origins for the idea that Jerusalem was inviolable may well have gone back to a time before David captured the city for Israel when it was still a Jebusite stronghold. When David was ready to attack the Jebusite city, its residents are reported to have thought, "You will not come in here, even the blind and lame will turn you back" (2 Sam. 5:6). The geography of Jerusalem made the city very difficult to attack with foot soldiers. However, beyond the logistical difficulties of capturing Jerusalem, it was believed that because the city was the place of God's earthly throne, it was unthinkable that the Lord would permit Jerusalem's destruction (see Psalm 48:12–14, but also Jer. 7:1–16 about the Temple particularly). Given the notion of the Lord's special protection of Jerusalem, perhaps the most compelling way to account for the destruction of the city was to attribute it to the Lord's wrath.

2. Beyond the Lord's wrath, Lamentations 4 also acknowledges that the religious leaders of Judah were to blame for the destruction of Jerusalem. This is quite similar to Lamentations 1–2, where Jerusalem's destruction was attributed to a combination of the Lord's anger and Judah's sin (see 1:5, 8, 13–14, 18; 2:1–8). In this chapter, the particular accusation against Judah's leaders is that they had shed "the blood of the righteous," by which they themselves had become defiled (vv. 13–16).

It is unlikely that we should understand this charge to mean that the religious leaders, prophets and priests, themselves committed murders outright. Rather, the accusation is more likely similar to that made by the prophets prior to the exile. In the book of Isaiah, for instance, the prophet links oppression of widows and orphans with the charge "your hands are full of blood" (Isa. 1:15 in the context of 1:10–17). In the Old Testament, blood means life. By allowing injustices, the life, that is, the blood, of the marginal was imperiled if not actually lost. We know, of course, that the poor in our world die of malnutrition and disease. Although no one directly murders them, we must recognize that their "blood" is on the hands of those (perhaps all of us) who perpetuate social and economic systems that harm the poor. The prophet Jeremiah, whose career immediately preceded the exile, also accused Judah and its leaders of shedding innocent blood by oppressing the poor (Jer. 2:33–37; 7:5–7; 19:4). Jeremiah particularly admonished Judah's kings in this matter (Jer. 22:1–19).

Lamentations 4 asserts that Jerusalem's destruction was the result of Judah's leaders shedding innocent (righteous) blood and then links this claim to Israel's laws of ritual purity. Blood, because it was associated with life, belonged to God and was not to be touched or ingested when eating meat. In this way of thinking, contact with blood rendered one unclean (see Lev. 17:10–16). When developed in relation to situations in which human blood was shed, these laws of ritual purity suggested that not only the one who shed the blood but the very land itself was made unclean by the shed blood (see Num. 35:22–34). Lamentations 4 follows this logic and asserts that Judah's religious leaders were rendered "unclean" (v. 15) by their involvement in shedding blood, and like lepers, they needed to be treated as outcasts in the community (compare Lev. 13:46: unclean lepers must live "outside the camp"; this law is evident in the way lepers are presented in the gospels, for instance, Luke 17:11–19).

In 587 B.C. when the Babylonians captured Jerusalem, it was the religious and political leadership, especially, who were deported to Babylon, who were forced to live "outside the camp." The conclusion reached in this section of Lamentations 4 is that the Lord "scattered" those who were unclean, citing in particular the priests and elders (v. 16). The prophet Ezekiel makes a similar argument. The land was defiled by shedding innocent blood, and the exile occurred when God expelled from the land those who had defiled it (Ezek. 22:1–22).

3. Another reason offered for Jerusalem's destruction is that allies did not come to Judah's rescue. Judah waited in vain for a nation that could

save them (v. 17). It is difficult to know how this failure is being interpreted, as desertion by allies or as flawed policy by Judah's political and
military leadership. In the book of Jeremiah, the prophet is quite critical
of Judah's leadership who turned to Egypt in the vain hope Judah's old
enemy might rescue them from Babylon. Jeremiah considered this policy
one that resisted the Lord's intention to judge Judah for long failing to
obey God (Jeremiah 37). It seems likely that verse 17 refers to this failed
effort by Judah's leaders to obtain help from Egypt during the Babylonian
siege of Jerusalem.

4. Finally, Lamentations 4 attributes the fall of Jerusalem to the overwhelming power of the enemy who defeated them (vv. 18–20). Hunting
images are used, and Judah became like stalked prey, so it was no longer
safe to be out in the streets (v. 18). So swift was Judah's enemy that there
was no escape, and fleeing was pointless (v. 18; see Jer. 4:13 for a similar
description of the enemy). Elsewhere in the Old Testament, the image of
"eagle's wings" is used to speak of God's rescue and protection (so, for
instance, to describe the exodus from Egypt in Exod. 19:4: "I bore you on
eagle's wings and brought you to myself"; also see Isa. 40:31), but that
image is reversed here. The pursuit concludes when the enemy captures
"the Lord's anointed" in a pit (v. 20). The Lord's anointed is the designation for Judah's king, the one who was to be God's agent for the well-being
of Judah and Israel. Compared to the highly critical view of Judah's kings
in many prophetic books (see Jeremiah 21–22, for instance), the Lord's
anointed is viewed quite positively here as the protector under whose
"shadow" God's people would live among the nations (see Psalm 91:1,
where assurance is given to those who "abide in the shadow of the
Almighty"). However, this positive view of the king could possibly be
intended as an expression of misplaced optimism, since it is the people
themselves who said of the anointed that they would live in his shadow.
Thus, this verse may suggest that the fall of Jerusalem occurred because
Judah held their kings in too high regard.

Lamentations 4:21–22

4:21 **Rejoice and be glad, O daughter Edom,**
> **you that live in the land of Uz;**
> **but to you also the cup shall pass;**
> **you shall become drunk and strip yourself bare.**
22 **The punishment of your iniquity, O daughter Zion, is accomplished,**
> **he will keep you in exile no longer;**
> **but your iniquity, O daughter Edom, he will punish,**
> **he will uncover your sins.**

The conclusion of Lamentations 4 moves beyond what had happened (vv. 1–10) and why (vv. 11–19) to a reflection about what Judah's future might hold. Edom, an old enemy of Judah, is warned that while for the moment they have escaped judgment, their time will come (the book of Obadiah concerns the difficult relationship between Judah and Edom). The reference to "the cup" from which Edom will be forced to drink echoes the vision of Jeremiah 25. There the prophet sees the Lord's judgment occurring as a "cup of wrath" passed from nation to nation from which they must drink and become drunk and ill. So, as Lamentations 4 thinks about the future, it imagines that Edom, Judah's enemy, will finally experience the same judgment that Judah suffered. Most of the prophetic books, in addition to announcing God's judgment on Judah and Israel, also herald the judgment of the nations as an indication of God's sovereignty over the whole creation (see Isaiah 13–14; Jeremiah 46–51, Ezekiel 25–30; Amos 1–2) and as a sign of hope for Israel's restoration.

As is also typical of the prophetic traditions just mentioned, Lamentations 4 links God's judgment of the nations with restoration for Israel and Judah. This chapter concludes with an indication that with Edom's judgment Judah's own exile will come to an end. While the Lord is not specifically mentioned in verses 21–22, the implication seems to be that the judgment of Edom and the restoration of Judah will be God's doing. Thus the poem of this chapter moves through a logical progression of ideas: a description of the judgment Judah has suffered (vv. 1–10); an analysis of why the judgment occurred that first attributes the catastrophe to God's wrath (vv. 11–19); and, finally, the poem imagines that God's wrath will be directed toward a traditional enemy of Judah, that is, Edom, and Edom's judgment will signal the end of Judah's exile.

Much of Lamentations is highly charged with emotion; it is a wail and cry. These verses are notable for their logical analysis of the causes of the exile. There is almost a dispassionate, objective tone that suggests an effort to step back and see the situation as clearly as possible. Again, Lamentations does not develop a single approach to attempt to explain the exile but is an untidy combination of many perspectives. In response to a catastrophe, there are times of emotional outpouring of grief, occasions when anger comes to bitter expression, but also moments when a community can step back and rationally account for what happened. Lamentations 4 is a more rational and objective reflection upon Jerusalem's fall, the reasons for this, and the prospects for Judah's future.

"Why Have You Forgotten Us Completely?"
Lamentations 5

After the largely descriptive tone of Lamentations 4, Lamentations 5 is once again an address to God, a prayer, a complaint spoken by the community (for similar prayers, see for instance, Psalms 44, 79). Prayers such as this one were part of the worship of ancient Israel and would have been used on occasions of national crisis. The rational and objective approach of the prior chapter vanishes, and this poem is an outpouring of pain and hurt. If Lamentations 4 suggests that the book is coming to some perspective that will bring neat and orderly resolution of the crisis of exile, such an expectation is shattered by the tone of this final chapter.

Not only is the tone of Lamentations 5 different from the prior poem, but the form of the poem is different from any other chapter in the book. Unlike the poems in Lamentations 1–4, this poem is not organized by using the letters of the Hebrew alphabet, and the disciplined order of the prior chapters is not evident. The only connection between Lamentations 5 and the prior poems is that it includes 22 lines, the same number of lines as there are letters of the alphabet. However, even in this there is a difference: Lamentations 1–3 included 66 lines (three lines for each letter of the alphabet); Lamentations 4 included 44 lines (two lines for each letter of the alphabet); Lamentations 5 is simply 22 lines. The breakdown of the disciplined order of the prior poems seems to reinforce the unraveling of any neat resolution of crisis hinted in Lamentations 4.

Following an address that seeks to gain God's attention (v.1), much of this poem recounts the hardships and suffering experienced by the people of Judah. The complaints are in two parts: what has happened to Judah's "inheritance" (vv. 2–7) and the harsh ways of Judah's captors (vv. 8–18). Each part of the complaint concludes with an acknowledgment of sin (vv. 7, 16–18). The complaints end, and the poem moves toward what seems to be a hymn praising God's rule (v. 19). However, the hymn of praise collapses into a question directed to God: ". . . have you forgotten?" While a plea for God to restore the community follows this question, the plea is not sustained either, and the poem and book conclude on an uncertain note: "Renew our days as of old—unless you have utterly rejected us . . ."

Lamentations 5:1–7

5:1 **Remember, O LORD, what has befallen us;**
     look, and see our disgrace!
  2 **Our inheritance has been turned over to strangers,**
     our homes to aliens.
  3 **We have become orphans, fatherless;**
     our mothers are like widows.
  4 **We must pay for the water we drink;**
     the wood we get must be bought.
  5 **With a yoke on our necks we are hard driven;**
     we are weary, we are given no rest.
  6 **We have made a pact with Egypt and Assyria,**
     to get enough bread.
  7 **Our ancestors sinned; they are no more,**
     and we bear their iniquities.

While Lamentations 4 concludes with an optimistic note that Judah's punishment will soon be ending, such confidence does not carry over to the beginning of chapter 5. There is instead a cry for God to remember. Such a plea is common in Israel's prayers of lament (Psalms 25:6–7; 89:47–50; 106:4–7; and outside the book of Psalms, Jeremiah's complaint to God in Jer. 15:15) and suggests the danger that the Lord will forget. In fact, near the end of the present chapter, the plea of verse 1 that God remember has its counterpart in the dreadful possibility, expressed as a question addressed to God, "Why have you forgotten us completely?" The initial verse of this complaint urges God to remember, look , and see what has happened to Judah. The verses that follow describe in some detail what happened to Judah and the disgrace into which the nation has fallen.

The reference in verse 2 to Judah's "inheritance" establishes the theme for verses 2–7. The Promised Land is described as Israel's inheritance (for instance, see Deut. 4:38 where the NRSV translates as "possession"; also see Josh. 1:6). However, there are broad implications of the word "inheritance," which include not just land but all that God had given to Israel. In its broadest sense, the people of Israel were themselves God's "inheritance," (see Exod. 34:9; compare Galatians 4, where Paul calls the church "heirs" of God). In complaining that "our inheritance has been turned over to strangers" the prayer has in mind the loss of land, to be sure, but also Judah's loss of relationship with the Lord, their sense of identity and vocation as God's people. Israel had once been aliens in the land of Egypt (see Exod. 22:21–24), and with the fall of Jerusalem, they had become aliens even while they remained in the land of promise (v. 2).

Other indications of Judah's difficult circumstances are also indicated. In Judah and Israel, widows and orphans were of particular importance. The origin of Israel was God's deliverance of them as a marginalized people who were slaves in Egypt. Because widows and orphans were persons on society's margin in the patriarchal cultures of the ancient Near East, their care was something of a litmus test of Israel's covenantal obedience and faithfulness. In this poem, Judah complains that they have all become widows and orphans, again marginalized and in peril and in need of God's protection. Further, the poem laments that in the land of milk and honey, water must be purchased (v. 4) and arrangements made with Assyria and Egypt to secure food (v. 6). The suggestion is that the Lord is no longer the generous provider known by Israel in the wilderness. A "yoke" (compare 1:14) was a symbol of social and political oppression (1 Kings 12:3–14; Jeremiah 27–28); thus, the people whom the Lord had once freed from Pharaoh's oppression were now under an oppressive yoke once again (see Deut. 28:48, where subjection under an "iron yoke" is a covenant curse). Many of the complaints seem to reflect a reversal of the Lord's care and protection known by Israel since the exodus from Egypt.

Judah's complaints about the loss of the inheritance conclude with a confession of sin (v. 7), though in a rather oblique way. Those who complain to God do not quite confess their own sin but, instead, acknowledge that their ancestors sinned and that they are bearing the consequences. A similar avoidance of responsibility among those who experienced the exile was sharply criticized by the prophet Ezekiel (Ezekiel 18).

Lamentations 5:8–18

5:8 **Slaves rule over us;**
       there is no one to deliver us from their hand.
   9 **We get our bread at the peril of our lives,**
       because of the sword in the wilderness.
  10 **Our skin is black as an oven**
       from the scorching heat of famine.
  11 **Women are raped in Zion,**
       virgins in the towns of Judah.
  12 **Princes are hung up by their hands;**
       no respect is shown to the elders.
  13 **Young men are compelled to grind,**
       and boys stagger under loads of wood.
  14 **The old men have left the city gate,**
       the young men their music.

15 **The joy of our hearts has ceased;**
   our dancing has been turned to mourning.
16 **The crown has fallen from our head;**
   woe to us, for we have sinned!
17 **Because of this our hearts are sick,**
   because of these things our eyes have grown dim:
18 **because of Mount Zion, which lies desolate;**
   jackals prowl over it.

The basis of the complaint shifts at verse 8, and the cruel character of the captors under whom Judah is subject becomes the focus. These captors are called "slaves" (v. 8). What this implies historically is difficult to determine. It may indicate that the persons assigned by Babylon to oversee Judah are viewed by the Judeans as Babylonian "slaves." Proverbs views quite negatively the idea that a slave should become a king (Prov. 30:22); the sense seems to be that this is a great humiliation. The claim that slaves are now the rulers of Judah plays into the theme of the reversal of God's exodus protection, the theme of verse 1. The once freed slaves are now oppressed by slaves. Further, Judah's situation is portrayed as hopeless; the poem sees no hope of deliverance (the end of verse 8). Clearly, the tone of this complaint differs significantly from the hopeful conclusion of Lamentations 4.

The other verses in this section develop the theme of the brutality of Judah's new rulers. These oppressors do not provide food, and there is famine (vv. 9–10; compare 4:7–8). Women are raped (v. 11), and the leaders of Judah are executed (v. 12). Grinding grain and gathering wood were regarded as menial tasks to which everyone was reduced to survive. The old men who sat in the gate were Judah's elders, and the city gate was where these elders carried out their judicial functions. These had ceased. The sense of verses 13–15 is that Judah's captors disrupted all of the normal routines of life. Such disruption of the community's life is exactly what the prophet Jeremiah had warned would be the consequences of God's judgment (for instance, see Jer. 16:5–9).

Like the first section of this chapter, these complaints also conclude with a confession of sin (vv. 16–18). This time, the confession is more direct and Judah's humiliation ("The crown has fallen from our head," v. 16) is linked to sin. Verses 17–18 reemphasize the point that has already been made, that sin is the cause of Zion's destruction (compare the imagery here and in 4:3).

Lamentations 5:19–22

5:19 **But you, O LORD, reign forever;**
   your throne endures to all generations.
20 **Why have you forgotten us completely?**

> Why have you forsaken us these many days?
> ²¹ Restore us to yourself, O Lᴏʀᴅ, that we may be restored;
>   renew our days as of old—
> ²² unless you have utterly rejected us,
>   and are angry with us beyond measure.

The hopeful conclusion of Lamentations 4 might lead one to expect the same in this chapter so that the book as a whole would bring resolution to the crisis of the exile. However, the conclusion of this chapter and of the book are quite ambiguous.

It begins with a hymn praising the Lord's enduring reign (v. 19). As a whole, Lamentations 5 is a prayer of complaint that raises serious questions about God's sovereignty. The poem has said, in effect, that the Lord cannot or will not even preserve the inheritance that has been given to Judah; the people God once freed from slavery in Egypt have been allowed to come under the yoke of cruel overlords. The praise of the Lord as an enduring sovereign suggests a resolution of the chaos that is the concern of much of this chapter and the book of Lamentations. However, the hymn does not proceed to some affirmation resolving the tensions of the book but, instead, to two questions that compound the difficulties (v. 19). "Forgotten" points back to the beginning of the chapter and the cry that the Lord remember. Why has the Lord whose reign endures forgotten Judah? As the book reaches its conclusion, this haunting question lingers, and it has not been resolved.

The uncertainty raised by verses 19–20 is reinforced by the final two verses of the book. Judah cries out, "Restore us to yourself, O Lord." However, the response to this plea is not an assurance that all will finally be well. Instead, Judah continues to speak and does so with a voice of doubt: "renew our days . . . unless you have utterly rejected us and are angry with us beyond measure."

With this the poem and the book conclude, and we do not know how it is between the Lord and Judah in this time of deep crisis. Has the Lord forgotten? Is God angry beyond measure? The poet of Lamentations is not sure, and the book does not speak with a single, clear voice about these matters. At points in the book, it seems as if the Lord's anger is "beyond measure," and with good cause, given the sin of Judah. At other places, there is confidence that the normative faith of Israel in God's steadfast love can be affirmed, and Judah's restoration will come soon. Finally, the book of Lamentations gives no clear answers, but before the Lord whose reign endures, struggles between hope and despair with no clear resolution in view.

Lamentations is at least honest, and it calls us to faith in God that asks us to trust the Lord in the ambiguities of our personal and communal life long before there is a clear answer whether life before God should be lived with despair or hope.

Works Cited

Gottwald, Norman K. *Studies in the Book of Lamentations.* Studies in Biblical Theology, 14. Naperville, Ill.: Alec R. Allenson, 1954.

Hillers, Delbert R. *Lamentations: Introduction, Translation, and Notes.* Anchor Bible. Garden City, N.Y.: Doubleday & Co., 1972.

Provan, Iain. *Lamentations.* New Century Bible Commentary. Grand Rapids: Wm. B. Eerdmans Publishing Co., 1991.

Re'emi, Paul S. "The Theology of Hope: A Commentary on the Book of Lamentations." In *Amos and Lamentations: God's People in Crisis,* R. Martin-Achard and Paul S. Re'emi. International Theological Commentary. Grand Rapids: Wm. B. Eerdmans Publishing Co., 1984.

Westermann, Claus. *Lamentations: Issues and Interpretation.* Translated by Charles Muenchow. Minneapolis: Fortress Press, 1994.